THE
UNARMED
TRUTH

My Fight to Blow the Whistle
and Expose Fast and Furious

John Dodson

THRESHOLD EDITIONS

NEW YORK   LONDON   TORONTO   SYDNEY   NEW DELHI

Threshold Editions
A Division of Simon & Schuster, Inc.
1230 Avenue of the Americas
New York, NY 10020

First Threshold Editions hardcover edition December 2013

THRESHOLD EDITIONS and colophon are trademarks of Simon & Schuster, Inc.

For information about special discounts for bulk purchases, please contact Simon & Schuster Special Sales at 1-866-506-1949 or business@simonandschuster.com.

The Simon & Schuster Speakers Bureau can bring authors to your live event. For more information or to book an event, contact the Simon & Schuster Speakers Bureau at 1-866-248-3049 or visit our website at www.simonspeakers.com.

Interior design by Ruth Lee-Mui

Manufactured in the United States of America

10   9   8   7   6   5   4   3   2   1

ISBN 978-1-4767-2755-4
ISBN 978-1-4767-2757-8 (ebook)

For my mother—I love you and miss you every day. So much in my life has changed since you passed, but one thing that hasn't is to whom I planned to dedicate this book. I was truly blessed to have been born your son.

Katie Elizabeth Dodson
February 22, 1946–January 19, 2013

I believe that unarmed truth and unconditional love will have the final word in reality. That is why right, temporarily defeated, is stronger than evil triumphant.

—Martin Luther King Jr., 1964

Contents

Foreword

Whistle-blowers are a special breed. They risk their careers to speak the truth, even if everyone around them is entangled in a web of lies. They do it because honor and integrity are more important to them than their own self-interest. The truth ruffles feathers. It upsets bosses and coworkers. But it needs to be done, and it takes someone with guts to stand up and speak out.

If it weren't for John Dodson, Americans would never have known the truth about Operation Fast and Furious and the death of Border Patrol Agent Brian Terry. A few people might have seen the press release from the Justice Department that announced the indictment of some gun traffickers in Arizona. But that wasn't even half the story.

The Justice Department didn't tell the public about the connection between that case and Terry's murder several weeks earlier. Dodson knew something that senior law enforcement and Justice Department officials desperately wanted to keep quiet. Guns found at the scene had been traced back to a government sanctioned operation.

That was a big problem for the Bureau of Alcohol, Tobacco, Firearms, and Explosives (ATF). Dodson was an ATF Special Agent on the case, and he knew that ATF had actually encouraged gun dealers to sell weapons to criminals for more than a year, even though its agents knew that the buyers were paid by gun traffickers. ATF also knew that those traffickers were reselling the guns to Mexican drug cartels. Rather than arresting the criminals, ATF merely watched and kept meticulous records of the serial numbers of all the guns being illegally sold to straw buyers for the cartels. The practice was known as "walking guns."

Dodson, and some of his fellow Special Agents, objected to the practice for months. Dodson actually confronted ATF officials and predicted that gun walking would end in a tragedy and outrage when the public learned about it. But no one listened.

Following the death of Border Patrol Agent Brian Terry in a December 2010 fire fight with Mexican bandits along a remote section of the border, it started to look to Dodson like the government was going to try to cover up the connection to Fast and Furious. That's when Dodson took his concerns outside the ATF, to Congress and eventually to the press.

Before the news coverage and investigations died down, every person in Dodson's chain of command had either resigned, retired, or been reassigned. Yet through it all, Dodson survived. He is still employed with ATF, and in the world of whistle-blowing, that is a minor miracle. The controversy ignited by his disclosures led to a stand-off between the Legislative and Executive Branches over documents and a bipartisan vote in the House of Representatives to hold the Attorney General of the United States in contempt of Congress for the first time in history.

More important, law enforcement officials had to answer publicly for their reckless pursuit of a big headline-grabbing case by any means. Because Special Agent Dodson spoke out, law enforcement officials might think twice next time before crossing the line between investigating criminal activity and encouraging it. For that and much more, the American people owe John Dodson a debt of gratitude.

When something has gone horribly wrong, the easy way out is to just keep your head down and keep your mouth shut. John Dodson didn't take the easy way out. This book is his story, a tale of the personal and professional journey of a man who decided to tell the truth, no matter the costs.

Chuck Grassley

Senator Chuck Grassley and Representative Darrell Issa
September 13, 2013

THE

UNARMED
TRUTH

PROLOGUE

No one likes the prick who says "I told you so."

But what we had done was so reckless, so dangerous, so wrong, that it didn't take some high-speed, low-drag "special agent" to figure out what was going to happen. I knew it from day one. I felt it in my gut. This was going to turn out bad.

They knew it, too. They knew it because I told them.

On an early morning in May 2010, sliding through the metal doors just as they were about to close, I encountered Hope Mac-Allister. She and I were both assigned to the newly formed Strike Force. Although comprising several federal agencies, including the Bureau of Alcohol, Tobacco, Firearms and Explosives (more commonly known as ATF), the Strike Force was located on the fourth floor of the Drug Enforcement Administration's building in Phoenix. Hope was the case agent for the ongoing investigation she had dubbed "Fast and Furious."

We were now nearly half a year into an epic battle I'd been waging over the merits of the Phoenix ATF office's most prized operation, one that the brass in Washington had taken an unusual interest in. I felt confused, frustrated, and pissed-off with my front-row seat to an impending train wreck. Sharing twenty awkward seconds with the person driving the locomotive did little to make it better.

I have always been fascinated by the human psychology displayed inside an elevator car; each person who boards usually gravitates to a position farthest away from the other passengers. Sometimes when getting on an elevator, I would intentionally stand right beside whoever happened to already be on board. Whether it was a friend, coworker, or a complete stranger, the reaction was always the same—visible discomfort. Having already done this to everyone I worked with, they would then enjoy watching the reactions of those unfortunate enough to have to share an elevator with us.

I guess even in the smallest of ways I liked to test the boundaries.

On this ride, Hope and I utilized standard elevator etiquette—each assuming a neutral corner and facing forward—waiting for that all too familiar jolt and "ding" that would signify our liberation. This time, it was Hope who would break with etiquette.

She turned to me and asked quite simply: "John, what do you really think about this case?"

My mouth opened and for a second or so I didn't say a word. *Really? What do I think about this case?*

For months now, our office had been watching known small-time criminals purchase hundreds of weapons . . . AK-47 variants, AR variants, .50 cals . . . all "weapons of choice" for drug traffickers . . . and then hand them off to drug cartels in Mexico. There was no question in anyone's mind that these weapons were being trafficked and that we were not only allowing it but in fact facilitating it. A few of us pleaded with our superiors to allow us to arrest these buyers—more commonly known as "straw purchasers"—interdict their load of guns, or seize their money before the purchase. To do something, anything to take some kind of enforcement action. To do our jobs.

Time and again, we were told—I was told—to stand down.

What did I really think about this case? I'd complained about Fast and Furious any number of times in Hope's presence. Was she really that clueless? I decided there was more to it than that. Maybe a part of her knew how screwed-up all of this was. Every once in a while, I thought, maybe the Kool-Aid had worn off.

As the elevator ascended, I looked at her. "Hope, don't ask me questions that you don't want to know the answers to."

"I do want to know," she replied. She seemed sincere. "What do you really think?"

The elevator doors opened, and we stepped off. While talking, we turned right, through the security access-controlled door, then made another right and walked down the hallway toward the ATF section of the Strike Force.

"We're walking guns," I told her. "How many guns have we flooded the border with? How much of the crime down there are we responsible for? We are just as culpable as if we had sold them ourselves," I said. "We're never going to get anywhere with this case. We're not going to climb the ladder. At best, you're only going to get back to the DEA wire. That's as high as you can go." Determined to take full advantage of the opportunity, I continued. "We haven't learned anything. The only thing that's changed from the very beginning is the number of guns we've let walk."

The two of us had entered the ATF space and were standing in the middle of the office, a good-sized room with cubicles all around us, the half-wall kind that didn't force anyone to have to stand up to see the person next to or across from them. For whatever reason, maybe it was the tension in my voice, our conversation had drawn the attention of everyone in the room. All the agents in our Strike Force Group VII turned to watch, as did the Gun Runner Impact Team (GRIT) guys who were there on detail from all around the country, called in to help us with Fast and Furious.

Even David Voth, our group supervisor, had stepped out of his office. Tall and stocky with the bearing of the Marine he once was, Voth had light hair tightly cropped with barely noticeable streaks of gray around the sides. We had a word for guys like Voth in the military. He was a "rock." In other words: if you didn't tell them to move, they would just sit there. Voth was a man who followed orders without question. He was good at it, too. I always wondered if that was why the brass had him supervise Fast and Furious.

My eyes were still focused on Hope, but my fury was directed more broadly to all of those complicit in Fast and Furious, a number of whom were within earshot, especially the guy who was now listening closely. "What you need to ask yourself is this: Are you prepared to go to a border patrol agent's funeral or a Cochise County deputy's funeral over this?" I asked. "Are you prepared to watch that widow accept that folded flag?"

Around me jaws dropped, fingers stopped jabbing at keyboards, all attention now intensely focused on us. I had just said what we all knew deep down inside. Everyone in that room knew this was what I thought, but no one had ever expected me to say it aloud, so bluntly, so publicly.

I knew what I was doing. I was telling the truth. We were going to get people killed.

Fully atop my soapbox, I finished with "It isn't a matter of 'if.' It's only a matter of 'when.' And everyone in this room knows it." It didn't take a clairvoyant. It was all too foreseeable.

Hope didn't respond. No one else said a word, either. The giant elephant in the room had just taken a shit right in the middle of it. I turned away, walked over to my cube, and started on my work.

If my name is known to you, it wasn't my choice. I didn't set out to expose corruption and wrongdoing on behalf of a major federal agency. But when I saw what was happening with Fast and Furious and its tragic consequences, I had a decision to make. It's the same decision every person faces when confronted with something they know is wrong, even if those acts are committed by colleagues and friends. To speak out or to stay silent.

Martin Luther King Jr. once talked about what he called the "unarmed truth"—the kind that survives cover-ups and denials and eventually triumphs over wrongdoers. When Fast and Furious made its way into the public consciousness, I knew the truth. And I went out and told it, unarmed and unaided, at the risk of ending friendships, long-standing relationships, and my career. I did what I did because it was the only thing I could do to sleep at night.

I spent my entire adult life swearing an oath to defend the Constitution, and it was heartbreaking to me to think about how far afield federal law enforcement had gone. "Protect and Serve" used to be the primary mission. Now it seemed we were no longer doing either.

I've heard all the theories about the Fast and Furious scandal among the press, among the pundits, among partisans. Frankly, from a hell of a lot of people who don't know a thing about it or law enforcement.

If I've learned anything over my twenty-year career, it is the uncanny ability we all have to create our own myths, to believe with every fiber of our being that we know what happened when the story is almost always more complicated. There are millions of people, for example, who believe a missile hit the Pentagon on 9/11. That's just not true. I know that because I was there pulling body parts from the wreckage of what had clearly been an American Airlines aircraft. In the Fast and Furious case, many people maintain that what happened in Phoenix was the result of a small group of misguided "bad apples." And that this sort of thing won't ever happen again. That's not true, either. There are also millions of people who believe the president or this administration masterminded a conspiracy to arm Mexican cartel members so that they could justify more gun control. It's simply not that easy.

Everyone, it seems, has a version of this story—their own version—a narrative all their own. But it's not the whole story. I know because I was there, I lived it, and it's dominated the last four years of my life.

Don't get me wrong. I have no great affection for the president or the attorney general, especially after the living hell their Justice Department has put me through over the last four years. But Fast and Furious is much bigger than the two of them. It goes beyond any one person, any one administration, or any one party. It is a symptom of a broken federal government and a broken law enforcement community that manufactures and exacerbates problems to justify their own missions, their own funding, and ultimately their own existence. Fast and Furious isn't about a person, but a system. A system that is broken. A system that has betrayed the very people that it is supposed to serve—the American people.

The media has missed the bigger story. Fast and Furious is not a grand conspiracy or cover-up—or at least it didn't start that way. Quite the contrary, it started as an all too normal occurrence in federal government, another example of the self-licking ice-cream cone. It was the result of good people, patriotic people, smart people even, trying to get credit for the big takedown in a press conference with bright lights and cameras, but not recognizing that the only reason they would get the accolades and attaboys for solving a problem was that they had exacerbated it to begin with.

In the drug cartels along the southwest border, America has a problem. But as Fast and Furious would prove, we made that problem a lot worse. At least forty thousand people have been killed since Mexico's president Felipe Calderón declared war against the cartels in 2006. The cartels are more violent and more dangerous than any organized crime syndicate that American law enforcement has ever faced. They exhibit total disrespect for human life and kill indiscriminately. They take over entire towns along the border and lay waste to anyone who disagrees. Driven by the almighty dollar, and beholden to no moral code, these thugs are some of the toughest, most vicious in the world. They are fueled by the multibillion-dollar narcotics industry, and the vast majority of their proceeds comes from the United States.

When our government agencies decided to join the Mexican government in waging war on the cartels, no one objected. We were promised fewer drugs on our streets and less violence along our border. It made sense.

The problem is that in the quest for glory, for medals pinned on by men in Washington with crisp suits and polished shoes, for favorable press headlines, we lost sight of the real goal—to protect and serve.

In Fast and Furious, three federal agencies—the FBI, DEA, and ATF—were running three different self-interested operations on a cloudless December evening in the Arizona desert. It was the night that led to Fast and Furious being exposed—and it took the death of a Border Patrol agent named Brian Terry to make that finally happen.

From what I know firsthand and the many things that I've learned since, my belief and opinion is this: With the exception of the squad of Border Patrol agents, everyone who was there that night in Peck Canyon was there at the direction of the Department of Justice. The DEA had information on, if not orchestrated, a dope load passing through Peck Canyon that night. According to press accounts, they passed this information to the FBI, who alerted their own group of informants, assets operating in a completely different drug trafficking organization, that a large shipment was coming through and that it was theirs for the taking. Stealing such a shipment would increase the clout of the FBI informants in the cartel organization they had penetrated, and thus lead to better intel for them in the future. I believe, based on what I have read in the press, that that was the thinking, anyway. And so a "rip crew," a group of armed men sent out to rip off the traffickers and steal the drug load, was dispatched. If that wasn't bad enough, as we would learn in the hours after the shots were fired, that rip crew had been armed with guns that the ATF provided through the Fast and Furious investigation. Worse still, the press would later report that many of them had even been paid for by the FBI.

In short, every person who was at the scene of Brian Terry's murder, both the good guys and the bad, was there directly due to the decisions of the United States government. Unfortunately no one bothered to tell this to the Border Patrol. No one told Brian Terry and his teammates that night to steer clear of a scene that would likely end in violence. As a result, an American citizen died a needless death. This was a conspiracy of ignorance. It was the result of separate government bureaucracies not talking to each other, yes, but of government bureaucracies manufacturing problems so they could claim credit for solving them. It was the inevitable result of hubris.

Just as troubling, those most culpable immediately worked to shield the American people from that ugly truth. This is the part of the story that I lived.

– 1 –

JUMP STREET

In 1989, shortly after finishing high school in Orange, Virginia, I left for the Army. My mother had driven me to Fredericksburg and cried as she watched me board a Greyhound bus. Uncle Sam spares no expense for his boys. After a quick overnight at the Military Enrollment Processing Station in Richmond, my next stop was Basic Training at Fort Leonard, Missouri. Nine weeks later, I then went on to my Advanced Individual Training at Fort Huachuca, Arizona.

Eighteen years old, I had never been off the east coast before, and never so far from home. Arizona was a different world for me; I may as well have been walking on Mars. The desert, the vistas, the desert, the mountains, the desert...there was a lot of desert. Not many people go through Fort Huachuca, or the thriving metropolis outside its front gate, Sierra Vista, and ever want to come back. It's a small, somewhat secluded town near the Mexican border. Not a whole lot goes on there. I imagine most would want to stay as far away as possible, but for me it was different. Something about Arizona resonated in me; I felt a connection with it, a kinship if you will. I was so captivated that after having to leave, for nearly the next two decades I was haunted by the words "Go west, young man, go west" and I was always on the lookout for some way to get back.

My job in the Army was intelligence, an unanticipated side effect of scoring well on the Armed Services Vocational Aptitude Battery. Although it sounds sexy, military intelligence (MI) isn't as cloak-and-dagger as you might think. A lot of it is book work, research, memorization, plotting, graphing, and even some statistics. As I was taught: "Information goes up—intelligence goes down." So you're always trying to find more, gather more, uncover more so that you can figure out more. It's a constant state of learning. But of all the things I learned in MI, the most important was to analyze. Not "how to analyze" or "how to think analytically"—but rather, to analyze . . . to be analytical.

After MI school I saw everything differently. I learned that everything is a puzzle—and every puzzle has a solution. In short, my job was to solve puzzles. So although not the super-secret, black-bag ninja warrior who teleports in and takes out all the bad guys with a paper clip and piece of gum, I knew how to figure out who the bad guys were, where to find them, and how to get into their heads.

After the Army, I went into law enforcement. It seemed a natural fit. At first I became a sheriff's deputy in Orange County, Virginia, where I had grown up. When I got the job as a "road dog"—a patrol cop—in Orange County, it was a very small department: the sheriff, chief deputy, one lieutenant, two investigators, two civil process servers, four or five court security personnel, and eight of us assigned to work the road in the Patrol Section.

My academy graduation was on a Saturday at noon. The following Sunday, just before midnight, I used the radio in my old Chevy Caprice patrol car to mark "10–41" (on duty). I immediately heard the others marking "10–42" (off duty). I was it—thirty-six hours after graduating from the academy, I was the only law enforcement officer for all 343 square miles. "Sink or swim" rang through my head. I'll never forget that feeling.

You see and deal with it all when you work as a cop in a small department. There's no *CSI: Orange* to call and have them come out to work the murder scene. No *Bones* to solve your case for you. You do it all. That, however, doesn't stop the large departments, big-city police, and especially the feds from looking down on us "Podunk" officers.

After the sheriff had hired me and during the months I was attending the police academy, the other road guys began referring to me as "one of us."

"How's it feel to be one of us?"

"Glad you're one of us."

I felt like I had just been picked to be part of some elite cadre, a coveted position on a special squad, an appreciated member of the team. It was a good feeling. It didn't take long after that first midnight shift to learn the true meaning of "one of us": a dead body floating in a pond—one of us (me) had to go in and get it. The town drunk with puke all over him who had just shit himself—one of us (me) had to take him to jail. The local crazy lady in her tinfoil hat screaming that her neighbor was controlling her mind . . . you get the idea.

Truth is, I garnered more experience in those first few years than many cops or agents do in their entire careers. Being one of only eight meant that there was no room to hide. You were always held accountable. The sheriff was also held accountable by the citizens he worked for. Those were the fundamentals of law enforcement. It was in Orange, Virginia, that what it really meant to be a "cop" was instilled within me.

I remember being told by my supervisor then: "Remember—protect and serve. Yes—you respond to calls, work wrecks, write tickets, arrest people, and we track all those stats. But the one thing we don't know, can't measure, and can never track is also the most important part of your job—preventing crime." Success back then wasn't judged on how many arrests we made, how many tickets we wrote, or who got the big case; we were successful when no one got hurt, no businesses got robbed, and no drunks were driving down the highway. When crime was down and people felt safe and were safe—that's when we knew we had done our jobs. Over the next two decades, however, what it meant to be a cop would change. An entirely new standard would be set.

After my time in Orange, I did a brief stint at the Newport News, Virginia, police department until being offered a job at the sheriff's office in Loudon County. The progression seemed logical to me; after five and a half years of working the street (pushing a cruiser), I grew tired of having to turn all my good cases over to some detective. So I put in for it, got promoted, and became a detective in the vice-narcotics section and street crimes unit.

I had a dual role when I worked narcotics: one as a detective with the county, the other with the federal government as part of the Drug Enforcement Administration (DEA) High Intensity Drug Trafficking Area (HIDTA) task force. County cases were mostly low-level narcotics enforcement and street crimes—the little guys selling dope out of their houses or hanging on the corner dealing. We also dealt with vice crimes like prostitution and illegal gambling. If I thought my first day on the road was sink or swim, my first day in vice-narcotics was more akin to "learn to fly or crash and burn."

The vice-narcotics (Narcs) office was located outside the Sheriff's Office. Disguised as a dummy corporation, it was a clandestine office, backstopped as a small business working out of a warehouse in an industrial complex just outside Leesburg. When I arrived that first day, I was handed a wad of cash and the keys to an old, beat-up Oldsmobile and told not to come back until I had grown my hair out, pierced my ear, and bought a bag of dope. Mind you, I was twenty-seven years old, had had four years of JROTC in high school, went straight into the Army, and then worked more than five years as a uniformed patrol officer. My hair had never before touched my ears.

Unlike the other detectives working property or violent crimes, those of us in Narcs essentially had to embed ourselves in the criminal element. We got to know the players, the hustlers, the dealers, and the crooks. All of it was undercover work, many times in deep cover, backstopped and supported with complete undercover identities, fake driver's licenses, phony vehicle registrations, and untraceable credit cards. We had secret apartments, got jobs in warehouses, on farms, or in bars, and then went about our mission and started to develop contacts.

Our first order was simple: buy drugs, as much and as often as we could. From there we tried to work every case up the ladder and back to the source of supply, to infiltrate the organization, identify the con-spiracy and all its conspirators, and then put a noose around its neck and bring it all tumbling down.

The minefields in doing so, however, are many: living that life, surrounded by that element, fearing you'll be found out, trying not to get killed, not to break the rules, not to get too deep, too close, or too drunk, all the while trying to build a good case that will withstand the scrutiny of some overpaid defense attorney.

Your goal is to get the information, get the evidence, make the case, and then get the hell out. Until then, there's no going home. No time-outs or do-overs. You can't risk blowing your cover. Occasion-ally, you'd meet other narcs in some darkened alleyway, vacant lot, or maybe a rest-stop bathroom and hand over some crucial pieces of evidence or information. You were always cautious that someone might be watching, that you would be recognized or outed. A degree of paranoia kept you alive.

My time in Narcs and on HIDTA had afforded me the opportunity to work some big cases, use all the expensive equipment, and deploy the most (for that time anyway) cutting-edge tactics on nearly every kind of criminal and criminal organization. As big cases often transcend different genres of criminality, it also allowed me to work hand in hand with just about every variant of "alphabet soup" that you can think of (DEA, FBI, ATF, INS, USSS, USMS, FPS, NCIS, DCIS, and on one case even—the BIA). What starts as a dope case may soon involve other crimes like money laundering, kidnapping, bank robbery, murder, and even terrorism.

My experience, both in law enforcement and MI, had brought me face-to-face with terrorism many times and I had worked with the FBI before on several occasions. One of the most profound memories I have in my life was when terrorism came knocking, right on our front doors.

I can recall exactly where I was and what I was doing that September morning in 2001. Working all day at DEA and most every night with the county, being a little late had become almost the norm for me. Driving down the toll road that links Route 28 and Dulles Airport to the Beltway, I was headed to my DEA office in Annandale, Virginia.

Like most mornings, the FM radio in my task force–issued vehicle, a small, black Mercury Cougar, was set to DC 101.1 and I was listening to the antics of Elliot and Diane. This morning however, reports were starting to come in from New York that a plane had crashed into one of the twin towers of the World Trade Center. Nobody really had a handle on what was happening yet; a piece of information from this station over here, a bit from this network over there—"fog of war" being made all the more thick by journalists and talking heads who spew out uninformed, unsubstantiated speculations in hopes they will at some point be able to say, "You heard it here first." The *Elliot in the Morning* crew were reaching out to their contacts, and even friends in New York, doing their best to try to put it all together for those of us listening so far away.

Mashing the accelerator into the firewall of the Cougar, I threw my blue strobe light onto the dash and cut through the barricade leading to the restricted-use Dulles access highway, which ran between the opposing lanes of the toll road. I had to get to the office; there I could maybe find out what was going on and there is where I had to be in case we were needed.

Our small office building just off of Little River Turnpike housed two DEA groups, two FBI dope squads, one IRS money laundering group, and a few other units. It was one-stop shopping for all things relevant to the war on drugs. When I arrived, the little black Cougar popping and belching coolant, I ran inside and found everyone in the central area just outside our group supervisor's door, huddled around a small portable television that someone had to help pass the time on those long nights of surveillance. In those days, we didn't have cable in our office, or even TV for that matter. Few offices did. One agent was frantically manipulating the TV's broken antenna, trying to find that perfect angle so that the picture didn't fade out into a fuzzy mess again. On the brink of being clear, it was just good enough for us to see the unthinkable: another plane hit the second tower. "Holy shit!" is pretty much the only thing I remember hearing anyone say.

While we stared, still stunned and fixated on that little eight-inch screen, thirty-four minutes later the office, the windows—the whole building—rocked. Knowing that something big had just happened, everyone ran for a window and began scanning the skies. Flung about from the four cardinal directions of the building was "Nothing on this side" or an "All good over here." Seemingly satisfied that Annandale was still on the map and yet still frantic for information, we all gathered back around that small, fuzzy TV. We would later learn that roughly two miles away, American Airlines flight 77 had been flown into the Pentagon at 535 miles per hour.

My supervisor had been juggling his "brick" (old-school government-issued Motorola flip phone) and his desk phone the entire time, sometimes getting a trickle of information, and sometimes regurgitating it out to someone else. Just as we had begun planning a response to assist at the Pentagon, he said, "Hang on," slamming his landline into its cradle. "We're ordered to go over and assist with protecting headquarters." For some reason, still unbeknownst to me, we had just been ordered to report to DEA headquarters in Crystal City, a high-rise neighborhood almost directly across 395 from the Pentagon, and help secure the building.

Seriously? I thought, *Why on earth would terrorists want to take out DEA headquarters? Was the White House not good enough of a target? The Capitol Building not make a big enough splash? Hell, even FBI headquarters, although still an outside chance, made more sense than DEA headquarters . . . nobody even knows where it is.*

Before leaving, I stopped just outside my boss's door. It was one of those moments when something pops in your mind, something that seems so simple, so completely obvious, that you second-guess yourself before voicing it because common sense mandates that surely it has either already been addressed or doesn't need to be because you should already know the answer. Pausing to quickly rummage through the filing cabinets in my brain, searching for what it seemed clearly should be there but apparently wasn't, I braced myself and asked the question. "Um . . . How exactly are we supposed to stop a plane from crashing into DEA headquarters?"

No answer, just a roll of the eyes and wave of the hand—off to headquarters we went.

Sometime later, well into the evening, while manning my post at DEA headquarters (prepared to do what exactly I still don't know) I got a call from my then father-in-law.

Jack was an FBI agent, just a few years short of retirement. He would joke about having worked for every director the FBI had ever had, including J. Edgar Hoover himself. An Ohio State grad and collegiate boxer, Jack had been stationed in the Washington Field Office his entire career, and at this time, he was working on a Joint Fugitive Task Force with the U.S. Marshals Service and Metropolitan Police Department. I always got along with Jack. We had our work in common, and between the two of us there was never a shortage of stories for the rest of the family during those many summer days and nights spent out on his back deck in Annapolis, Maryland, cracking blues and drinking beer.

Jack told me he was at the Pentagon and tasked to one of the many teams that the FBI had dispatched there. Heading up his team was another FBI agent who was assigned to HIDTA that I knew and had worked with. Jack said that they were short on people and asked if I could break away and help out.

After assuring my boss that it looked like we had everything pretty much "protected" and locked down there at the DEA building, I went over to help at the Pentagon. I quickly badged my way through security set up at the perimeter, but while trying to make my way through the chaos looking for Jack, I was taken aback.

Still smoking and smoldering, that odd, almost burning sensation of JP-4 jet fuel permeating the nostrils, it looked like a war zone. There were uniformed Defense Department personnel running about, orders being blared from megaphones, debris seemingly everywhere, roaring generators, light trees, a triage, medics, Red Cross vehicles and humvees . . . And right there just across the river, the night sky yielded, surpassed by the city glow of our nation's capital and pierced by the giant obelisk of the Washington Monument. It was utterly surreal.

Fortunately, the FBI command post wasn't hard to find. They were there in full force, as were a number of other agencies. I may bust the FBI's chops once in a while, but on that scene, I'll give them their due—they did a good job. Soon I found Jack, sitting together with the rest of his team on makeshift chairs and benches. Introductions having been made, I fashioned a seat of my own from the mounds of equipment and supplies that were dumped in piles nearby. Expecting at any moment to get the okay to go in, and with no one daring to wander off too far for fear of missing it—the chance to help in some way, to do something—we just waited.

Mid-morning on September 12, our okay finally came. Ours was the first investigative team to enter the Pentagon after it had been deemed safe to do so. Our mission: body recovery. It didn't come as a surprise; we knew what we were assigned to do.

Prior to our entering the building that first time, the FBI had mandated we wear big white Tyvek suits, hooded, with thick puncture-proof rubber gloves, boots, goggles, and a full face-protective mask. I was still working undercover at the time: earring, goatee, ponytail . . . the whole nine yards. I had no chance of actually getting a good seal with the mask (so that it would actually be effective), so I tucked my ponytail away under the hood, loosened the straps on the mask so that it didn't drive my earring into my mastoid process, and was ready to go in.

Eight figures, standing in line against the huge granite wall of the Pentagon's outermost ring, all clad head to ankle in white Tyvek. In a last bit of preparation, every other person was handed a roll of silver duct tape and a Sharpie marker with the instructions to tape the seams of each other's suits at the ankles and wrists and have your last name written in large letters across your back. "Don't think for a second that since we said it was okay to go in that that means it's safe in there. If something goes bad, we don't need any more bodies to identify."

I quickly ran the tape around Jack's ankles and wrist a few times, turned him around, and wrote his last name across his back. Jack turned back facing me, grabbed the tape and Sharpie, made a few quick spins of the tape around my ankles and wrist, and then spun me around. I felt the point of the marker press hard on my upper left shoulder and then . . . a pause . . . and ten seconds later it dawned on me—my father-in-law had forgotten my last name.

"It's Dodson, Jack. You know, your daughter's husband . . . same last name as her?"

"Oh—shut up. I got it," he said and I spell-checked him as he scribbled the letters across my back.

For the next two days, we pulled bodies out of rubble, trying to identify each before placing them into bags. Some were easy: a wallet, name tag, dog tags, etc. . . . others, not so much. Fortunate were the times an entire body was recovered.

Somewhere in the second ring, I believe, on one of the upper floors, there was a conference room with some minor damage: a few fallen ceiling tiles, pictures knocked off walls . . . disheveled, but in no way destroyed. Seated around a large wooden conference table in the middle of the room were seven or eight people, each covered in fine particles of dust and debris, slumped over in the high-back chairs or collapsed forward on the table, but none with any trauma. No visible injuries or wounds, no burns, no blood . . . bodies perfectly intact. They were in the middle of a meeting one second—dead the next.

Closer to the impact site, almost right in the middle of all the devastation, there stood this large, perfect square, a big box with nothing left standing near it, debris all around and leaning on it, seemingly untouched by the flame and exempt from the carnage. It was obviously a room of some kind, and this being the Pentagon and all, I thought: *SCIF? War room? Bunker? Vault maybe?* Crawling through tons of debris, over mounds of rubble and under felled girders, we made our way to it. It was a bathroom. If that hadn't been odd enough, the inside was immaculate—the mirrors weren't cracked, it wasn't dirty or dusty, nothing. Standing there, I remember thinking about the contrast: the microcosm of that pristine bathroom environment compared to the perdition of the world surrounding it.

A little over a year later, in October 2002, I again found myself in the tempest—the D.C. sniper case. Whereas anger and revenge were the predominant reactions to 9/11, this time it was fear that had gripped the Washington, D.C., area. Dragging on for nearly a month and spanning from southern Maryland to Ashland, Virginia, the investigation meant hundreds of us—cops, troopers, and agents alike—running down lead after lead, shutting down Interstate 95 and the Beltway, jumping Jersey barriers and median strips while chasing every "white van" that dared show itself to anyone with a cell phone. Sleep was rare those three weeks.

I thought about those victims a lot: coming out of a Home Depot or Michael's craft store, pumping gas, waiting for a bus, doing one of those things that we all do on any given day. Everything normal one minute—dead the next.

After several years, similar frustrations to those I had developed while working the street began to arise: making good cases only to have to turn them over to some fed. Thinking I'd finally put an end to that pattern—I put in my application. The Bureau of Alcohol, Tobacco, Firearms and Explosives—more commonly known as ATF—hired me in June 2004 and assigned me to a two-man, satellite office in Harrisonburg, Virginia. I had a great boss, made some good friends, and worked some good cases over the next five years.

Meth was the *dope du jour* in the Harrisonburg area and we filled the dockets with large, armed drug-trafficking conspiracy cases. One of my favorite cases there, however, had nothing to do with drugs at all. It started on a Saturday morning in the summer of 2007: a local bank was robbed by a masked man armed with two stolen Glock pistols and a hoax bomb device. After brandishing the pistols at the tellers and ordering them to hand over what cash they had, he placed a device in the middle of the floor. It consisted mainly of a cell phone duct-taped to a small box and had several wires seemingly establishing a circuit between the two. "This is a bomb," he announced. "If anyone calls the cops in the next thirty minutes—it's going to go off." And out the door he went.

A lot of law enforcement folks will tell you that ATF really stands for "After the Fact." Actually, that isn't too far from the truth. The FBI exerts jurisdiction over bomb threats that meet a threshold for federal prosecution. A real bomb (ticking or otherwise) is handled by a real bomb squad, which generally consist of state and local officers—although the squad and its members can only be certified by the FBI. A hoax device (fake bomb) is handled by a bomb squad until deemed a hoax device, which then would constitute a threat to bomb and thus fall back to the FBI. It isn't until something goes *boom* that ATF can exert its authority and muscle in and try to take the lead from FBI. ATF doesn't defuse bombs; our expertise is in working bomb scenes.

Regardless, we all know from the movies that the FBI is still the lead agency on a bank robbery. That's true for the most part: the FBI has jurisdiction over the robbery of an FDIC-insured financial institution (bank). However, if the bank robber uses a firearm then it becomes a federal crime of violence—ATF shares jurisdiction equally with the FBI.

More important, the most vital causative factor leading to my involvement in this case—the robbery happened on a Saturday morning. Ever try getting an FBI agent to come out after 5 P.M. Monday through Friday, or on a weekend or a holiday?

The local detective called the FBI and was referred to the duty agent, who advised him that he couldn't make it out there that day. Graciously, however, he said he would come to the PD on Monday and pick up copies of the reports and the evidence if they could have it all boxed up and ready to go for him by then.

I had no desire to work a bank robbery case, but one of the detectives there that day was assigned to the local drug task force that I worked with regularly. He called my cell phone, told me what he had, and I headed that way. Having been a real cop, I knew his frustration. I had been pleasantly surprised after meeting my ATF boss for the first time back in 2004. He was a true "agent's boss" who took care of his people and knew how to do the job. He had explained to me that my mission in Harrisonburg was to assist local law enforcement; if federal prosecutions came from that, then great, but if they just needed an extra body to stand a post on something or direct traffic— my ass better be there. He understood the importance of relationships, and how taking the time and effort to establish and maintain those would yield true results.

After I got to the bank and got brought up to speed, I told the PD guys there was no sense in them booking all the evidence into their vault on Saturday, which required a hell of a lot of paperwork, only to have the FBI agent come over on Monday and pick it all up from them. So I took the evidence back to my office and secured it for the FBI agent.

By Monday there was no escaping it. Having briefed him about the Saturday callout, my boss assigned me to work with the FBI agent on the bank robbery case. Over the next four weeks, it became a serial bank robbery case. Same suspect, five different banks, all but the very last one robbed on a Saturday. My summer was ruined: every weekend spent at crime scenes and every week spent bringing the FBI up to speed on what they had missed over the weekend.

That Monday after the first robbery, I met the FBI agent working the case with me for the very first time. I gave him copies of everything and turned all the recovered evidence over to him. "First thing," I told him, "send that cell phone from the hoax device to your lab and get it analyzed." I knew they could easily fingerprint it and perhaps trace it back to the purchaser.

A few weeks in we got our first break: the FBI had a composite sketch drawn up and soon a suspect was identified. A local guy, early twenties, worked as a groundskeeper at a shop in Harrisonburg. It was a Friday afternoon, and if he was to keep to his schedule, we'd have another robbery the next day. The order came down from the FBI brass that their field agents could not hit the suspect's house due to the "risk involved." They wanted a full-time tactical team to do it. The FBI's team, however, was unavailable. Quickly I offered up that we, the ATF, would do it.

I and the other agents assigned to my field office, which was in Roanoke, maintained our own area tactical team and trained regularly.

I called my boss and said, "Send up the fellas: we're landing on this guy—tonight."

Surprisingly, he was hesitant. Citing the "risk involved," he wanted to use ATF's full-time Special Response Team (SRT) from D.C. Although I understood his concerns, it made no sense to me.

"Everyone we deal with is armed and dangerous . . . violent felons, armed drug traffickers," I said. "We're the 'violent crimes police,' remember? That's what we do. When the local cops need help or can't handle it because the guy is such a badass, they call us. Our job is to go after these guys who are too dangerous for everybody else."

He tried to talk me down: "John, I understand what you're saying, but it doesn't work that way. If we can wait on getting SRT, then we should let them do it."

"But that is the way it works. You tell us we can hit the door, we hit it, the bad guy goes to jail . . . it's over with," I said.

"No, not this time," he responded.

Hindsight being what it is, I'm thankful that he shut me down that day. It turned out that the FBI had identified the wrong guy. Without missing a beat, however, the FBI quickly created a "serial bank robber task force," and I found myself immediately assigned to it.

Frustrated and unable to wait for the FBI lab any longer, I decided to track down the phone company from which the cell phone on the initial hoax device had been purchased. It was a typical burner—a temporary pay-as-you-go phone favored by a lot of criminals because there were no long-term phone records and, more than likely, no real way to track down the purchaser. I called up the company; the phone manufacturer could only tell me where and when it had been purchased—a local Wal-Mart a week or so before the first robbery.

So I rolled up to the Wal-Mart and found the manager. I asked him for the surveillance footage from the date of purchase and the transaction records. The video wasn't available but the manager said he could try to pull the register receipts. Within minutes, the manager walked out of his office and handed me the receipt.

The Wal-Mart receipt had no name or anything on it but, surprisingly, it did have a credit card number. Leaving a record like this is a rare mistake, usually avoided by criminals at all costs. I went straight over to the Bank of America across the street and had the manager put me in touch with their corporate security office. Due to the severity of the situation, within minutes I had a name and an address.

There wasn't a shred of doubt as to where I was headed next. On my way to the suspect's house, I called my partner at the office with the FBI agents and informed them. Driving along, I saw several marked cruisers go screaming past me, sirens blazing.

"He just hit the Patriot Bank," my partner told me. "The calls are coming in now."

"I'm almost at the house," I said. "Get someone headed this way."

I pulled onto the street and rolled by the address. Nothing. When I got to the end of the block, I turned around and was about to park on the street, where I could keep an eye on the residence, when I saw the suspect pull up. I watched him as he parked. Still wearing his gloves from the bank robbery he had just committed only moments before, he reached into the backseat, grabbed a backpack, and went inside.

A few short moments later, backup having not yet arrived, I saw him come out of the house carrying the backpack and walk toward his car. My choice was either get in trouble for acting alone and without backup or watch him get away. Without hesitating, I chose trouble.

I got out of my car and started walking toward him. As soon as I got close enough, I wrapped one arm around his neck, threw him on the ground, and pressed the barrel of my pistol to the side of his head.

"Police!" I told him, "If you so much as clinch a muscle, I will splatter your brain all over this sidewalk."

The cavalry came in a few short minutes later. Cop cars and FBI vehicles, sirens screaming and lights flashing, skidded into the neighborhood and slid to a stop. All told, we recovered seventy-two thousand dollars in cash and the two stolen Glock pistols. We transported the robber back to our office and the FBI case agent and I interviewed him.

The interview room was small, with concrete block walls from the tile floor up to the white drop ceiling and one door leading only to a secure hallway on the other side. It had one tinted window, behind which other agents could observe the interview from an adjacent location. Furnished only with a small, rectangular table and three chairs positioned around it, it was stark to say the least. I sat the suspect down in one of the chairs at the middle of the table and then walked around to the other side and sat on the back of one of the others. With my feet in the seat of the chair, leaning forward with my elbows resting on my knees, I looked at him. He was in his early twenties, seemed healthy and fit, with short brown hair and dressed just like any other kid I had seen around town. Since I first introduced myself to him there on the sidewalk in front of his house, he had been compliant and respectful, polite and well-spoken. He just seemed normal.

I couldn't help but wonder what had happened. What event had caused his life to spiral down such a path as it had? These questions were nothing new to me; I posed them to myself many times in many similar situations. Each time, I was able to draw but one solitary conclusion: there but for the grace of God go I.

Mere moments passed until the FBI case agent walked in and sat down. He introduced himself to the kid, showed him his FBI credentials, and then spread open a large folder in front of him. Following all the procedures, the FBI agent produced the appropriate bureau interview and consent forms, read each aloud, made sure they were all clearly understood, and then obtained all the required initials and signatures on each one.

Finally, I thought to myself, *we can start the interview.*

While neatly putting the pages back into his folder, he fired off his first question.

"So?" he asked, "Why did you rob those banks?"

Uncontrollably, my head snapped toward him.

Quickly, my mouth began to move as I began my attempt to utter something to spare my FBI cohort from the folly of his question.

His gaze still squarely fixed on me but speaking directly to the FBI agent, the suspect answered: "The same reason anybody would rob a bank . . ."

I cringed, knowing that the obvious punch line to the joke that my FBI counterpart had inadvertently made himself the victim of was about to be delivered.

"For the *money!*"

The next morning, I walked into the office and, after getting my morning cup of coffee, sat down at the small table in the break room. My partner slid the local newspaper across the table to me. Front page: "FBI Arrest Serial Bank Robber—Minutes After Robbery." Seconds later, a local TV news reported the same. "Breaking news"— they had an exclusive interview from one of the serial bank robber's last victims, of less than twenty-four hours ago—a teller from the Patriot Bank.

After her short narrative describing the robbery itself, the teller concluded with "and then I pushed the emergency 'holdup' button and then, just seconds later, the bank and the parking lot were filled with FBI agents. They told me that they had the guy under arrest already. Just like that. And I just want to say, thank God for the FBI!"

In 2007, while I was still based out of Harrisonburg, there was the horrific shooting that left thirty-one dead and shocked the campus of Virginia Tech. Others will argue that the death count was thirty-two; I don't count the shooter. Our Roanoke office is less than two hours from Blacksburg, Virginia. When my partner in Harrisonburg and I first heard about it we knew that our Roanoke guys were already on their way down there, and we knew that we wouldn't be far behind.

When we got to the campus, FBI, ATF, and state police were already there en masse. They had already locked down everything and were wrapping up searches of the other buildings. It was one of those scenes where you don't really know where to begin. There was so much carnage—and no real playbook for something like that.

The scene in Norris Hall, the epicenter of the violence, still haunts me. To this day, every time a cell phone rings, I am immediately taken straight back to that place and time. The ringing wouldn't stop. Emanating from everywhere, the ringing of cell phones as they sat in motionless pockets, or buried down in a backpack, or lying somewhere on the cold, tiled floor. Worst were those still clutched in the death grip of their owner's hand—ringing . . . and ringing. You knew that on the other end was someone's boyfriend or girlfriend or mother or father or sibling. Some loved one trying frantically to reach someone they loved. They had seen the news and only wanted reassurance that the person they cared about was okay.

The scene was horrific: some victims were still seated at their desks; others lay where they had huddled together in the corner of a classroom. It was saddening to see that so many of them had just given up, had watched as their killer came through and methodically executed classmate after classmate. Some just sat there and awaited their turn to die; others held their hands and arms up over their faces as if to try to shield themselves from the bullets somehow. In class one minute—dead the next.

And then there were others: those who did something, got up, ran, jumped through windows, anything to get out of there. Although still very much victims, they had at least survived.

Shortly after the scene had been secured, we began identifying the survivors and witnesses, tracking them down and interviewing them. We had to make sure there weren't multiple shooters or other accomplices who had managed to flee by disappearing into the crowd of others.

When you go through experiences like those, one after another after another—terrorists, lunatics, mass murderers—you begin to think that there isn't much to life that you can't handle. Life, however, seems ever determined to prove to you otherwise. I was blindsided and caught completely off guard when my wife abruptly ended our marriage. The next year and a half was consumed by a hellacious divorce that affected every facet of my life: my children, my finances, my work, my own self-esteem and confidence. Working deep undercover, recovering bodies, or witnessing things that would make your skin crawl all paled next to the toll that the divorce took on me. At the end of it, though, I was able to keep a hold of the most important things in my life—I had primary custody of my children, I had parents and family who loved and supported me, and I still had a great job that I loved. In what seemed my darkest hours, I still had things to be grateful for.

Like so many times in life, one thing leads to another—one door opens as another one closes. While I was still recovering from the trauma of divorce, ATF offered me an opportunity and a transfer. I was more than ready. The timing couldn't have been more perfect. Since I had to start all over again anyway, why not do so in a brand-new place? "Go west, young man—go west."

– 2 –

THE PHOENIX WAY

Soon after I got my transfer orders in September 2009, I was sitting at my desk in Harrisonburg, Virginia, when the phone rang.

"This is David Voth," said the voice on the line. "I'm going to be your new group sup when we get to Phoenix."

Like me, Dave hadn't yet reported to Phoenix; he was still in Minnesota at the time he had gotten the nod to head up Group VII—the newly created gun trafficking group I had just been assigned to. He had already been out to Phoenix and met with the bosses—including the Special Agent in Charge (SAC), Bill Newell. So he gave me the skinny on what he knew about the area and the division.

I had been told that Newell had handpicked the people that he wanted to fill the ranks of Group VII. I'm not sure how I made the cut. I didn't know Newell, never met him. I had no juice at headquarters or anywhere else for that matter. Maybe my file showed that I knew what I was doing, or maybe he just threw darts at a list of names on the wall. Newell's deputies, the two Assistant Special Agents in Charge (ASAC), were Jim Needles and George Gillett. Group VII would fall under Gillett's side of the house, making him Dave's immediate boss. Coincidentally, or perhaps not, George and Dave had worked together before in Minnesota and were good friends.

Group VII was poised to be one of the first Strike-Force groups. The "Strike Force" concept is billed as the next generation of the "Task Force." Tried and true, the Task Force concept consisted of cops from different agencies (local, state, federal), all cross-designated, cross-sworn, and cross-credentialed (with members carrying two, sometimes three different badges), and all working together to achieve a single goal: get the bad guys.

I had experienced this on the DEA task force. Back then the participating agencies all brought something to the table: local departments had a place to take cases that transcended their municipalities (multijurisdictional) and had access to federal resources; federal agencies had streetwise local cops who knew their home beats.

Another benefit of the task force approach was federal funding. Washington has an uncanny way of coming up with an alphabet soup of ideas to fund certain priorities that it deems worthy at any given time. The Office of National Drug Control Policy and Department of Justice handed out blank checkbooks through programs like HIDTA and OCDETF (Organized Crime Drug Enforcement Task Forces). These and other funding programs were specifically designed for specific types of cases that agencies and task forces could apply for. Through participating membership, the task forces concept helped smaller, local departments that otherwise would not have the ability to spend $20,000, much less $100,000, on a single case or even a single narcotics purchase.

Most important, a good task force knows how to get things done. We called it the "okey-doke." If you were working a case and had to front money for a dope buy, DEA regs wouldn't allow you to do it. So you could structure your case through one of the task force agency's local departments whose policy did allow for it. You whipped out your local badge, still used task force funds, personnel, and equipment, and when it was over you wrote the case on the back end through the task force and prosecuted it in federal court. All of this had one fatal flaw by government standards: it worked too well.

The Strike Force, in theory, was based on those same concepts proven effective by the task force: multiple agencies, working together, sharing information, each bringing something to the table for all to utilize and benefit from. However, as I would find out later, it lacked a simple foundation—rather than being put together by cops who identified a problem and came up with a solution, it was put together by bureaucrats and lawyers as a solution sent out to find a problem. The Strike-Force was mandated by the Justice Department to be "prosecutorial lead." Cops would no longer run the investigations— lawyers would. Preventing, deterring, and solving crime would take a backseat (if still allowed to ride at all) to successful prosecutions, which, as we all know, come with press conferences, media attention, awards, and other attaboys. No longer would the resolve be on actually making a difference; it was now corrupted into merely showing that a difference can be made.

Before I left for Arizona, Dave called me again, around early November 2009, to tell me about the great case we would be working on when we hit the ground in Phoenix. He explained that three agents already stationed in Phoenix had begun working on a firearms trafficking case. Dave seemed very excited. He told me how the rules on OCDETF requirements had recently been changed and now allowed for firearms trafficking cases. Previously, as the program's name implies, only organized crime and drug trafficking cases qualified. Just to be clear, OCDETF is a funding program that law enforcement agencies apply for and when approved, it basically gives them an un-limited amount of funds to work a case.

"This is a great OCDETF case and a great wire case," he told me.

A "wire," as it's commonly called (or T-III), refers to an electronic intercept (wiretap) used to eavesdrop on the communications of sus-pected criminals and/or criminal organizations. It's a highly invasive tactic and is normally only used as a last resort in law enforcement. I thought it strange that Dave was already talking about this as being a wire case. A wire is a tool to work a case. You don't work a case to get a wire.

Every cop knows that "big cases equal big problems" and before such an intrusion into someone's privacy is authorized, there are many well-defined prerequisites that must be satisfied, numerous checks done, and layer upon layer of reviews conducted, all in place to act as safeguards. To ensure all these prerequisites are satisfied, there is a whole chain of people who have to offer their two cents and get their paws all over your case. Your entire chain of command has to approve, HQ must sign off, the local U.S. attorney's office (USAO) must sup-port it, funding has to be secured, additional manpower obtained and brought in, facilities set up, equipment procured.

Aside from the constitutional requirement of probable cause, policy and protocol dictate that all wiretap applications/affidavits be approved by the highest levels of the requesting agency and by the Department of Justice. The last and highest hurdle is Justice's Office of Enforcement Operations (OEO). OEO must review and authorize before it can even be submitted to a judge.

Wires are also very costly and laborious. Not only do you have to get the actual wiretapping approved, but you must get funding authorization as well (such as OCDETF), which means even more people asking more questions about your case. Most important is the legally mandated requirement that before the court can authorize an electronic intercept, and before one should even be asked for, law enforcement must "exhaust all other investigative means."

I told Dave that it might have wire potential now but that a lot could change before we even got out there to Phoenix, and that based on my experience and all the hoops that must be jumped through, "We don't want to do a wire unless we have to."

Dave waxed nostalgic, explaining how he had done a wire on a gun trafficking case out of Minnesota and what a huge success it had been. I'd later learn that he won the "Agent of the Year Award" for that case. He lamented that we weren't on the ground in Phoenix already. I assured him that we would both be there soon and we could figure out where to go from that point.

Later that month, the day after Thanksgiving, I gave my mom and dad a hug and loaded my sixteen-year-old daughter, seven-year-old son, and two-year-old pain-in-the-ass dog into my black four-door Toyota Tacoma.

I stopped at the end of my parents' driveway, clutching the steering wheel, and I thought about it. *Is this my test?* So far away, such a different world, no friends or family for thousands of miles, no one to help me—but most important, no one to help the two kids in the seat behind me. It was a feeling of total loneliness. In that moment, everything seemed to be riding on my shoulders. What if something happened to me? Who would care for the kids or get them back to their family? What would they do?

I thought about turning around and calling the whole thing off. Instead, fighting off the fear that had tried setting in, I reached through the gap in the steering wheel and pushed the reset button on the trip meter. Two thousand, three hundred forty-six miles later, on a Sunday afternoon, we pulled into the driveway and saw our new home for the very first time.

A week later, on December 7, 2009, I reported for my first day at ATF in Phoenix. The Division Office was located in the Bank of America building in the heart of Phoenix's bustling downtown district, with a five-story parking garage underneath the building. The first floor contained an area sectioned off for banking customers only, strictly patrolled by security. On the very bottom floor, a small section was fenced off for ATF and accessible only via a secure card reader.

Our offices were upstairs on the sixth floor and half of the ninth where the bosses held forth: Newell, his deputies, their support staffs, the public information officer, and a small workspace for the senior operations officer (SOO).

Dave and I reported to Phoenix at about the same time.

One of the first people I met that day was Hope MacAllister. Originally from North Carolina, Hope had been with ATF for several years and had been assigned to Phoenix the entire time. That same day, I also met two other Group VII agents whom I would be working with: Tonya English and Jose "Joe" Medina. Both were relatively new to ATF, and as with Hope, the Phoenix Division had been their first and only ATF duty station. The three of them had been moved over to Group VII as soon as it officially came online. They all seemed like good people, and in those early days we all got along fine.

Tonya and Joe were still on their probationary status. Upon being hired by ATF, you are considered a probationary trainee for your first three years. Until you hit the three-year hurdle, ATF can fire you at will for any reason—or none at all.

Tonya had moved around several of the groups in Phoenix since graduating from the academy, and now Hope was her field training agent. The two of them formed a close kinship, always looking out for the other; what was said to one you knew would be immediately passed to the other.

Joe had been a policeman in Toledo, Ohio, before joining ATF. The way he spoke, how he handled himself, it was obvious to me that he had been a real cop in his pre-ATF life. Before arriving in Phoenix, I had gotten word that I had originally been assigned to be Joe's field training agent. But when Fast and Furious (F&F) started up, Hope signed off and approved Tonya's training, making her available to take Joe under her tutelage. Joe told me that it was explained to him that he could get a lot of "great experience" on this "really big, really great case" and this way he would be trained by an "expert in firearms trafficking investigations."

With Hope as case agent on the F&F investigation, her protégé Tonya was appointed co–case agent. Joe, the best cop of the three, was often relegated to bitch-boy and charged with only the most trivial tasks.

On Friday of that first week, Joe had been sent down to Naco, Arizona, to pick up some ammunition that the local police department had seized from one of the F&F suspects. Joe didn't make it back until late that afternoon. As I began making my way out for the weekend, walking down a long corridor on the sixth floor, with cubicles along the windowed exterior side of the building on my right and large multipurpose rooms defined by off-white Sheetrock walls on my left, I saw Medina hunched over in the middle of one of the rooms, his face barely visible above the flipped-up screen of his laptop and his two index fingers feverishly punching at keys. I poked my head in to bust his balls about being in the office so late on a Friday afternoon.

"You ever hear of 'Fed Friday'? Factoring in the three-hour time difference, headquarters was a ghost town before we even started talking about where to have lunch today."

He rolled his eyes. I noticed that stacked all around him, on the table, on the floor, atop nearby chairs, were boxes upon boxes, cases upon cases, of ammunition. As I drew closer, Joe looked up, glanced at the door behind me making sure no one else was in earshot, and softly said, "I can't leave until I count all this ammo, enter it in NFORCE, and then book it into the vault." NFORCE was our computerized case-management system.

"Like hell!" I said, in a not-so-soft voice. "Says who?"

"Ssshhhh . . ." he cautioned. "Tonya."

"Seriously?" I had to be sure.

"Yep, I have to open all the boxes and count every round." I chalked it up to Tonya's inexperience with the ATF regulations. She simply didn't yet know the ropes.

"Joe, you don't have to count every round. First of all, an unopened box or case that says on it 'quantity: fifty rounds' means there are fifty rounds inside. 'One thousand rounds' printed on the side means there are a thousand rounds. Second, you don't have to do it tonight. You can store all of this in the outer vault until Monday, and process it and book it in then."

Joe shook his head. "I know. That's how they taught us to do it at the academy," he said, "but I'm on probation. I have to do what she tells me to do."

"You're supposed to listen to your field training agent and Tonya's not your FTA," I exclaimed. "Did you tell Hope?"

Still shaking his head, he answered: "It was Hope that told me I had to listen to Tonya. She sat right there when Tonya was telling me what I had to do with all of this."

"I'll be right back." I turned and walked out the door.

Heading down the long corridor, taking a quick left between two rows of cubicles, immediately after passing by Tonya I stopped at Hope's desk.

"Hope," I said. "Hey, I just talked to Joe. Since it's six thirty on a Friday, I told him to secure that ammo in the outer vault for the weekend. I will help him process it and get it into NFORCE first thing on Monday morning, ten-four?"

Before Hope had even looked up from her computer to answer, the words "We can't do that!" came from the other side of the cubicle wall. It was Tonya. "They won't let us do that here."

"We can't store evidence in an evidence vault?" I asked incredulously.

Tonya belted out, "Not in the outer vault. They won't allow it."

I looked down at Hope with an unmistakable facial expression that said "I'm asking you—not her." I raised an eyebrow for emphasis.

"Yeah, it has to be booked into the vault," Hope said.

Conceding that perhaps such a rule could vary from one division to another, I adjusted my dive angle. Still addressing Hope, I said "Okay. Well, he is under the impression that he has to count each individual round as opposed to just tallying the numbers of the un-opened boxes and cases."

Again came Tonya: "That's how *we* have to do it," she said, her inflection on the *we* dripping with contempt for however it was that I thought it should be done. All the while I kept my gaze fixed on Hope as she appeared to punch only the left and right arrow keys with her right hand and the spacebar with her left as, I believe, she played some bootleg game on her computer that had somehow been embedded in an Excel program as a way to defeat our computer protocols.

"No it isn't," I objected.

Tonya jumped to her feet. Her attempt to talk down to me was diminished by the fact that only her eyes and forehead were visible above the five-foot cubicle wall.

"Um, yes we do," she demanded. "They said that we have to count every round, each individual one."

"Who the hell are 'they'?"

Surprised at the question, all she could muster was a stammered-out "What?"

"Who are 'they'?" I asked again. "You keep saying 'they.' Whoever 'they' are, I'm sure that 'they' don't trump ATF policy. I know 'they' can't contradict ATF orders. And unless you can tell me exactly who 'they' are—I don't give a rat's ass what 'they' say or what 'they' have told you about how we are supposed to do a damn thing."

Fixing my gaze back on Hope, I said, "As his FTA, I can only assume that you want him to do things the right way, in accordance with the orders—correct?"

She nodded her head yes. Turning, I walked past Tonya and returned to where Joe was working.

"I just talked to Hope," I told him as I passed through the doorway.

"And?" he asked.

"And, we are going to do this the way it is supposed to be done." In a matter of minutes, Joe and I had the boxes and cases of ammunition separated, itemized by caliber, and labeled, and the numbers totaled and uploaded into NFORCE. After we stacked it all on a large metal pull cart, all that was left to do was to get the vault custodian—who happened to be Tonya—to open the vault and wheel it in.

"You got it from here?" I asked Joe.

"Yeah," he said. "Thanks, man."

"Any time, brother," I told him. "Do it, get the hell out of here, and have a good weekend."

It usually took me about forty minutes to get home from the division office. That was nothing compared to any Northern Virginia or D.C. commute. I took Interstate 10 west to Estrella Parkway and then up the Hill—what the residents of my neighborhood called our little part of Estrella Mountain. Still a recent transplant, I was awed at the nearby peaks of the mountain range. As I took a right off the parkway my cell phone rang. It was Joe.

"You're not going to believe this," he said. Joe went on to tell me how Hope and Tonya had confronted him right after I left. They told him that regardless of how things might work in other divisions, Phoenix had its own ways of doing things. One of them was opening every box, every case, and individually counting every round of that ammunition, and then closing and resealing them before putting them into the vault. And all of that had to be done before he could leave.

The concept of "the Phoenix way" was beginning to take shape for me. I'd hear that phrase a lot over the next few months, and it never sat very well with me.

Joe's ammunition incident did little to dampen my enthusiasm the next Monday. It was week two, and I was read into Jacob Chambers et al.—the unassuming name of the case that would become Operation Fast and Furious. Hope briefed me on it. She had earned the reputation of being *the firearms trafficking guru* for not just Phoenix but all along the southwestern border and even back at headquarters. As I sat through the briefing, I had a hard time understanding why.

She confirmed something that Dave had said during one of our pre-Phoenix phone calls—that the genesis of the case was information provided by local Federal Firearms Licensees (FFLs). In other words, a gun shop owner had called the ATF office and described how suspicious buyers were picking up sizable quantities of the same firearms, sometimes adding up to thousands of dollars, and always paid in cash. The gun shops were suspicious that several individuals, one of whom was named Jacob Chambers, were buying guns on behalf of a criminal organization. The law enforcement term is called "straw purchasing"—when people without a criminal history buy weapons for people who would otherwise not be legally allowed to do so or who don't want the purchase to be traced back to them.

Drug trafficking organizations or cartels are laced with people with criminal records, a disqualifying factor for a legal gun purchase. So they'll find people with clean records, generally young people, underlings, maybe addicts, or anyone in need of some quick cash and willing to fill out a form with their name on it. The only qualifications for the position are a basic level of discretion and being able to pass a criminal background check.

While there's no federal law that expressly says straw purchasing is illegal, it's relatively easy to make the case. Anyone who purchases a firearm from a legally licensed gun dealer has to fill out a form stating, among other things, that the weapon is for his or her individual use. That's how we prosecute the straw purchasers. Lying on the form is against the law.

My experience before I got to Phoenix was that gun shop owners were valuable sources of information. The ones I had known were pretty sharp, patriotic, law-abiding small business owners. They'd often chat about their PTA meetings and their kids' school functions. I've known several who also held elected positions in their communities. Many are prior service military, National Guard reservists, or local police officers. I had even known one FFL who was a magistrate in Virginia, issuing warrants and setting bonds.

We never used FFLs as confidential informants (CIs) or agents of the government, but they worked with us. They would tip us off to suspicious activity or purchases that, although legal, didn't pass the smell test. Sure, any business is driven by profit, but they also knew that if their guns ended up in the wrong hands, the blame could boomerang back on them, and their industry as a whole could suffer the consequences.

Hope explained in her briefing to me that the FFLs knew these purchases were hinky and strongly suspected they were straws. It was obvious—if someone is dropping ten thousand dollars in cash to buy ten or fifteen of the same gun, and you see through the front window that they showed up driving a piece of shit, it's not hard to figure out what's going on.

So convinced and concerned were the FFLs that they weren't going to allow the sales anymore, and with no obligation whatsoever to do so, they called ATF and reported it.

This was about as routine a case as it got in ATF. In ATF offices all across the country, once agents were tipped off about straw purchases, they would thank the FFL for the information and affirm to them that whomever they chose to do or not do business with was entirely up to them and the standards and regulations of their industry. If the FFL was willing (they almost always were), the ATF would then ask them to call back if anything new developed. Agents would open a case with the information provided, conduct background checks in different databases to find out about the suspected straw, and check to see if any of the firearms they purchased had been recovered in crimes. This was Investigation 101.

Fast and Furious, at that point, had all the makings of a standard ATF case. I still didn't see what Dave had been excited about. My first assignment was to put the names and identifying characteristics of forty-two suspected straw purchasers into the "Suspect Person Database." Again, most of these names had been provided by local gun dealers, and some of their guns had already been recovered in crimes, sometimes within mere days of them being purchased. We should have been landing on people—not filling in a database. I had been with ATF since 2004 and I had never used the database before, nor had I known anyone who did. But, as it was explained, this was the Phoenix way.

Lee Casa, another transferee to Group VII, had arrived in Phoenix around this time and, both being new to the area, we partnered up. A full-blown Italian from Chicago with the matching accent and vernacular to pull it off, Lee could have just as easily been in the Cosa Nostra as in ATF. He was a pretty fit guy and sported a mid-December Chicago tan, which only got darker after he moved to Phoenix and spent his weekends on the side of his pool baking under the Arizona sun. Above all, though, Casa was a blast to work with.

We'd been provided with a list of names, all straw purchasers from the "Fast and Furious" investigation, and we were sent out to the various FFLs to check their books for purchases. It was possible, if not likely, that straws had hit up multiple stores beyond the ones we already knew. Sometimes Joe would tag along with us, but most of the time Hope or Dave had him doing more menial tasks back at the office. Riding in Casa's brand-new Chevy Impala, exactly like mine in every way except dark blue instead of black, we bounced around from FFL to FFL. We would walk in, ask to see their "book," and search it for any of the names on the list of straws. The "book" referred to a ledger mandated by ATF that must be maintained by all FFLs. It must record the origin and disposition of every firearm that enters inventory or transfers through the business. The owners are required by their licensing agreement to make it available to ATF whenever asked.

Hope and Tonya had warned us to check the records ourselves for the names and to provide as little information as possible to the FFLs about the investigation. "They might be dirty or let something slip," they had warned. We were also told not to visit some stores—such as the Scottsdale Gun Club—because they were already working directly with Hope and providing information.

One day in early January 2010, Joe called Casa and me and advised that Hope had sent him out to the Scottsdale Gun Club to retrieve some transactions records, called an ATF Form 4473, and copies of the store's internal surveillance video that showed some of the primary targets during their most recent purchase of firearms. Joe suggested we coordinate our travels so as to be near the store around lunchtime, and we would all grab a bite together when he was done. Agreeing, Casa and I called an audible and started making our way to Scottsdale.

Taking in the sights as we made our way through town, we got a call from Joe. "I'm having an issue here and I can't get a hold of Hope or Dave. Can you guys meet me out here?"

We pulled into the parking lot within minutes. Joe had made his way out of the store and walked through the lot to meet us. "They don't want to give us anything," Medina explained. "They keep asking for something in writing."

When I was briefed into the case, I was told that the Scottsdale Gun Club had been cooperating with Hope and ATF for some time. Recently they had notified her that one of the suspected straws had made a big purchase of firearms and she had sent Joe there to pick up the 4473s and a copy of the store's closed-circuit video footage of the purchase. Joe explained how he had done this many times already, but now, for some reason, store management wanted something in writing before they would release it to him.

Sitting in the parking lot, Casa and I exchanged puzzled looks. I had never had an FFL not cooperate unless they were dirty. And I knew Scottsdale Gun Club wasn't dirty. As I understood it, they were one of the FFLs at the genesis of the investigation. Something wasn't tracking.

Joe walked us inside. The SGC was an upscale gun shop with high-dollar, quality inventory, sales counters sectioned off by firearm types, uniformed staff, an indoor range, and a restricted area reserved for dues-paying members—dues that my GS-13 salary wouldn't allow me to afford. We were escorted into a back room to speak to the manager.

"We understand that you guys are working on a case," the manager told us. "But the owner and our legal department have some concerns. We still want to cooperate and work with you, but they just want something in writing from you guys that says it's for your investigation and what it is that you're asking for."

Bewildered, I asked, "Why the change? Joe here says that you guys have previously provided him with copies of the surveillance footage and it was never a problem before."

"Well," he explained, "like I said, the owner and the lawyers have some concerns."

"What concerns?" I asked.

"Well," he answered, "they just want something in writing."

It continued this way for a few minutes more. Finally, I deemed it just another incident of overeager lawyers complicating an otherwise simple thing. I figured if they were going to play the lawyer card then I would, too.

"Okay," I told him. "The 4473s belong to ATF. Those are our forms and you are merely a custodian of them. We will take those now. As for something in writing, if I have to put pen to paper to get a copy of that video, it will be in the form of a grand jury subpoena that will require you to bring it to me downtown at a date and time of my choosing. Now, where can we find our forms?"

There was an icy silence.

After obtaining copies of the 4473s, we were walking out when a female employee called Joe back over to the office door. Casa and I continued outside. Before Lee could even get the car started, his phone rang. It was Joe. They had just given him a copy of the surveillance video. *Problem solved,* I thought as we followed Joe through the North Scottsdale streets and found our way to a local restaurant.

But something still gnawed at me. Why something in writing saying we were working on a case and what information we wanted? It just didn't add up.

A week or so later, we were on our first op out in the field—conducting surveillance on one of our suspected straw purchasers. Andre Howard, the owner of the Lone Wolf Trading Company on the western outskirts of Phoenix and one of the original cooperating FFLs, had called Hope and told her that one of the known straws was in the store and about to make a purchase. Andre was cooperating fully with ATF and following the directions given to him by Hope, Tonya, and later, Dave. He continued to sell to the straws, notifying ATF in real time (often ahead of time whenever he could), providing detailed records of who (names, addresses, and all identifying information) bought what (make, models, serial numbers) and when (dates and times), and stalling the purchasers until we could get there and get in position if need be.

Hope told us about the tip. Casa and I jumped into our g-rides (government issued vehicles) and hurried out of the division parking garage. We drove up Interstate 17 a few miles and a few blocks west on Peoria Avenue, then hurried into the shopping center parking lot and took up good vantage points. A few minutes later, at roughly 2 P.M., the radios started coming to life as Hope, Tonya, and Joe all descended on the area as well. Marking our locations and ensuring that all exits were covered, we set the trap.

Hope, on her cell phone with Howard, was relaying the events inside the store over the radio to us as they happened. "NICS check is done."... "He's at the register."... "Deal is done—he's on his way out."

This was one of the most prolific straw purchasers in the case. We had already documented several multiple-firearm purchases by him; some guns had already been recovered in crime scenes on both sides of the border. And now we were watching him as he walked out of Lone Wolf with fifteen or so AK-variant rifles. It took him three trips to load them all into his car. There was no question that he was a straw purchaser and we already had ample evidence that these rifles were going to be trafficked to the border or into Mexico in no time flat. With what we had been able to put together thus far, he was already "bagged and tagged." It didn't get much easier than this.

Game on! I said to myself as I clipped on my gun belt and thigh rig. My ballistic vest was at the ready, flipped over the driver's seat at my back. I slid my SIG Sauer P229, showing its wear more than ever from having been carried stuck inside the front of my pants for the past five years, into the polymer Serpa holster. I heard the familiar click as it reached bottom.

Casa and I, both driving our Chevy Impalas, windows not even tinted yet, hung back, since our cars screamed *police.* As the car pulled out of the parking lot, we fell in behind him. Not too close; we didn't want to burn the FFL as having tipped us off. That's how trusted sources end up as former sources—or worse yet, end up dead. Common practice is let 'em get some distance, but don't let 'em get away.

We followed for some time, checking in periodically with Hope. Casa and I were waiting for the word to pounce, noting suitable locations to execute the takedown as we neared them and then watching as we passed them by. Still no word.

We started asking: "Okay, we don't want to run out of road here; when are we going to take him?"

Hope responded: "We're not. We know where he's going— probably the house over on Seventy-Fifth." In our hurry to get to Lone Wolf, I thought that Casa and I must have missed it when the plan for our vehicle interdiction had been changed to a residential search warrant. "Oh—ten-roger. We'll keep eyes on the house and make sure the guns don't leave. Who's writing the paper and what kind of turnaround time are we looking at?"

"No paper," she responded. "Just follow him to the house and come on back to the office."

Not understanding or believing what we were hearing, I replied, "Umm . . . say again?"

"We have a pole camera up on the house. Just make sure that that is where he goes and then come back to the office," she told us. A pole camera is a live-stream video from a hidden camera. It could see the front of the house from the outside but not much else.

Several phone calls later, one to Hope confirming her radio traffic and then questioning the logic of it, followed by ones to Casa and Joe, each beginning with "What the hell?," it became clear that we wouldn't be authorized or allowed to make an arrest, do an interdiction, or conduct any enforcement action whatsoever. We began making our way back to the office.

I couldn't believe we had just followed the suspect to that house and then left. God knows how many different ways they could get the guns out of there without it being seen on the pole camera. Even if we could see it, we couldn't get back there in time to do anything about it.

What was going on? I kept thinking that there had to be a reason, something I hadn't been briefed on. Maybe Phoenix PD was on the house? Maybe the house was being run as an undercover op? There had to be an explanation.

We had more than probable cause, the legal standard to make an arrest, and in my opinion enough to convict criminally where the standard is proof beyond a reasonable doubt. Worst-case scenario would have been that we start a civil proceeding in which we'd need only to prove something beyond a preponderance of the evidence, a much lower threshold.

Regardless, I would have damn sure taken those guns that day. And to all the Monday morning quarterbacks I say, if a judge gave that turd his guns back, then that's on the judge. Or if a jury found him not guilty, then that's the jury's call. Either way, I would have done my job.

After arriving back at the division, my inquiry into what exactly had just taken place was answered by the trio of Hope, Dave, and Tonya. In short: We know better than you, shut up and do as you're told, and this is Phoenix—you're just a new guy here.

Sometime later that evening it all came together in one moment of sudden enlightenment. My mind flashed back to that Scottsdale Gun Club manager wanting something in writing a couple of weeks earlier. Knowing that ATF had told the store to open the floodgates and let these straws buy all the weapons they could afford and getting no real assurances that they would be interdicted, someone at the gun shop foresaw the catastrophic potential. If one of their guns that they had sold to a suspected straw purchaser ended up being used in a violent crime and then traced back, Scottsdale Gun Club management knew the size of the gigantic shit sandwich that they would have to take a bite out of.

I felt like such an ass for being stern with them that day. But why didn't they say something to me? Of course I knew the answer. To them I was ATF—just another part of the problem.

The bigger question was why. Why would we do this? Who ordered it? What was the reason? It didn't make an ounce of sense. One thing I knew for sure: I felt like a stranger in a very strange land.

THE GODS DEMAND
A WIRE

"It's like the underwear gnomes," Casa told me one time as we recounted the latest bizarre goings-on in Phoenix.

"What?" I asked.

"You ever watch *South Park*? There's this episode where all the boys get their underwear stolen by these underwear gnomes. They track them down to get it back and one of them asks why they are stealing everyone's underwear. The gnomes break out this PowerPoint and reveal their master plan: Phase One: Collect underpants ... Phase Two: ? ... Phase Three: Profit."

"We're doing the same thing," he explained. "We know Phase One is 'walk guns' and Phase Three is 'take down a big cartel!'" Both of us were laughing now; a more fitting and appropriate allegory could never be found. Casa concluded, "Just nobody can figure out what the fuck Phase Two is!"

What was happening did at times almost seem like a spoof. Letting guns "walk" was a tactic that I had never before seen or even contemplated. It simply wasn't done. The definition of walking guns would later become a point of contention. Those under pressure to explain the strategy and excuse their actions often hid behind the lack of any recognized definition for the term—the tried-and-true "what is 'is'?" argument. For me, there was never a need to define it; everyone in law enforcement knew what it meant. It wasn't until later, during my first in-person, transcribed interview with the Congressional investigators, that I was asked for a definition. As I explained then, "when it was in or could have been in and quite possibly should have been in law enforcement custody, a decision is made, a conscious decision is made to not take it into custody or to release it. Then it is walked." Under normal protocol, we would have confiscated or interdicted the guns. I couldn't understand how anyone could argue that allowing guns that ought to have been in law enforcement custody to go to known or suspected criminals—people who shouldn't have been near a gun, people who almost certainly would be passing them on to Mexico's most brutal drug cartels—wasn't gun walking.

As the weeks went on, it was the same routine. Hope would get a call from a gun dealer advising that one of our low-level knuckleheads was in the store or on their way there, and purchasing high quantities of the same make and model weapons all at one time. We'd rush out to the respective gun shop, set up in the parking lot, and watch, taking pictures or video as they exited the store, arms full of boxes containing weapons. Sometimes there would be so many they would have to wheel them out on a store cart. Then we watched as they loaded them into their vehicles and then casually drove away. One of the suspects purchased as much as forty AK-variant rifles in the same day. Our coping mechanism was to joke about it. Joe regularly speculated about when that record of forty in one day might be broken, and how we would simply watch it and do nothing.

As had become our routine, we would follow the straw purchasers to a stash house or other location. On occasion, they would meet up with another vehicle and pass box after box from one car to the other. I struggled to reconcile us knowing what was in each one of those boxes, where the guns were headed to, and what they were going to be used for, with how could we just watch them drive away. There were several times we actually saw money change hands. We were ordered to always stay on the known straw purchaser, the one we already knew everything about, rather than follow the new player who left with the guns. We recorded everything we witnessed, wrote reports about it each time, and kept every document involved. Other than that, we just allowed it all to happen month after month. In all we watched thousands of weapons leave, all bound for the carnage-riddled *frontera,* the Mexican border.

We knew where they were going because from the very beginning of Operation Fast and Furious, the guns that we had facilitated them to purchase, the ones we directed the gun shop owners to sell, were regularly being recovered at crime scenes in both Mexico and the United States. Sometimes the recoveries were within merely a day or two after their having been purchased. The term used to describe this is called "time to crime," and a short one is indicative of firearms trafficking. It wasn't mere coincidence. When multiple guns purchased by one individual show up at different crime scenes, it's basically prima facie evidence of trafficking. In short, from the get-go these firearms were meant to be used by criminals.

One rung above this group of straws, and still very much a pawn by cartel standards, was Manuel Celis-Acosta. Short and stocky, in his mid-thirties with dark hair atop his full face, Acosta was a first-level manager and organizer. Acosta was running his own straw-purchasing ring. He appeared to be a subcontractor for various drug trafficking organizations and drug cartels. He wasn't a cartel member himself, although he probably wanted to be, but he was responsible for receiving the orders for weapons, recruiting straws to help fill them, and then arranging their deliveries. He knew good and well that the guns he and his straw ring were purchasing were going straight to one cartel or another.

We had Acosta identified from the beginning. We knew who he was and what rung of the ladder he occupied. We even had his network mapped out. One of the frequent purchasers on his behalf was Jacob Chambers (before being dubbed "Fast and Furious," after the movie of the same name, our investigation was titled after him). In that beginning phase, Hope had done a routine query of several federal law enforcement and phone number databases to see if any of our targets had pinged any other agency's radar. They had.

In December 2009, DEA agents were working a separate case involving a suspect named Manuel Marquez, a Phoenix-based courier who was involved in drugs and firearms trafficking. Several elements of our case had already been identified in theirs.

On December 15, 2009, the DEA agents working the case met with Hope, Dave, and Tonya. Dubbed a "deconfliction" meeting, it became clear that we, ATF and DEA, were working some of the same people. Due to operational security issues, unauthorized disclosures, or simply not wanting your case to get stolen by another agency, it's normally the nature of law enforcement to keep things tightly compartmentalized and as few people in the know as possible. This meeting, however, was designed to be the exception.

The DEA agents told us that a month earlier their wire had intercepted communications between their target, Marquez, and another suspect who was involved in firearms trafficking. Having previously made purchases of AK-variant rifles for Marquez, DEA already had identified him as Jacob Chambers.

Hope then shared with DEA that our investigation had identified Chambers as well, and that we knew he was working for Acosta. The connections now compounding, the DEA agents let out that they knew, through their wire intercepts, that Marquez was working with a guy named "Manuel" but they had not been able to fully identify him yet. Comparing records, it became clear that their "Manuel" and our Acosta were one and the same.

I had worked with DEA long enough to know this: If a suspected offense is not found in Schedule I or II of the Controlled Substance Act, DEA wants nothing to do with it. After all the work, effort, time, money, and headaches involved in building a good case, the last thing they wanted was some other crime rearing its ugly head and screwing up their well-planned dope conspiracy. True to form, the DEA agents were eager to punt whatever information they had about firearms trafficking to ATF, and fortunately, Hope and Dave asked them to do just that. Fully expecting their ATF counterparts to act on it, DEA agreed and in return asked only that they be kept in the loop of any significant events. Shortly thereafter, DEA called again and dropped a fresh new nugget of intel. Acosta was planning a transfer of thirty-two semiautomatic AK-variant rifles to his cartel contacts in El Paso who would then take them the rest of the way into Mexico.

The break of all breaks—it doesn't get any better than that. The brass ring that you're reaching out and trying to grab hold of has just been placed in your lap by another agency that wants no part of it. You see, if the purpose of the case is to stop firearms trafficking, then you interdict this load and shut the group down. If the purpose was to get evidence on Acosta, DEA had just provided all that was needed to catch him in the act. If the purpose was to do a wire, DEA was already up on one and intercepting Acosta's calls on the other end. If the purpose was to take down a cartel, DEA had just given us the chance to jump one rung of the ladder higher than Acosta before we ever even got up and running.

However, four days later, on December 19, 2009, when DEA called with more information about the pending weapons transfer, Hope told them that we were too short on bodies because of Christmas to staff a surveillance team and so we wouldn't be covering it. She never asked DEA if they could help or cover it themselves and they made no attempt at it on their own, either, because it was only a firearms transaction and did not involve narcotics. As had been requested of them, they yielded to ATF as the lead on the gun trafficking aspects. DEA later learned through their case that the delivery had in fact taken place, just as their sources said it would, in El Paso, Texas, on December 22. They even learned the first name of the suspect Acosta had delivered the guns to. And like before, they forwarded all of this information over to Hope.

Later, in March 2010, DEA again contacted ATF with yet more intelligence. Agents from another one of their divisions had fully identified the suspect to whom they believed Acosta had delivered the weapons in El Paso. They had also identified an accomplice and informed Hope and Dave that both of these suspects had been receiving multiple weapons deliveries from Acosta. Then DEA dropped a bomb: through their own deconfliction protocols, they had learned that those two suspects, both above Acosta in hierarchy, were already subjects of a joint DEA-FBI investigation being worked out of another division that had begun back on December 9, 2009.

This was major news, or at least should have been. If those higher than Acosta were already being investigated by other federal agents, then, like it or not, our case had a ceiling imposed. There was no reason to keep following Acosta because we couldn't get to his bosses; they were already wrapped up by the other investigation, which had priority since it involved a higher level of criminal element. Later we would learn from press accounts that these folks Acosta was reporting to weren't just targets of the joint DEA-FBI investigation; they had been cultivated as informants and were in fact assets of the FBI. More shocking, they had been using FBI money to ultimately purchase a significant portion of the firearms. To put it in perspective: According to the press, the money we had seen exchanged for the firearms was FBI money. For these reasons, I believe the FBI assets were ordering the firearms (possibly even at the FBI's direction) through the DEA target, who was the subject of a DEA wire, from Acosta, the subject of our wire. We, ATF, had facilitated the whole thing by coercing the FFLs to go through with the sales, declaring prosecutorial priority so that U.S. Immigration and Customs Enforcement or some local department couldn't actually do anything that might impede or stop the thousands of firearms that we were allowing to be trafficked by the organization.

You can't make this shit up!

Take the government out of this equation and nothing gets done. No guns get ordered by the FBI's assets; no guns get purchased, because there is no FBI money to pay for them; no guns get sold, because ATF is not coercing the FFLs to sell them; and no guns get trafficked, because ATF is not using the guise of a "big case" to allow it all to happen. And a Border Patrol agent named Brian Terry makes it home to Michigan for Christmas because there are no armed bad guys in Peck Canyon, Arizona, that night. None of it ever happens.

Acosta was now ours to arrest. Before another week would pass, we had more intercepts and even actionable intelligence of Acosta personally trafficking firearms—the chance to catch him in the act.

We also had enough to indict him since there was evidence aplenty that he had already trafficked a couple of hundred weapons by this point. The only reason we had waited this long, Hope and Dave constantly reminded me, was so we could work our way up the organization. Now we knew we couldn't have gone any higher—our case was capped. Working past Acosta would only have taken us up through DEA's wire case and then to the suspects of the joint DEA/FBI case whom he was delivering the weapons to, and that case was already two steps ahead of ours.

That made their decision to continue with an ATF wire on Acosta all the more baffling. "What is the point of this?" I asked them regularly. "He's just going to take us back to the DEA targets. Those guys at the DEA are already up a rung; you're just going to get the underlings and straws who we already have identified and the case is already made on."

Their tone was always the same: arrogant and dismissive. It seemed as though I wasn't worthy of an explanation, and so they apparently saw no reason to provide me with one.

Dave's and Hope's minds were dark and mysterious places where I preferred not to venture. But still I searched for answers as to why they seemed as clueless as they did, seeking to build a case against someone who we could already prove was guilty and whose bosses we couldn't get anyway because they were either already bagged and tagged or on the payroll of a sister agency. There wasn't an ounce of logic in any of it.

I would ask them if I could question some of the straw purchasers: interview them, get them to give up something, or maybe even flip them so they would work for us. The answer was always "No, we can't let them know we are on to them, it will jeopardize the wire." They bragged how this case was being watched closely by headquarters and that main Justice in Washington was involved. We were doing what D.C. wanted—going after the big fish and getting this wire was the way to do it. It was circular logic: we had to do a wire on this case so we could get to the guys that were already being investigated in two other cases, by two other agencies, who were already up on at least one wire.

Dave and Hope had briefings and meetings seemingly all the time. They were communicating almost daily with the U.S. attorney's office in Phoenix. From the U.S. attorney himself, Dennis Burke, down to the lead assistant U.S. attorney assigned to Fast and Furious, Emory Hurley, they were all on a first-name basis with Hope and Dave.

The Strike Force was the Justice Department's new pet project, the shiny new crown placed upon DOJ's head, and Fast and Furious was to be its prominent jewel. One of the first major strike force cases, if not the first, ATF and the USAO wanted to show D.C. they could deliver the goods. Perhaps they thought putting a wire up on Acosta would be their way to do it? Perhaps they wanted credit for spearheading something new? Perhaps there simply weren't enough brain waves among them all collectively to toast a piece of bread? Who the hell knows.

There was also the fact that Justice was trying out another bureaucratic experiment—the Organized Crime Drug Enforcement Task Force (OCDETF), which for the first time, beginning in 2009, could include firearms trafficking cases. If a case was given OCDETF status, it was effectively a blank check for ATF to throw as many resources at the problem as it deemed necessary. Money was no object. The Justice Department would foot the bill.

I remember Dave had to go to Washington, D.C., and headquarters to brief the case, at least once—maybe twice. He briefed all the brass: Acting Director Kenneth Melson, Assistant Director William

Hoover, Deputy Director Mark Chait, Deputy Assistant Director William McMahon, and several others. He was so well-received that they also had him brief suits from main Justice, the DEA Special Operations Division (SOD) in Chantilly, Virginia, and, on a subsequent trip, personnel at the El Paso Intelligence Center (EPIC). Dave was at the helm of ATF's flagship case that was going to pop the cherry on the Justice Department's new OCDETF rule change, whether the case actually warranted it or not.

Often state and local law enforcement or the U.S. Border Patrol would seize weapons that traced directly back to Fast and Furious. When weapons were recovered, the serial numbers would be entered into the eTrace system operated by ATF (the only entity in the United States that handles tracing data) and provided to other agencies for the purpose of tracing firearms recovered or seized by law enforcement. The National Tracing Center (NTC) in Martinsburg, West Virginia, has an enormous amount of data; it is able to trace the firearm from the manufacturer or the importer of the weapon, through the wholesale distributors, to the specific gun shop that received it, and then obtain the name of the person to whom the firearm was sold. The system has its limits, however, and contrary to popular belief, there is no database of firearms ownership or sales. No system to just put in a serial number, click enter, and see who owns that gun or put in a name and see how many firearms John Q. Public has bought. Conducting a trace is a somewhat laborious task and it can only give you the first point of retail sale—who bought it new from that dealer and when. It cannot tell you if the weapon has been resold or traded.

The eTrace system can be a very useful tool in criminal investigations, but here's how the system got hijacked by ATF Phoenix. Because we were watching and tracking all of the firearm purchases in the case, we were able to quickly get all of the guns entered into the Suspect Gun Database (SGD, or Suspect Gun). Suspect Gun was created in eTrace so agents could enter a firearm suspected of being trafficked and then find out contemporaneously if it was ever traced as a result of being recovered in a crime somewhere. Although I had never used it before Phoenix (or really even heard of it), it made sense. However, as it was being used in this case (and some others) it was a gross perversion of its intended design. Before being traced, every firearm submitted through eTrace is pinged against the Suspect Gun Database first. If it hits, the trace stops and the agent who submitted it, the case agent (if different), and the group supervisor are all immediately notified by an email from the NTC. The agency that is trying to trace the firearm is not told any of this. They only receive a generic "Delay" notice from the NTC and, by rule, the trace will not proceed any further unless the case agent who listed the gun allows it to.

So, whenever a gun we had put on the list, purchased by Acosta or one of the straws, was recovered and traced, the trace was halted when Hope, Tonya, and Dave were all notified immediately by email. Then they would go or send Joe down to wherever the recovery had occurred, flash a badge, and say "We need that gun because it's part of our big bad federal case that we're working." The outside agency, not knowing the true goings-on, would never actually find out who purchased the gun unless Hope ultimately decided to tell them. She, Tonya, and Dave would then consider that gun as an "ATF seizure" and add it to the stats for the group and the Phoenix division.

It chapped my ass every time. After facilitating these guns to be sold in the first place, monitoring them as they were purchased, all the while knowing that they were destined to be trafficked, tracking them as they were being recovered in violent crime after violent crime, ATF was then claiming credit for seizing them even though we hadn't actually done a damn thing to recover them except take 'em from some good cops who had actually been doing their job. Manufacturing a problem to fit the established solution.

Every time we had one such of these "recoveries," Group VII's trio of sycophants exchanged high-fives while prancing around the office. They saw these weapons seizures as proof that their suspects were directly linked to the cartels—the more violent the crime, the stronger the link. They couldn't see, or chose not to see, that their quest for the big fish was actually causing some of the very crime that we were supposed to be trying to stop. In our pursuit of gun traffickers, we facilitated and allowed gun trafficking.

I offered idea after idea on how to utilize other methods, proven investigative tactics, to achieve the stated goal. Early on I had suggested that we use GPS trackers so that we could better track the weapons and ensure their interdiction before making it south of the border. When they agreed, I felt a sense of relief. Finally we were going to start doing something.

Dave had arranged for EPIC to construct a hidden GPS device into an AK-variant rifle. What should have been a relatively easy task for any full-time technician to perform ended up taking a few weeks. What finally arrived was a rifle with the GPS built into it, but a slightly different variant. This was pretty much useless, since we knew from our observations and statements from the gun shop owners that the suspects only wanted "under folders," which is an AK-variant with a metal frame shoulder stock that could be folded up under the receiver, thus making the rifle more portable and easier to conceal.

Frustrated, but knowing that something is better than nothing, we had the rifle with GPS put into play by one of the cooperating

FFLs. As the straws came in to make purchases, the FFL offered up the bait. Each time they passed on it, insisting only on the under-folder models. Even when the FFL offered it to them at a substantial discount, still they passed. The straws were just filling orders, not allowed to deviate, and different variants weren't on the grocery list. One time, on a transaction of twenty or so rifles, the gun dealer, at our insistence, slipped it into the stack of boxes as one of the purchased rifles. Within an hour, the straw was back in the store exchanging the rifle for an under-folder.

Finally, one of the straws took the bait and purchased the rifle harboring the GPS along with a group of others. As so many times before, we had enough to arrest him on the spot, but we let him drive out of the parking lot with a trunk full of guns. This time, at least, we could track the guns.

The GPS tracker was now in play. EPIC could then notify Hope and Dave where it was, when it moved, and in what direction—even how fast it was going.

We were told to keep a loose surveillance; no need to risk heating them up—to let the GPS tracker do its job.

"Seventeen South," Hope said over the radio as she relayed the information she was getting over the phone. "Still southbound— Passing Camelback Road."

Unknown to Casa and I, there was a delay in the information we were getting; the GPS was being monitored by a technician at EPIC who was then relaying the information to an analyst, who then relayed it over the phone to Hope in the Strike Force office, who then relayed it over the radio to us. Although it was ridiculous that so many links need to be in the chain in the first place (we should have had the capability to monitor the GPS directly), it wasn't overly problematic, until . . .

Hope's voice came out over the radio, "Does anyone have eyes on the vehicle?"

Shaking my head, I thought, *You told us to stay back so we couldn't be seen; if it can't see us—we probably can't see it.*

Someone answered, "Negative."

After a brief pause, the radio crackled again as Hope's voice broke the static: "We've lost the tracker. It may have went down or gone somewhere where the signal can't get out." Looking around as I drove the last known route it was headed, I saw warehouses, storage facilities, acres of tractor trailers parked alongside each other as if someone had sat out a giant set of dominoes, and nearly an entire city block covered with shipping containers and Con-Ex boxes stacked thirty feet high, three or four deep.

My head on a swivel looking around for the vehicle, I pressed hard on the mic key and asked, "Last known location?"

"Fifty-First near Buckeye," she answered, "eleven minutes ago."

Eleven minutes ago! Do you have any idea what can happen in eleven minutes? How far a vehicle can travel in eleven minutes? Needless to say—it was gone.

The maiden voyage of our EPIC tracker had lasted less than an hour. Back at the office, the only concern expressed was for the loss of the GPS equipment and their having to account for that. The guns getting away . . . well, that was business as usual. It was another example of futility, and of a government agency slowing things down, making things difficult, and creating problems rather than solving them. The brains at EPIC could have given us the tracker and the ability to track it directly, but like every other federal agency, their primary mission is to justify their own existence. To do that, they needed to stay relevant by bogarting the one small piece of the puzzle that they had their hands on. It happens every day.

• • •

A few days later, the following Sunday morning, I was driving down the Hill to meet Lane. Lane was the Immigration and Customs Enforcement (ICE) agent assigned to Group VII. Since most international trafficking cases, by their very nature, can transcend traditional agency boundaries and land firmly within those of another, agencies like to protect their interest (God knows that none of the brass ever wants to miss the chance to be hailed at some press conference). The F&F investigation was no exception.

Inherent in any international firearms trafficking case is the potential for violations of ITAR (the International Traffic in Arms Regulations) or AECA (Arms Export Control Act). Although the Department of State and the Department of Commerce's Bureau of Industry and Security may have a dog in the fight as well, physical enforcement of import and export laws at the border falls to the Department of Homeland Security. ICE wanted to protect their stake in the case so closely, Lane had been task-forced over and inserted into Group VII. In an attempt to placate ICE, ATF anointed Lane as "co–case agent" in the Fast and Furious investigation. Rest assured, however—it was in title only.

Lane worked Operation Fast and Furious closely, but like the rest of us, Phoenix ATF would never have let him call any of the shots, either. To them, Lane was a necessary discomfort, allowed only to appease his ICE bosses so that they could help ensure the continued retrieval of weapons from other DHS entities (such as Border Patrol when they would recover some of our weapons), so our suspects were allowed to cross the border unabatedly, and so ICE would pull the reins back on any of its trafficking groups should they happen across any facet of our case.

Unlike DEA, whose mission is very specific, ICE's is much more broad—and they were reluctant to turn over everything that they already had, or might get, to ATF when it involved crimes that they arguably had jurisdiction over. ICE couldn't be ignored or simply bullied to stay out of it for long. Their size and budget were too big, their influence too much in play along the southwest border, and, like it or not, their claim to any international firearms trafficking case was just. Lane was to be their anchor point; he was privy to it all and made sure that a separate ICE report, with a specific ICE case number, was written as a shadow to every one that ATF did.

Lane knew about my gripes with Fast and Furious all too well. He knew I thought it was a clusterfuck. He listened to me politely, never signaling disagreement or agreement. As a new agent, he was reluctant to rock the boat with his chain of command—I could understand that. A good guy in what I perceived as a bad situation, he was a friend and we even played golf together occasionally. We had a tee time that Sunday morning and I was driving on my way to his house when my BlackBerry rang.

"Hey, I can't make it," Lane told me. "The tracker is up. It just started pinging a few minutes ago. It showed up just south of Tucson and is right now on the Tohono O'odham Indian reservation heading south toward the border."

"Shit," I responded. "I'm turning around to switch vehicles. Who else is going?"

"Nobody," he said.

"Okay," I told him, "I'm hurrying and will let you know when I'm southbound in the g-ride."

There isn't a lot of south left between Tucson and the Border. The Tohono O'odham Indian reservation lies about fifteen miles from Tucson and covers the remaining fifty miles to the Mexican border. It's a vast reservation in the middle of the desert, about the size of the state of Connecticut; it has its own communities and its own tribal government, which oversees the roughly twenty-eight thousand tribe members who live there. Essentially, like many other reservations, it is its own separate nation.

Still wearing a polo shirt, shorts, and sandals, I pulled into the driveway at my house. No time to change, I just jumped in my g-ride and started zipping back down the highway.

I always maintained a wardrobe in the trunk of my government car suitable for nearly every occasion. I had a pair of Tru-Spec tactical pants, short and long-sleeve T-shirts, a full battle-dress uniform, raid jacket, a polo, a button-down, extra belt, socks, underwear, and boots. I even kept things like a highway construction safety vest, shirts, and jackets from various utility, Internet, and cable companies in there as well. I had learned a long a time ago to try to be ready for whatever the job had to throw at you. You can find yourself digging through some pretty disgusting places when executing a search warrant—it's nice to be able to change clothes. Sometimes you end up going from trying to stay awake at your desk to kicking in a door in less time than it takes most people to have lunch. Having all your tactical gear with you makes it all the more easier. Sometimes you need to get a little better look at something or have a reason for just hanging out in the same area all day while doing surveillance. If you've donned utilities or some other worker garb, nobody looks at you twice. Working dope and undercover for so long taught me that the best place to hide is often right out in the open.

As I pulled out of the neighborhood, I fumbled around for my BlackBerry to call Dave.

Before I could utter a word, Voth was talking. "Yeah, I know what's going on," he said. "I think Lane is going down there."

"I just talked to him. I'm going with him so that we have some of our people down there," I said.

"Oh, no, don't worry about it," Dave replied nonchalantly. "ATF Tucson is going to help them out."

"Okay," I said, "but wouldn't it better to have someone from Group VII there also?" It was, after all, our case. "I'm already in the car and southbound just a few minutes behind Lane."

"No, don't go," Dave told me. "We've got enough already."

Frustrated, I called Lane and told him about my call with Dave and that he'd be on his own until our Tucson guys caught up with him. Lane informed me that he had spoken with Hope while I was talking to Dave, and that the tracker was now located at a house that was previously part of ATF Tucson's Wide Receiver case, and that was why the Tucson office would be handling it. All I had ever heard about Operation Wide Receiver was that it had been a large case involving firearms trafficking to Mexico, had been worked by our Tucson office, and was a real shit sandwich all its own.

After hooking up with Lane, the Border Patrol and ATF Tucson stopped the car with the GPS tracker rifle inside. It was one of forty-seven guns (the majority of which were F&F guns that we had previously let walk) that they recovered in that load. They also interviewed the driver of the car.

Finally—police work! Exactly what we should have been doing with every load of guns. The interview was an absolute gold mine. The driver, a member of the tribe who lived on the reservation, told how she hauled dope loads for the drug cartels north into the United States and ran guns back south into Mexico. She described how the entire thing worked: who she met with in Mexico and who in the States, how they utilized the reservation to avoid Border Patrol and other law enforcement, how many trips she had made, how frequently she made them, and how much they had paid her for doing it.

But no one was arrested that day. After the interdiction and the interview, the female suspect was released and the agents went on their way. The only exception: firearms were actually seized.

During my entire time in Group VII, this was the only seizure that occurred as the result of any proactive measures, or action of any kind, by ATF. It would always anger me whenever I would hear Dave or Hope or Tonya or Gillett or Newell say how we had seized hundreds of guns in this case. *No,* I would think, *good cops who had been out there doing their jobs had seized those guns . . . All we did was just took the credit for it.*

Even granting the Tohono O'odham seizure to ATF gave me heartburn. To see them all pace around the office, worried and voicing their concern over having lost the GPS tracking device, whose fault it was, and how they were going to explain it, only then to see their relief and happiness upon its recovery, with never a mention of any of the other guns in that load or the countless loads before. I will always contend that what occurred that day was an equipment rescue mission and the only reason we took any action to seize that load of firearms was to recover the tracker. The other forty-six weapons were merely by-product . . . the price that had to be paid for doing so.

After that incident, I decided to see if I could install my own tracker. I went to a local electronics store and bought a small, slightly larger than a pager GPS tracking unit, and then went to Cabela's and purchased a replacement grip for an AK. After a few late nights around my kitchen table with only a Rotozip mini saw, a file, and some epoxy resin, I had done what those full-time government technicians at EPIC had been unable to do—I had built a working GPS tracker that would fit an AK under-folder. (And I did it in two days, not weeks, and for less than two hundred bucks.)

Utilizing the included software, I set it up to where anyone with the passcode could log in and see its whereabouts, even with our smartphones, and have it immediately at our disposal as we were actually in our cars conducting surveillance. As an added bonus, it could notify us by text if it had laid up somewhere and then went on the move again. I took the homemade tracker to Lone Wolf and, with the owner's consent, installed it on an AK under-folder. Andre agreed to try to include that rifle in the next load that our straws purchased.

Since the EPIC tracker had been recovered during the seizure on the Tohono O'odham reservation, it too was placed back in Lone Wolf's inventory and was to go out with the next shipment. Both trackers went out together with the next load.

The ad hoc tracker worked perfectly as some of us watched on our smartphones and it led us to a previously unknown stash house, out in the Surprise area of the west valley. Eleven minutes later, the EPIC tracker led the others to the exact same place.

Normally, discovery of such a stash house meant we were kicking in a door before anything had the chance to leave. But, since "this is Phoenix," we were told to call it a night and go home. They would let us know when EPIC called and advised that the tracker was moving again. Reluctantly, we again drove away from yet another prime warrant opportunity and yet another load of weapons destined for somewhere south of the border.

When I got home, I immediately jumped on the computer and set up the alert to notify us if the low-budget tracker went mobile. Having only a single battery as a power source, it had done its job by leading us to the stash house that night, but now, after more than three days, the battery died and it went offline. However, EPIC continued to advise that their high-speed/low-drag tracking system had not moved from the location.

A few days later, amid worries that the battery had died in it, too, there was a feeling of relief when we heard it was back up and on the radar. Until, that is, we learned it had signaled its position as being fifty miles south of the United States border. I asked Hope and Tonya if they were at least going to notify Mexican authorities of its location so that they could attempt to interdict the load. But then I was told that the battery in that tracker had died as well and they no longer had any way to know its whereabouts.

My anger and frustration continued to grow. As the days and weeks went by, we stockpiled more and more of the same information. Knowing where these guns were going, we still did nothing. We just sat by and watched.

I agonized over our inappropriate relationship with the gun dealers, encouraging the sales of firearms that we knew were unlawful and that we did not intend to seize. I would think back to that day with the manager at Scottsdale Gun Club. It had become obvious by this point that the owner of the club, having been in it longer than I, had already realized that what we were doing didn't pass the smell test. His shop, a well-respected local business, had been cooperating with ATF Phoenix for years now and was just seeking some assurances or protections. Now, as I had become suspicious of what we were doing myself, I wondered what else he knew that I had yet to learn.

We were putting the gun shop owners in a very bad position: encouraging them to make sales that they normally wouldn't have made, when all the while we knew that the guns were going to various drug cartels. We were not stopping or interdicting them in any way, or even trying to.

The FFLs genuinely believed they were doing the right thing cooperating with our investigation. The natural assumption was that ATF was preventing the guns from being trafficked because they were no longer turning up at crime scenes and being traced. Dave and Hope perpetuated this myth by assuring the dealers that, although it was ongoing and "sensitive" in method, we were on it, making every effort and seizing the firearms. Truth is, it was a fixed ballgame.

Because the gun shop owners were cooperating with us, we could enter the weapons purchased by the straws into the Suspect Gun Database within hours, or days at the most. When they were recovered at the border or in Mexico, many after being used in violent crime, and traced, they would ping on the database—which immediately halted the trace by the National Tracing Center. No longer getting trace requests meant to them that the guns were no longer being recovered at crimes. Therefore the gun dealers were none the wiser and would conclude that ATF must have a handle on it; must be doing something.

The owner of the Scottsdale Gun Club, however, became leery about what his shop was being asked to do. Seeing what, again, was all too foreseeable, he expressed his concerns in an email to Dave. "I have friends with the Border Patrol," he wrote, "and wouldn't want any of these firearms to be used against them."

Having requested a meeting, the owner of the SGC met with and was assured by Dave and the Phoenix U.S. attorney's office (USAO) that he needn't be concerned—ATF and the USAO would never allow any of those weapons to end up in the wrong hands.

When a sense of duty or obligation wasn't enough, and their assurances were no longer placating the concerns of gun dealers, ATF Phoenix and the USAO, so invested in the success of Fast and Furious, didn't hesitate to apply a little pressure. ATF handles not only the enforcement side of federal firearm laws, but also the regulatory side. Gun shop owners know that their ability to operate their business, their very licenses, and even their industry as a whole are regulated solely by the ATF. Not cooperating with an ATF investigation could mean that regulatory problems, inspections, fines, and even loss of license may be coming down the pike. Again, it was a fixed ballgame.

As I later found out, during one meeting with the owner of the Scottsdale Gun Club, when he seemed reluctant to continue "helping" with the investigation and again asked for some assurances, he was told, "You know, we're not on the regulatory side of the house [meaning ATF], but we do have lunch with those guys." Veiled though it was, everyone in the room understood it to be exactly what it was, although the real intent of it will probably forever be denied.

The owner of Lone Wolf, Andre, was one of those who really thought he was helping us out. He was patriotic and motivated by a sense of duty, right and wrong, good guy versus bad guy. ATF Phoenix took full advantage of this. Andre had been a helicopter pilot in the Army and looked every bit the part. Having logged more time in the back of helicopters than anyone should ever have to, I had gotten to know several "Army aviators" during my time. It's not hard to pick out the helicopter pilot, in any crowded bar, anywhere in the world.

Lone Wolf was the store where the majority of the purchases we were tracking took place. Andre had been instructed to keep far more inventory of AK-variants than he ever would have normally. He let us behind the counter when our straws were in purchasing and ATF put cameras up in his shop so we could watch, in real time, without the daily bother of even having to be in the parking lot. At one point, Melson, our then acting director of ATF at headquarters in Washington, had the IP address so he could watch the live camera feed as well. For what reason I don't know, nor can I even think of one.

Over time, I noticed it appeared that the agency's relationship with Andre grew more and more inappropriate. Several of us guys in the group remarked about it. Sure, we had all gotten tips from gun dealers before, had asked them to call us if someone came in their shop, had seen this person, things like that. But we had never before seen an owner working as a confidential informant on the hook daily and embedded into an investigation. I didn't even think it possible since it seemed clearly a conflict of interest—ATF regulating the industry and all. I remember once when Andre asked about all the profit he was recording due to the high volume of the straw's purchases and whether ATF would be collecting it. He was told no, it was his to keep, and even advised on his obligations to report transactions over ten thousand dollars to the Internal Revenue Service. It was all so unheard-of.

– 4 –

MAKING THE OMELET

Inside the Group VII Strike Force, two camps began to emerge. There were the minions of leadership—Dave, Hope, and Tonya—who all insisted that we continue ahead with the plan and had full support up the chain of command up to and including the acting ATF director and main Justice itself (it was so often pointed out how much they loved this case). Then there were those of us who opposed or questioned the logic of the strategy being employed and argued that we pursue a different one.

At first that latter group was limited to just Casa, me, and Joe Medina, whenever his FTA wasn't around. Around March, we were joined by another. Transferred in from Tennessee, Larry Alt was as good as they came in ATF. Besides being a part-time instructor at the ATF National Academy and a former major in the Army Reserve, Larry was a bona fide, card-carrying member of the bar association.

In his former life, he had been an attorney and even a prosecutor with the Maricopa County Attorney's Office. Like me, he quickly sensed that what we were doing wasn't right. But unlike me, Larry possessed a certain amount of couth.

When members of our group voiced objections, we would do it in our own ways. Casa would often go into Dave's office and close the door, only to come out frustrated. Alt would be more diplomatic, but still ended up frustrated and irate. As for me, being somewhat challenged in the art of diplomacy, I was more inclined to just call things as I saw them, a trait that more often than not led to Dave and I butting heads.

I'm the guy with the broken Kanuter valve. The neurons fire, the brain formulates a thought, then the thought passes unabated through the defunct Kanuter valve (which is supposed to catch or filter such things and thus allow for an evaluation of some kind) and straight to and out of the mouth. By this point, we all knew that this ill-conceived plan was going to get somebody killed.

There was also a third group—not cheerleaders for Fast and Furious, but not vocal opponents, either. They simply went with the flow. But there was more to it than just taking the easy way out. They wanted to believe that those in charge deserved to be there. That they were experienced enough, smart enough, capable enough to reach the proper determination and make the important decisions. They wanted to believe that the brass, including those at main Justice, knew what they were doing, and so they trusted in the system. Their default was to the status quo.

When your bosses, those in the chain of command, tell you over and over again something that you know isn't true, you would think that the resolve of even the most loyal employee would begin to wane. That so many people, agents, and prosecutors, from the rank and file in the Phoenix Division, through those at ATF headquarters, and finally up to main Justice itself, failed or refused to speak up or put a stop to the program was one of the most damaging things that could have happened. Apathy is what allows things like gun walking to be possible.

I too tried to find the logic behind our leadership's actions. As a cop, especially working undercover, I had made the determination that sometimes the ends do justify the means. I'd already faced those hard decisions. But until Fast and Furious, the measure had always been a sliding scale of ends versus means; with each end capped by a red zone that the other was never allowed to penetrate. What we were doing in Phoenix was to achieve the ends by whatever the means.

Dave and the others tried to sell us on this approach, so much so that once my challenge of this strategy was countered with the argument, "If you're gonna make an omelet, you've got to scramble some eggs." Easy to say when you're the chef, not so when you're just a little oval sitting in a carton with eleven of your buddies.

But the more I saw of the leaders at the top of the operation, the more I understood where this mind-set came from. When I met Bill Newell, the Special Agent in Charge—the top dog in the ATF Phoenix office—I understood how vacuous the leadership actually was. Newell was the "golden boy" of ATF. He spoke fluent Spanish and had been with ATF for years. At headquarters he was considered an up-and-comer. It looked to me like he had come up too quickly, without logging sufficient time in the field actually doing what agents do—working cases.

I didn't exactly meet Bill Newell so much as encounter him. Tall and thin, he had short blond hair and small, wire-framed glasses. He reminded me of Lurch from the old *Addams Family* TV show. The first time, he was walking through the office on the sixth floor one day looking for Hope. If I hadn't learned before that Hope was Newell's favorite, I did this day. "Where's my sunshine bear?" Newell shouted as he stalked down the hall, leaning and peering through doors and over cubicle walls.

After finding Hope seated at her desk and saying a word or two to her, he turned to Casa and me, and announced, "You know, if I had six more agents like her, that'd be the only group I'd need here in Phoenix." That was it. That was also when I knew we weren't going to get any help from the top of our chain. We lacked strong leadership. And that all appeared to be fine with the golden boy who was in charge of it all. Tensions continued to mount—so much so, it could no longer be ignored.

Although the email came from Dave, more than likely it was George Gillett, the ASAC, who decided it was time to address the matter. The general consensus was that Dave wouldn't wipe his ass without checking with Gillett first. The guy didn't have an ounce of initiative and could seldom muster an original thought.

"It has been brought to my attention that there may be a schism developing amongst the group," Dave wrote. "This is the time we all need to pull together, not drift apart. We are entitled to our respective (albeit different) opinions however we all need to get along and realize that we have a mission to accomplish.

"Whether you care or not," it continued, "people of rank and authority at HQ are paying close attention to this case."

His aside again confirmed D.C.'s involvement in the case—and it definitely bolstered the confidence of people like Hope and Tonya. The Fast and Furious case was a big moment for ATF, especially the Phoenix office. The leadership basked in the attention they were getting from ATF headquarters and from main Justice. Dave, Hope,

Tonya, Gillett, and Newell all saw the national recognition of Fast and Furious as their ticket up. And none of them wanted to miss the ride.

The purpose of the Friday evening email was to call a meeting of the whole group for the following Monday. Some wondered what would happen at the meeting. Me—I simply assumed that I would be receiving yet another ass-chewing. They had become somewhat regular by that point. My main concern was trying not to be goaded into saying something that could get me fired.

On Monday morning at nine thirty, George Gillett sauntered into the office. He had a goatee and wore an earring. Not a little thing either; it was one of those that you couldn't help but notice. I had heard a comedian say once: "If you're a man over forty and you have an earring in your ear, you better be a pirate." Since hearing that, every time I saw George I laughed to myself and thought, *Arrr, matey.* Earring aside, he was always well-dressed: nice suits, silk ties, expensive shoes, everything matching, everything fitted, everything pressed.

Dave stood with Gillett in the front center of the room. The rest of us were seated at our desks and I couldn't help but feel that I was back in the sixth grade again.

Dave began the meeting introducing Gillett as if he were some hard-to-book celebrity guest, praising and thanking him for trudging all the way down to our office, in reality barely a two-mile trip.

Then Gillett started his monologue. It was largely a rehash of the email Dave sent on Friday, which bolstered my suspicions that Gillett was the true architect of the email and the one who had called for the meeting.

"We all need to come together," he said. "This is a great case. Everybody knows what a great case it is. You guys aren't going to ruin it by pissing around and arguing and fighting."

Although Gillett was speaking before the whole group, Casa and I glanced at each other in acknowledgment that we both knew he was talking to us.

Gillett's tone became more stern. He turned his gaze on me, squared his shoulders and leaned his torso slightly forward, raised his right hand and extended his index finger, pointing at me as if lining up a set of sights.

"I don't want to hear any more talk about walking guns," he demanded. "You don't know what walking guns is."

Staring down the barrel of his finger, I wasn't angry as much as I was impressed. It is rare in government work that a supervisor will dress down an employee in such an open forum. Protocol suggests that it be done behind closed doors; it's more common to simply stab him in the back, put him on the "shit list," and make his life hell until you can get rid of him somehow—all the while telling him face-to-face that there's really no problem at all. For Gillett to do it in this manner—I had to give him credit. The way I saw it, although he was misguided in his aim and supporting the wrong cause, it did demonstrate a level of leadership that has become all too rare in federal law enforcement. Right or wrong, at least he had made a decision and then acted upon it.

I just sat there and took it. To them, I was a nobody, insignificant and expendable. There was no way they were going to tolerate me standing in the way of the biggest case in ATF: the "flagship case" that they were at the helm of.

When the meeting ended and Gillett made his way out, it became clear that there was no point in trying to change the direction of this case. The course was set. It was full steam ahead, and we could either get on board or get run over.

Word of Gillett's appearance—and my getting reamed—quickly spread throughout the division. Sometimes it was said directly. Sometimes I could just sense people were thinking. *Man, Dodson got his ass handed to him.* Regardless, it was clear what to expect if anyone dared voice any objection. With all that was happening and all that I was witnessing, losing battle after battle, day after day, I began to notice a change in myself. I had always been confident. Now, even though I had these strong gut feelings, I began to second-guess myself. Maybe there was something I didn't know? Maybe I should do what everyone was telling me to do, what so many other people were doing. Maybe I should just go along—to get along.

The confidence I once had was fading fast and the beginnings of a little voice in my head began questioning everything, telling me that I couldn't do anything right.

A few weeks later, Dave got his wish. The Justice Department had approved the affidavits of our wiretap request. We were but a switch throw away from him having his wire.

The most important thing to know about our receipt of a wiretap authorization was that it could not have happened without the oversight, involvement, and approval of senior officials in the Department of Justice. The process for a field group in ATF to receive wiretap approval is lengthy and complicated, requiring clearance from a long laundry list of higher-ups. I believe that the affidavits clearly spelled out the tactic of gun walking. At any step in the process, someone could step in, ask questions, and put a stop to it. No one did.

The assistant U.S. attorney for Arizona assigned to work the Fast and Furious investigation was Emory Hurley. He could have blocked the wiretap. He didn't. As the lead prosecutor for the Strike Force, he had every reason to earn brownie points and get some face time with the folks back in Washington. As soon as his boss, the United States attorney for Arizona, Dennis Burke, read the request and accompanying affidavits, I was sure he would shut it down. Didn't happen. Finally, I knew it would never make it past the deputy attorney general's office in Washington, D.C. Not only would they shut it down, but someone would be collecting scalps over it. That didn't happen, either.

My last thought, knowing that we hadn't met the legal requirement of "exhaust all other investigative means," was that a federal judge would for sure shut it down. That didn't happen, either. The judge may have personally recognized the ill-conceived nature of the strategy and even disapproved of it. But lacking any legal basis to the contrary, if he found probable cause, he would grant the order. That was part of the problem: the murky waters of federal law do not prohibit gun walking as an investigative tactic; neither did ATF and DOJ regulations at the time. The practice was simply so stupid that no one ever thought we needed some rule to say that it couldn't be done.

Hope had never had an OCDETF or wiretap case before, and she asked me, and the others who had, a number of questions about it. We tried our best to help her, especially Casa and I. Knowing the fecal tempest that lay ahead for her, we told her what to prepare for, how to lay the groundwork, and to delegate what responsibilities she could because she would soon be overburdened and spread entirely too thin. Working a wiretap is very laborious and consumes loads of manpower. You always have to have an agent in the wire room and must maintain a full surveillance team 24/7. If you get some chatter on the wire, your surveillance team is tasked with making the actual observation or taking whatever enforcement action is necessary. That said, we needed help.

As a result, Phoenix requested that headquarters authorize a GRIT (Gun Runner Impact Team) deployment to help us. Gun Runner is yet another funding initiative whereby money is allocated to be thrown at a specific problem. Once approved, agents from all over the country, some volunteers, some volunteered, descended on

Phoenix for a hundred-day deployment. This was a win-win for the
brass. Not only would they have the splash, accolades, and good press
from the F&F case, but now they could pad the numbers for GRIT
(deployments, arrests, seizures, etc.) and go back to Congress and say,
"Look what a great job we did with that money. Now we need more
so we can do an even greater job."

For the detailees, however, it was a mixed bag: Yes—one hundred
days of per diem was a significant amount of extra change, and staying in a nice hotel, or even a resort if you could get the government
rate, was always cool. But it was one hundred days away from home
and friends or family, and it was one hundred days in Phoenix—in
the summer no less. At times in the summer you could make a good
argument that Phoenix was somehow millions of miles closer to the
sun than the rest of the planet.

Adding to the challenges for them was the fact that Fast and
Furious was, by that time quite literally, a hot mess. Misguided and
mismanaged, it continued to grow and sucked the life out of everything that happened to cross its path. The GRIT detailees were im-
planted throughout the division: some in Group VII assigned to work
F&F with us, some in Group II to assist with their new "storefront"
operation, others assigned to various other enforcement groups, intel
groups, and the regulatory side.

The detailees assigned with us in Group VII were but a representative sampling of agents everywhere, I suppose. Some saw what we
were doing and asked questions or voiced their objections about it,
some saw it and simply tried to avoid it, others simply continued with
"go along to get along." A rare few saw it and seemed to not have a
problem with it (or the would-be feather in their cap from working
on ATF's flagship case), and some others either didn't recognize what
was going on or simply didn't want to. Ironically, the GRIT agents
who I saw voice objections to us walking guns were soon off the F&F

case and found themselves working much smaller lead cases, which were sent out from the intel shop.

A lead case is just that, "a lead" that needs to be followed up on. The intel group developed them when a firearm was recovered, whether in the United States or Mexico, but Group VII was only given those with a nexus south of the border, purchased in the Phoenix area, and had a relatively short "time-to-crime." We were issued these leads and then ordered to go out and interview the purchaser as part of a potential trafficking investigation.

I was stunned. Interview the purchaser? A seizure with a short time-to-crime was a lead to possible trafficking? Why the two playbooks? Two different sets of rules? Over here we have interviewing the purchaser as a good thing, a mandated thing, done so in furtherance of an investigation to try to develop a case and/or take it to the next level . . . and yet over here, on this side of the room, the F&F case, where that is not allowed, forbidden even, we are told that it never works, the "straw purchasers won't cooperate," and "even if they did we would only get the straws and they are a dime a dozen," easily replaced, and we'd have no chance of reeling in the "big fish." I was living in Bizarro World.

With our ranks now swollen by the influx of GRIT and the wiretap up and running, we set out on our busy summer. Dave prepared the team's schedule. Rather than assigning those of us who knew our way around the city and were familiar with the suspects, their residences, their vehicles, etc., to the surveillance squads, he assigned the GRIT detailees, all from different parts of the country, to that. Casa, Alt, and I found ourselves working eight-hour shifts in the wire room.

The wire room was located on the fourth floor of the DEA building, just down the hall from our Strike Force office. Accessed by security card reader and requiring special authorization, it was a large open room, taking up a little less than half of the entire floor, with different computers and various other electronic workstations along the exterior walls. Several tables and desks were grouped together in the room's center regions, forming three different pods or islands. These pods, tabletops full of computer screens and keyboards, notepads, phones, and headphones, is where the wire intercepts actually took place. One pod was working our ATF case, the other two on DEA wires. As a call was received or placed on a monitored line in an investigation, the screens of that pod would flash a banner and an alert would ring out. The intercepted call could either be listened to through headphones or over an external speaker. Every call was logged, time-stamped, and recorded by the computer's wire-intercept software and transcriptions and notes were added to round out each logged entry.

Hanging on the wall adjacent to the access door leading to the hallway was a large flat-screen television. Wired for both watching cable broadcast channels and as a computer monitor, we had dialed up the IP address of the pole camera covering Acosta's house. From the wire room, we could watch via live streaming video all the comings and goings and whatever activity might happen to take place in the front yard.

The law requires that all wire intercepts be monitored—someone actually has to listen to it as it happens. The investigative idea behind doing a wire is not to get the "dirty call," one bad guy talking about criminal activity with another, but rather to get the evidence that the "dirty call" leads you to—who is involved, what is happening, and exactly when it happens. That way surveillance units can be dispatched and either observe and document the activity firsthand or take enforcement action if possible.

Ideally, agents or task force officers (TFOs) are assigned the duty of monitor. But in many cases, the targets of the intercept may be speaking in a foreign language, requiring the use of translators. Such was the case in ours. There are companies that exist solely for the purpose of providing this wire-translation service. (Most of them, coincidentally, happened to be owned by retired DEA or FBI agents.) These companies are contracted on a case-specific basis and they must ensure that their monitors/translators meet certain language proficiency standards, have gone through an extensive background investigation, and have obtained (or be qualified to receive) the needed security clearance as required by the case's classification.

Of the wires I had worked on before, two required translators in the wire room: The first were Spanish speakers because we were working a large Colombian trafficking investigation. The second was Patwa (from *patois*), as we were trying to take down a violent Jamaican posse, as they were called back then.

Working the wire room was a welcome change. For one of the few times in my career, I had set hours, was home every night with the kids, and had plenty of time during the day to get caught up on paperwork. Knowing exactly when you're getting off work and will be home is a luxury little known to field agents and grossly underappreciated by most people.

Plus, I was surrounded by some wonderful folks. Taking full advantage of my assignment, I got to know the monitors and even made a friend or two. We had fun and laughed a lot. I would make drink and snack runs to the vending machines or Circle K for them. They would share their lunch or bring some in for me—keeping me filled with some of the best home-cooked Mexican and southwestern food you can imagine. They helped me work on my Spanish, sometimes including things no gringo should ever know how to say.

Case-wise, the wire was an abysmal failure. My first day in the wire room I learned that, in spite of all that talk about "moving up the chain," we weren't even targeting Acosta's phone. For some reason still unknown to me, the first two lines we went up on, wiretapped and began to intercept the content of their calls, belonged to an underling of Acosta. Even knowing only what was explained to them in their initial briefing, this didn't add up for the monitors either. They couldn't make sense of why we hadn't included Acosta's phone from the start and asked me for an explanation. As had already become the custom, I had none.

Although they were not agents or law enforcement, the monitor's full-time job was working wires: one after the other, case after case, contracted by nearly all the different federal agencies. Besides speaking the language, their experience had taught them the lingo, what was important, what was a code word or secret message, and how to decipher much of it. Sitting on wires, all day every day, they knew how these investigations were supposed to go from the minute we flicked the switch until the second we took it down. They were true experts in wiretap investigations and had more experience working actual live wire intercepts than anybody in the building. Any agent worth his weight in salt would have recognized this and utilized them as the true assets they were. Not so in this case.

As the first two weeks progressed, I recall only one phone call coming over the initial two lines—telemarketing that went straight to voice mail. The monitors, having literally nothing to do all day and all night, kept asking me, "He's obviously dumped these lines; did they get the new ones?" "Do they know how to get the new ones?" "Are they going to go up on the new ones?" "Why don't they go up on Acosta's?" All good questions—and I still didn't have any answers for any of them.

As time went on, I found that I was being assigned to the wire room less and less. The monitors and I joked about it being because Dave must have realized that I wasn't miserable enough in there. Even though I began working on other things, I would stop by the wire room and catch up with my new friends, run to the store for them, have lunch with them, or just help them out if I could. I wanted them to know that they were considered, even if only by me, valuable assets. They would bring me up to date on the progress of the case, traffic on the new lines as they had gone up, anything else that might be going on. And oh yes—they had more questions for me; plenty more.

After going up on several dead lines, Hope, Dave, and Tonya finally hit on a couple that were being used. However, as the criminal element seldom deviates from trends among the popular culture, these guys communicated either in person or via text message—they weren't talking on the phone much. The monitors showed me as one text message after another alerted across their screens but they could not read any of the content because the intercept order didn't allow for it. Visibly frustrated, they asked me, "Why don't they get the text messages?" Meaning, why weren't we getting the authorization to monitor them.

When writing up a warrant or affidavit, a lot of it is simply boilerplate. The only original writing involves case-specific details (who, where, when) and establishing your probable cause. One of those boilerplate paragraphs covers text messaging. If you have probable cause that your suspects are using an electronic communications device (in this case a cell phone) in furtherance of their criminal activity, it's an easy lay-up to get approval to monitor the text messages; it requires little more than pasting that paragraph into your affidavit. Surely, ATF headquarters knew this. Main Justice is staffed almost exclusively by lawyers, all government prosecutors no less; certainly they knew it as well. Why had no one told them to include it in the affidavit?

I went to Hope and Dave and asked them about it. "We don't have enough probable cause," I was told. No probable cause? Disagreeing, I presented to them a more than persuasive argument to the contrary and clearly demonstrated that we did in fact have probable cause. Our suspects were text-messaging to cooperating FFLs about their firearms purchases! Once, while one of the straws was texting as he was buying a load of guns at one of the cooperating FFLs, their security staff had zoomed the store's surveillance camera in so close that you could actually read the messages, which clearly indicated gun trafficking. The FFL had even given us copies of that video.

It was utterly ridiculous. We had active text-messaging occurring between known suspects, before and after firearms transactions, being logged in on the active wire we were up on already, and they were telling me that we didn't have any probable cause to intercept text messaging.

Providing no argument, no evidence, and no point of fact to the contrary, they refused to waver.

I began pressing the issue now, feeling that if this had truly all been about obtaining a wire, then by God we should at least do it right and try to get some evidence from it. "Why not just include the text-message paragraph the next time it's up for renewal, or in the next affidavit we do for any additional lines we spin off on? The verbiage is the same; all you have to do is cut and paste it in there, no extra work, no extra writing. Just put it in there and we'll let the judge decide." Bothered by my persistence, and perhaps even more so by my unintended suggestion that an independent arbiter might in fact rule against them, Hope and Dave dismissed my idea entirely.

The same held true for tracking the location of the targeted phone by either its built-in GPS tracking device or triangulating the signal tower information. The intercept software used on the computers in the wire room was designed to handle it all: phone and number identification, voice recordings, transcriptions, notes and comments, text messages, and even the GPS tracking. "Why didn't you guys include tracking in the order?" the supervising monitor asked me. Pointing to her screen, she showed me how the software divided it all into sections, kept it organized and stamped, logged, and tracked it all as the information would come pouring in. Only in our case, it was barely a trickle, and her many different sections weren't all processing information—several displayed a banner that simple read "No Intercept Data." Again, as with text messaging, a single boilerplate paragraph included in the affidavit would have allowed for us to track the movements of every active phone we intercepted—down to the meter. And again, they didn't include it when obtaining the order because, as they again explained, "We didn't have enough probable cause."

Like the military, law enforcement has its own jargon. Each has words, phrases, or acronyms specific to the vocation, but many cross over and are applicable to and used in both fields. *Snafu* is one such example. Almost always used improperly in the modern vernacular, it doesn't mean an encounter with an error or problem that is significant and unexpected. Those of us who know and have experienced situations that it describes usually just roll our eyes in condemnation when we hear things like "We've hit a snafu." Believed to have first been used by American GIs during World War II and probably best defined by Frederick Elkin in 1946, a SNAFU, as it was originally spelled, is "a caricature of [government/agency] direction. The [agent] resignedly accepts his own less responsible position and expresses his cynicism at the inefficiency of [agency leadership]." SNAFU is "situation normal: all fucked up."

As more time passed the status was the same—SNAFU. This frustrated the monitors even more. Not only were they listening to the intercepts as they occurred and watching the live video feed from the IP camera pointed at Acosta's house, but the monitors were also privy to our radio traffic. So they would hear known straws talk about an illegal firearms purchase and hear over our radio system how we had agents watching the purchase. Then they would listen as Hope relayed information received directly from a gun shop owner—

"Surveillance team be advised: suspect has——————AKs and is walking out the door." They would turn their heads and watch on the large flat screen hanging on the wall in front of them as the straw occasionally unloaded the guns into Acosta's garage—sometimes it already having gun boxes stacked four or five feet deep inside. After seeing, hearing, and knowing all of this, their jaws dropped as they heard the agents clear the area over the radio, go to lunch, or go off duty entirely, and then Hope, Dave, and Tonya would stick their heads into the wire room on their way out, smile, and say, "See ya tomorrow."

Most of the monitors were of Mexican descent and some had family on both sides of the border. "Why, John?" they asked me. "Why aren't you guys doing anything?" Their questions would always hit me hard: "You know where these guns are headed and who's getting them. You know what they're going to be used for! How can you guys just let this happen?" I felt helpless and sick about it, sick about still not having any answers, and sick about our perpetual status—SNAFU.

At one point, all the wires had gone down. Hope hadn't submitted the renewals in time and so had allowed the intercept orders to expire. Missing my friends, I swung through the wire room at least once a day hoping to find them back at their pod. On one such trip, I found Hope seated there instead, a folder open in front of her as she scribbled something on a piece of paper. "Any word on when we'll be back up?" I asked her.

"No," she said. "We have to wait for Breuer to get back to D.C. He's been out of town."

Her blatant attempt at name-dropping completely lost on me, I said, "Who's Breuer?"

"DAG Breuer?" she asked in mocking disbelief. "Head of the Criminal Division and OEO?"

I didn't know who Deputy Attorney General Breuer was, and honestly, I didn't give a rat's ass, either. What I did know was that if any other agent in any other division had failed to submit a renewal order in time to keep an active wire from going down, they would have had a piece of their ass gnawed off and another case agent would be running the show before the seat of the chair even began to cool. Another thing that I knew: I had never before seen the DAG sign off on a wire or renewal application; usually, such things are delegated out. So she was either full of shit (which is entirely conceivable) or DAG Breuer was so invested in the case, he gave the order that he wanted to review the applications personally.

I was still struggling with everything by this point, trying to keep my mouth shut because it seemed every time I opened it, all it got me was more trouble. I felt isolated. My ideas about law enforcement, being an agent, being a cop, were constantly being challenged. Everything seemed so different to me now: right was wrong, wrong was right, up was down—it was all chaos.

– 5 –

RENEGADE

In May 2010, soon after my very public declaration to Hope that we were going to get someone killed, I found myself starting to be cut out of the F&F investigation and ostracized from Group VII as a whole. Dave had started giving me a few lead cases to run down, assigned me to do several nexus reports for other agencies, and relegated me to handle some of the group's more mundane duties. He farmed me out to every other agency that asked for a hand with something. Truthfully, I didn't mind that part. I enjoyed working with DEA, FBI, and BP—at least they were all out there actually doing something.

At some point that spring, a friend of ASAC Gillett who ran a local gun shop in town called him with some information on a suspected straw purchaser. Gillett passed it to Voth; Voth assigned it to me.

I drove out to the shop and got all of the info from the owner. The suspected straw had come in and purchased some firearms on several occasions. The last time, after the sale, he had jumped into a car with a Hispanic man that the owner had never seen before. Something just didn't seem right about it to him. I began with all the usual things: driver's license check, criminal history, background check, previous traces, etc.—nothing. So, my options limited, I drove out to the guy's house and rang the doorbell. (The legal standard I needed for just talking to someone: none.)

Answering the door, he stepped out onto the carport with me when I identified who I was and why I was there. He struck me as an average, blue-collar kind of guy.

"Hey, you bought a few firearms recently," I told him, as we stood in the carport. "We have a problem with firearms trafficking here in the Southwest. If you wouldn't mind, I'd like to check and just make sure that you still have them."

He gave it up on the spot: "I don't want to go jail; I just needed the money. I've been buying for this guy named Fernandez." (I recalled in my head what Hope had said to me so many times: "Straw purchasers won't cooperate with you." *Bullshit!* I thought.)

He gave me the whole story, all the details that he was aware of. The guy wasn't holding anything back. I didn't want to wrap up some poor, sickly dude for straw purchasing; I wanted to climb the ladder. Not only because I thought that that was what we were supposed to do, but because I wanted to show Hope and Dave that it could be done. Hoping to take the next step, I gave him the "ninety seconds to change your life" speech, or sometimes called the "Come to Jesus." Regardless, it always ends with the question "Witness or defendant? Which is it going to be?"

I was asking him to become a confidential informant (CI) for the ATF, and he agreed. Most people think CIs are all criminals who are only trying to help themselves. That's true for many, but not for all. Some are just normal folks who, for whatever reason (unforeseen circumstances, financial troubles, addiction, stupidity, what have you), find themselves having made some bad decisions and landing on the wrong side of the law. Others still have committed no crime but volunteer to be CIs out of a sense of civic duty or desire for justice. Lastly, some are professional CIs that do it solely for the money—and the good ones make a lot of money. These are the ones that give me the most concern, but that's another story.

I knew this guy wasn't working for the cartels, but whoever he was buying for might be. I went back to the office and briefed Dave on what had happened. Much to my surprise, he liked the case and seemed excited about it. For the first time in a long time, I felt a sense of comfort. I had done what I had always done, how I thought something should be done, and I didn't have any teeth marks in my ass for doing it! Maybe the world was righting itself?

Having briefed the CI that he couldn't do anything with Fernandez until I could get a plan laid out and approved, I told him to keep me informed of any developments. He called me on the following Saturday; Fernandez was on the way to his house and he wanted him to go buy a couple of guns for him.

"Shit!" I said. I told him to just sit tight. Our entire group was out working that day. Group VII's number had come up to help work the gun show that weekend.

Casa, Joe, and I were assigned to the parking lot. How Joe escaped the tutelage of his FTA that day, I'm not sure. After speaking to the CI, I called Dave, who was, naturally, hanging out at the command post. I brought him up to speed and asked him if we could break away, cover the CI during the meet, and then land on Fernandez either when he fronted the money or when he showed back up to get the guns—whichever worked best.

"No," Dave told me. "There's too much going on. We can't break away from the gun show to deal with this." Standing in the parking lot where the three of us had been parked all day fighting off the boredom, I looked down into their cars. Both lay back in their driver's seats, fully reclined, their faces barely visible above the window line. Casa was fast asleep, an audible snore growling out of his window; Joe was texting and playing games on his new smartphone. Hell, right before the CI called, I was half asleep and playing solitaire.

Seriously? I thought to myself.

"Can't I call some of the GRIT guys to come out?" I asked. "That way I'm the only one who has to bug out for a bit."

"No," Dave said again. "They're all busy with Hope's case"—in other words, Fast and Furious. "She has some stuff going on."

Defeated, I told him, "Okay, I'll just scrub it. I'll see if he can buy us enough time until we can get people free, set it for another day or something."

"No—do the deal. Just tell him to do it."

I couldn't believe what he had just said. I had to make sure I heard it right, so I shot back, "You're telling me to tell the CI to go buy for the dude?"

"Yeah," he responded, unperturbed.

"We're, we're not even going to cover it?" I asked in disbelief.

"Just make sure he tells you where he buys 'em from. You can go by there afterward and grab the 4473s."

Whatever feeling of comfort I had was now replaced with panic. My mind was inundated with a flood of thoughts, each one sparking its own specific emotional response, all seemingly contrary to the one before. *Do I? Don't I? What do I do? Tell him okay? Tell him to kiss my ass?* In that moment, with confusion and fear pulling me to one side, better judgment pulling me to the other, I compromised myself by deciding on a modified go-along-to-get-along strategy. I would do what they wanted but still continue to argue and fight against it.

"Okay," I said to Dave. "If you say so."

If I was going to have to do this, I was going to do it the best way that I knew how. I called the CI back. "I need to meet you—now," I told him.

I slipped away from the gun show and met the CI behind a nearby gas station. I gave him my digital recorder, taught him how to use it, and told him that every word he and Fernandez spoke to each other had better be on it when he gave it back to me. I told him to text me or call me every step of the way and gave him a signal to use in case something went bad and he needed me to pull him out.

The CI went and waited for Fernandez. I took a position nearby and watched as he arrived, met with the CI, gave him some money, and then left. The CI called me and filled me in on the conversation: Fernandez told him which gun store to go to, what to buy, and to call him when he was headed back with guns.

"Meet me back at the same place before you do," I instructed him. Unbeknownst to the CI, I watched as he made the trek and filled the shopping list. We then met back behind the gas station. I took the purchase receipt from him and photographed the pistols, making sure to document the serial numbers of both. I listened as he placed the call to Fernandez and then sent him on his way. Back to my previous position, I again watched as Fernandez arrived and put the pistols in his car, I watched again as he drove away. I then retrieved the digital recorder from the CI and I was back at the gun show in less than an hour. I hadn't missed a thing.

I called Dave. "It's done," I told him.

"Okay," he said. "Do you know where he bought them?"

"Yeah. I'll go by later and grab the 4473s."

"Make sure you put 'em in Suspect Gun," he told me, referring to the database.

"Ten-roger." And I hung up the phone.

When Monday morning rolled around—I barely made it into the office—Dave was there waiting for me in the hallway. We had been through this God knows how many times before, so I was familiar with the routine. I plopped down in my regular chair on the other side of his desk, he in his.

I only half listened to Dave's latest rant. These rants had become so common that I don't remember the specifics of this particular one. I managed to stay quiet until he said something that compelled me to bring up yet again how we were walking guns. However, now not only were we doing it in Fast and Furious, but we were doing it in the Fernandez case as well. I argued, as I had so many times before, that the gun dealers making these sales were no different than a CI doing it at our direction. And since the gun dealers were doing it on our behalf, that made them all *agents of the government*, and we were just as culpable as if we had sold them ourselves.

It's like this scenario: A neighbor suspects that the man who lives down the street is selling drugs, he breaks into the man's house, takes some pictures and a small amount of drugs, and turns it over to the local police as evidence. Although it was illegal for the neighbor to do this and he'll probably—or at least he should—get arrested himself, the cop can use the evidence against the drug dealer and obtain a search warrant for the man's home. The police haven't violated anyone's rights or committed any crimes (the Fourth Amendment protects from unreasonable search and seizure by the government—not by your neighbor), so the evidence is admissible. Now alter the sequence slightly: The neighbor goes to the police and says he suspects the man who lives down the street is a drug dealer. Not having any evidence, the cop instructs the man to break in, take some pictures and a small amount of the dope, and bring it back to him. The neighbor does so, but in this instance, none of it can be used as evidence against the suspected drug dealer. Because the cop had instructed him to, the neighbor was acting as *an agent of the government* when he broke into the house—a violation of the other man's Fourth Amendment rights since now it was a government intrusion into his privacy, and thus the evidence is inadmissible against the man.

In Fast and Furious, when we would tell gun dealers to conduct sales to straw purchasers that they'd normally, independently choose not to conduct, they were acting as agents of the government. Similarly, when the CI in the Fernandez case completed a straw purchase at our direction, he was acting as an agent of the government. I couldn't understand why Voth didn't realize that. He didn't see how that made us responsible for every gun that was sold under our direction.

"This is no different than if we were selling them ourselves," I said to Dave.

This was one of the few times Dave actually focused in on me after I made that statement. Perhaps I had finally gotten through, finally made the point?

Dave, apparently done with our argument, asked me, "Can this guy introduce you as an undercover?"

"Probably," I answered. "When I debriefed him, I went over several possibilities, ways we might want to take the case. Doing an intro was one of them."

"Have him introduce you as a straw purchaser," Dave ordered. I could see the wheels turning in his head.

"I had run that by him," I explained, "but the problem is we'd have to buy-bust him [arrest Fernandez on the spot] and we haven't had time to find out all we can yet."

"No we don't," he said. "We don't have to bust him."

"Okay. You want me to have a CI introduce me to Fernandez as a straw purchaser so I can straw-purchase guns for him?"

"Yeah," Dave responded. What he was asking was if we could actually cut out the middleman and have me deliver the guns myself, and without landing on Fernandez right away. His intent was to allow Fernandez and the firearms to walk away—unabated. My argument had backfired against me. True, I had finally gotten through to him, finally made a point—but absolutely the wrong one. Rather than proving a wrong, I had inadvertently created a worse.

When I walked out of Dave's office I grabbed Casa and Alt. "You're never going to believe what Dave just told me to do."

I recounted the story.

"Well, that's crazy," they both said. "What are you going to do?"

"I'm going to do it," I answered coolly. "He's the supervisor; that's what he wants me to do. What other choice do I have?"

A couple of days later I called the CI back up and told him to make it happen.

Over the next few days, I amassed a stack of the regular paperwork that I needed to get done, some reports on the Fernandez case, and some other stuff. As on occasion, I had been scheduled to work the wire room for the Fast and Furious case, so I planned on knocking it all out while I was in there. Sitting there chatting and joking around with the monitors, my fingers poking at the keys on my laptop, I managed to get it all done. I don't think we got an intercept at all that day.

Dave had walked in and out of the wire room several times throughout the day, frantically checking if there had been any activity. "Nada," I told him.

I had no way to access the secure net from the wire room, so as soon as I finished my shift, I carried my laptop back to my desk and docked it in its station. I ignored the many alerts notifying me that I had new emails until after I was done uploading the reports to NFORCE.

Finally done, I thought I'd clean out the inbox real quick before heading home. Weeding through it, I saw an email from Dave. Rude and unprofessional, it chastised me for not having turned in the reports from the Fernandez case and said I needed to "make better use of my time" until I did. I checked the time stamp on the email.

"That son of a bitch!" I said—aloud. I had those reports done since lunchtime. On one of his strolls through the wire room, I had told him that they were done and that I was going to upload them as soon as my shift in there was over. He had walked straight out of there, back to his office, and sent me that email, making sure to do it before I could get the reports in and uploaded. He was on a witch hunt against me, manufacturing a paper trail of bogus crap so he could justify some punitive action against me sometime in the near future. Pissed off, my first instinct was to walk into his office and punch him in the throat. But knowing the win-win that would be for him (I get fired and arrested), I refrained.

Figuring I needed to calm down, I started to leave. Before I got out of the seat, though, I hit the reply button and started banging at the keyboard. I was careful not to cross the line; I knew he was keeping paper on me and I wasn't about to give him any free ammunition. I carefully crafted an email explaining how I had been "utilizing" (making sure to use quote marks) my time "wisely" and that all the reports were now in NFORCE. Lastly, I ended by pointing out how his email was unnecessary since we had seen each other and spoken multiple times that day when he had come in the wire room. I hit SEND and left the building.

I couldn't have been more than ten minutes away from the office when my cell phone buzzed. It was Dave: "I don't know what you think you're doing. I don't know who you think you are!" He was irate.

Screaming into the phone, using his big-boy voice, he said, "You go home and stay there. You're on leave tomorrow. I just checked with the ASAC [Gillett] and I *can* put you on leave. So you're on leave and you better have your head straight before you come back in. Got it?"

Having not said anything since "Hello," and feeling somewhat proud of myself because for a change someone had flown off the handle and it wasn't me, I asked him very calmly, "So, I'm on leave tomorrow?"

"Yes!" he screamed back. "You are!"

Me, still calm as ever: "Am I getting paid or am I on the beach?" (suspended without pay).

There was a long pause; I pictured him on the other line asking Gillett while covering the receiver. Finally, and in a voice much different than before, deflated, he was confused and stammering, "Uhm . . . yeah," he said. "I can put you on leave but I can't give you days off [suspend without pay] or anything like that."

Tactical situational recognition (TSR) is having the uncanny ability to quickly identify your immediate status, interpret both the tangible and intangible factors at play or affecting it, and utilize that to achieve or, if having achieved it, to exploit your tactical advantage. I like to think of it as a gift.

"So I'm off tomorrow, getting paid for it, and it's not costing me any leave?"

"Well, um . . . yeah."

"See ya on Thursday." And I hung up the phone.

I spent Wednesday donating two sleeves of golf balls to the desert surrounding the course near my house. I left my cell phone at home and just tried to put everything out of my mind.

When it was time to go back to work, I met up with Dave first thing. He was having breakfast at a restaurant near our office; I walked in and sat down at the bar beside him.

"What's the problem here?" I asked earnestly. I wanted to try to understand what had sent him over the edge. "I saw you ten different times when you walked into the wire room. You saw me writing the reports. I even asked you a question about one of them while you were standing there and later told you that they were done and only needed to be uploaded. And then you go right out and send me that email. Are you witch-hunting me here?"

Still eating and trying hard to not have to look at me, Dave said, "There's no witch hunt. I just didn't know about your email but I get it now." He gave off the impression that everything was fine, like there was no problem at all.

Over the next few months, every couple of weeks or so I'd get another email from Dave telling me that I was late on something. Every field agent doing his or her job is always late on one thing or another. The amount of bullshit involved with doing anything in federal law enforcement is all but overwhelming. I don't contend to be a paperwork guru and openly admit that it has always placed well below catching the bad guys on my list of priorities, but I always managed to get it done, a few days late maybe—but done and done right. The odd thing was, if Dave was so concerned about the time-liness of our paperwork, why was I the only one getting these emails? And why send them when he was sitting in his in office ten feet away from me—often having just spoken with me about it? I told him that morning at the restaurant and two other times when I tried talking to him, "I know I can't survive the witch hunt." I'd seen it done to good agents and to bad ones. When the bosses come after you like that, you can't win; you can't even end up in a tie. The best you can do is buy yourself a little time.

"Look," I explained to him, "I know I can't win. If you want me gone, help me find a place to land and I'm gone. I won't fight it. I just don't want to go to some shithole somewhere."

"I don't want you gone," he would tell me. I'd get to my desk, sit down, and *ping*—another bullshit email.

As tension was growing around the office, so too did the Fernandez case. I first met Fernandez, the gun trafficker my CI had been purchasing for, at the Cabela's in Glendale, Arizona. It's a huge building, two high-vaulted floors filled with nearly everything you could imagine for the hunting, fishing, camping, or other outdoor enthusiast. The store had not only firearms but boats and ATVs filling a large section of the ground floor and continued outside along one entire side of the building. Cabela's was part of WestGate, an entertainment complex connected by an outdoor mall full of shops, restaurants, and coffeehouses. It also included the University of Phoenix Stadium, where the Arizona Cardinals played, the arena where the Phoenix Coyotes hockey team took the ice, and the largest IMAX theater I had ever seen. I had been there many times before. Being Glendale, it was west valley and close to my house. Many times at night, I would find myself standing on the small wall behind my pool in the backyard, looking out over the west valley and seeing the lights from WestGate as they illuminated the desert sky with a large amber dome.

I had set the meeting there because I knew there would be enough parking and foot traffic for the cover team to safely deploy and still be able to blend in. Also, we knew the capabilities of Cabela's store surveillance cameras—and they were much better than anything we had. Casa was tracking our every movement using their system.

I sat out in front of the store on a large, wooden bench waiting for Fernandez. We had already identified his black Mercedes-Benz and saw it as soon as it pulled into the lot. He walked up and sat down on the bench beside me.

Hispanic, in his late twenties or early thirties, slightly on the stocky side, he had come straight from work at some construction job. Fluent in English and Spanish, he was intelligent and easy to talk to. He was no moron, no gangster, no thug; he was just a regular guy, like so many others. I had done my homework and already knew much more about him than he would ever know about me. He lived with his wife in a nice house on the south side of town; they had a couple of kids and, as far as I could tell, were living within their means. For whatever reason, whatever turn his life had taken, he now needed a way to make some easy extra cash and this is what he had come up with.

He talked a good game, implying that his "people" were the real deal, that money wasn't an object, and that his volume was huge. One thing was for sure: throughout my years of working undercover, I had been on both sides of meetings just like this one—many more times than he had. It was evident he was peacocking. We talked, strolled around a bit, and then parted ways after setting up our next meet. The surveillance units followed him out of the area and then broke off and headed back downtown.

Countersurveillance is always a concern in undercover (UC) ops. The last thing you want is for the bad guy to follow the UC back to the office, or to a staging area, or anywhere that makes him as the police. Or even worse, follow him home, find out where he lives, and identify his family. So measures are used to defeat it. They say experience is a good teacher, but I can attest that bad experience is the best. Knowing that Fernandez had driven away, my concern fell to the unknown: Did he have others there as I did? Were there folks we hadn't identified who were watching everything I did and where I went next? Cognizant of this, when I left Cabela's I took a cleaning route—I went the long way, making quick and unpredictable turns, backtracking here and there, sometimes stopping on a green light and sometimes going on a red. Once satisfied that no one was following me, I headed back to the Strike Force office.

Fernandez and I were still in our courtship stage. We hadn't yet developed any trust. So a few days later, on a Saturday, he called the CI again and wanted him to purchase a couple of Draco pistols, high-powered pistols modeled on an AK-variant rifle. The CI immediately called me, and I immediately called Dave. My plan was to have the CI do the purchase, disable the guns, and then interdict Fernandez after they were in his possession. Maybe arrest him, maybe not—recovering the guns and keep the arrest in the bag for when we needed to use it later. I'd make that call after it all played out.

Dave, however, had another plan. He told me that no one was available because of things happening with F&F. I argued that I could get it done with just the help of two other guys, but still he said he couldn't spare them. Frustrated, I told him that I would just have the CI pull the plug on it then. Dave told me not to, and instructed me to let it go—just like before. Reluctantly, somewhat sickened, I told him okay and let it happen—just like before.

My case with Fernandez was progressing; we were talking and texting almost daily. Dave called me into his office one day and told me that he needed me to write up a proposal about it because we had to submit it to the new ASAC, Jim Needles, for approval. There had recently been a realignment in the Phoenix Division. Needles had taken over for Gillett after Gillett was suspended for forty-five days. With Group VII now falling under Needles and him no longer reporting directly to his close personal friend Gillett, Dave overtly displayed his displeasure with the realignment.

He said I had to describe why we needed to do the straw purchases for Fernandez and what we were hoping to get from the whole case. Admitted micromanager that he was, he told me what points to use, which ones not to, how to lay it out, what language to have in it, the order I needed to quote that allowed for it, everything. He might as well have written the damn thing by himself.

My TSR tingling, I asked him, "You ... [pointing at him] ... want me ... [pointing at me] ... to write a proposal ... [pointing at his computer] ... asking the ASAC ... [pointing south, in the direction of our Division Office] ... for authorization for us ... [finger pointing up and circling] ... to straw-purchase firearms for Fernandez?"

"Yeah," he responded, obviously confused by my feeling the need to have to clarify.

Uncontrollably, a small grin began forming on the right side of my mouth. *Finally!* I thought. Finally I would spell out in writing, right there in black-and-white. Finally somebody would see how stupid Dave was and finally put an end to this. The mere fact that our new ASAC had suddenly ordered the proposal in the first place I took as a sign of something heretofore unseen—someone in leadership challenging Dave and this strategy. If not challenging yet, at least asking questions instead of just drinking the Kool-Aid.

"I'm on it," I told him.

"Good," he said. "I need it right away."

I walked back to my desk and had barely sat down before Dave emailed. "Here is the order we need to include." Attached was the ATF order with part of its language highlighted. The order said essentially that ATF agents do not immediately have to make an arrest upon witnessing a straw purchase. The intent of the order is to let the purchase happen and then arrest the straw when he delivers the firearm to the actual purchaser in the parking lot or other nearby location. Again, Phoenix was distorting the rules, using the system in ways so absurd, no one ever thought a need to spell out its prohibition—and headquarters, the USAO, and the Justice Department were not only allowing it, but encouraging it and applauding themselves for the results.

I drafted the proposal and sent it to Dave. He walked out of his office and over to my desk. He had printed it out, made corrections all over it red ink, and handed it back to me.

Two more times this played out, until finally, after inputting all of his corrections, I sent him the third draft . . . no more red ink.

I've never seen the final draft, so I don't know what else Dave changed, added, or took away. Sometime later, he told me he had sent the proposal up to Needles.

Several days later, Needles wanted to meet about the proposal, and we headed over to the division office. Dave, Alt, GRIT team member Gary Styers, and I waited in the conference room up on the ninth floor. Needles was running late. Dave moaned about having another meeting that he had to run off to soon.

Needles finally arrived and we started going over the proposal. After several minutes, Dave excused himself and left for his other meeting. The rest of us continued. With Dave gone, I felt I could speak more freely. I told Needles how we had argued with Dave about Fast and Furious, how the gun dealers were agents of the government, how we were just as culpable, and how we might as well be selling them ourselves. I presented the proposal as evidence of the ridiculousness—I didn't want Needles to approve it. I never thought in a million years that he would. I wanted him to see the folly I was pointing out in Fast and Furious.

Much to my surprise however, Needles didn't ball up the proposal and throw it the trash can. Instead he said he'd have to get with SAC Newell, who was out of town, and run it by him. *Holy shit,* I thought *Can anybody in this outfit make a decision?*

A few days later, Dave raced out of his office. Excited, he pointed at me and said, "I just heard from Needles. It's a go! Set it up!"

Have you ever heard the expression "banging your head on the desk"? I did nothing to slow it down, either, just a straight frontward fall from a sitting position in my chair—with a loud bang as my skull crashed on my keyboard and sent it sliding into the monitor.

Casa sat directly across from me. The half-wall cubicles allowed us to see everything the other did. He leaned forward and whispered, "Document ev-er-y-thing."

Lifting my head a few inches, I banged my forehead twice more—signifying my acknowledgment.

I thought of pulling the plug, sabotaging the case, or just simply refusing to do it. But honestly, I feared the repercussions. Feeling I had no fight left in me, I had succumbed. Giving in, giving up, going along—whatever you call it—is so much easier. To be swept up with the herd of your fellow lemmings as they dash for the cliff's edge is much easier than trying to stand your ground. Letting the ocean's wave take you as it rolls and crashes on the shore is much easier than trying to keep standing with your feet planted on the bottom. Sometimes the allure of what's easy can seduce us. Sometimes it seems everyone is taking the easy way. Sometimes easy just doesn't seem that bad. And sometimes, when things have become too much and you just can't do what's hard anymore, easy is all that's left.

Whenever I met with Fernandez, he had said his connections to the drug cartels also wanted military-grade stuff: hand grenades, automatic weapons, etc. I decided to try to exploit that angle. Military-grade weapons are not available on the open market and what is available is strongly regulated by the National Firearms Act (NFA) and ATF. If you deliver one, somebody goes to jail as soon as they pick it up. So, if I could get the deal to happen, we'd have to buy-bust Fernandez immediately and avoid the whole straw purchase aspect.

However, the process to get weapons allotted for the sting was so overly complicated, if not intentionally delayed, that I couldn't get approval in time to use them.

The day of the deal came. Still conflicted, now more than ever, I felt a knot growing in my chest. At the office, Dave gave me the funds to purchase the firearms that Fernandez wanted—six Draco pistols. He told me to use my undercover ID to purchase the weapons.

"No," I said, "I'm not going to use my undercover driver's license on the forms."

Besides the fact that I didn't want to compromise my undercover identity for future cases, and it was a pain in the ass to get a new one set up, there was something else. I suddenly remembered Casa's words. Though only uttered as a whisper, they now echoed loudly in my head: "Document ev-er-y-thing."

Whether a warning, prophecy, or merely good advice, they had planted a seed in my mind that quickly sprouted: this was a trap. In an ironic culmination of the witch hunt being orchestrated against me, they were having me build the very pyre upon which they'd tie me before igniting it. If the shit hit the fan, they could say I went out and bought the guns with my undercover ID and sold them to Fernandez on the side, to make money, against their knowledge. I was rogue, or dirty, or whatever. Regardless, I feared the trap was being set.

I demanded that Dave sign "dealer letters" for the guns. A dealer letter is on official stationery and has to be signed by a supervisor. It states that the firearms are needed and being purchased for official government use by ATF (the agency—not the agent) and as such the buyer is exempt from having to fill out the 4473 form and from the background check requirement. Covering my ass, I wanted it on record that ATF was buying these guns—not me. Before I left the office, I got with some of the others on a takedown plan. If I was going to act like a straw purchaser, I needed their help to make sure that these guns were not going to get away from us—whether Dave agreed with that or not.

The plan: I would buy the weapons, call Fernandez, meet up with him, and deliver the guns. I would borrow a car that didn't reek of "cop" to do the deal—a rental from one of the GRIT guys. They would cover it and then stay on Fernandez until I switched back to my g-ride and caught back up with them or, if need be, they'd take him down sooner. That was their call to make. As soon as Fernandez headed south or passed the guns off to someone else, we would stop them to interdict and at least recover the weapons. If we could manage making it look like it was unrelated and maintain my cover—great. If not, oh well. Either way, we were landing on those guns.

With the plan drafted, I set out on step one. I thought it would seem odd to the gun dealers for me to actually buy guns—they knew me too well. I was right. It wasn't like I was there off duty picking up something for me; I was there buying Dracos for a trafficking investigation. Andre at Lone Wolf, where I bought four of the Dracos, offered me a discount. I declined. I didn't want to have to go through the paperwork nightmare of returning unspent cash. Same at the second gun dealer, where I picked up the last two. I gave them each an original dealer letter, signed by Dave, to file in their records. I pulled each one close, leaned in, and said, "Whatever you do, don't lose this." Stressing the point as much as I could, I added, "If anyone ever comes asking about these guns or wanting this paper, give it to them. But make sure you keep a copy. Don't give them anything until you make a copy of it." Though confused by the whole thing, they nodded and agreed.

I was running late to meet Fernandez. I got back to the office, switched vehicles, and hit I-17 north. I had borrowed a red Ford F-150 pickup truck from one of the GRIT guys. Since they were deployed on temporary duty, they all had gotten rentals. I put the guns on the front seat, hid my badge and wallet in one of the console compartments, and pulled out my Gerber multi-tool. I dragged each pistol into my lap, partially disassembled it, and tried to clip, file, or bend the firing pin—anything to retard it enough to keep them from striking the primer, preventing the gun from firing. I wasn't sure if it would work, if it would be enough, but I had little time and I had to try something.

I whipped into the parking lot of the gas station where we scheduled the meet. I met Fernandez and we put the Dracos in the trunk of his car while surveillance watched our every move. Fernandez gave me the cash for the guns plus an extra hundred dollars for each one— my payment for having done the deal.

With some amount of street cred now established, I was still trying to steer Fernandez away from me being a straw. I told him I was an expert at putting secret compartments into vehicles. I was thinking if all the smugglers in Arizona came to me to install their compartments, we could put anything in there, including GPS trackers and listening devices. Fernandez seemed to like the idea and said he would talk to his people about it. All in all, it was an oddly normal meeting: fast, not too much talk, and then we went our separate ways.

The surveillance team followed Fernandez to a storage facility in Glendale. I got back to the office, switched back to my Chevy Impala, and headed out there. On the way, I heard them talking via the group-talk feature on the phones that Dave had procured for us with Strike Force funds; they were headed back to the office. I hit the transmit button of my phone. "What's up? Where are you guys going?"

They had been pulled off to assist in the F&F case.

My blood was boiling. I went to the storage facility, determined to work this case as it seemed it would have to be: by myself. I maintained vigil on the facility for several days, waiting for Fernandez—or the guns—to make a move. I immediately started working the phone, trying to get the prop guns so I could set up the buy-bust before he had a chance to deliver them. That endeavor proved more complicated than need be and ultimately moved too slowly to effectively be put into play.

The following week, I was scheduled to return to Virginia to attend my niece's graduation. It would be my first time back since arriving in Phoenix. It was originally planned for ten days but I changed the itinerary. I couldn't in good conscience leave those weapons unobserved. I left the storage facility and drove to the airport on Friday afternoon. I returned from Virginia on Monday and drove straight back there.

I had no clue whether the guns were still there or not; anything could have happened while I was gone over the weekend. The next day I changed tactics and shifted my focus to Fernandez himself, becoming his shadow. Still frustrated with the prop gun situation, I finally managed to "appropriate" one from the other Phoenix group. I set up the buy-bust with Fernandez and then briefed Dave.

"Can't do it today," he told me. "Too much other stuff going on." Over the next ten days or so, twice more it played out this way—I'd set it up and Dave would shoot it down, each time citing a more pressing event, a more important need.

As bad as all this was, it had actually helped me. By pushing me over the edge, polarizing me finally to one side, the constant struggle inside me to either ride the train or be left at the station was resolved. I felt more personally responsible than ever and guilt joined the long list of emotions that now percolated inside me.

I was working completely on my own, so much so that some started calling me "Group 7.1." Noting that I was actually trying to recover guns in a case, Casa referred to me as the "Renegade." The moniker didn't bother me at all.

– 6 –

DEFEATED

I had never felt so isolated in my job. Fortunately, even though my professional life was circling the bowl, my personal one was just starting to climb out of it. Keri worked for the DEA, on the third floor in their fiscal department. I had introduced myself a couple of months earlier when I saw her and one of her coworkers up on the fourth floor near our Strike Force office. I spotted the two of them around the office together on several occasions. Both were very attractive and personable, and I enjoyed running into them whenever I could.

Keri had long dark brown hair, brown eyes, and a radiant smile. Her outward glow instantly caught my attention. Lovely and over-flowing with energy, she seemed to beam with happiness. Her beauty was captivating, her charm infectious. You knew instantly she was genuine in every way.

I had a couple of conversations with her. I learned that we both lived in the same neighborhood. It was mostly young families, so to find another single person living there seemed unlikely. Finding one that was also beautiful, had a great personality, and worked in the same building seemed downright lucky to me.

One Friday afternoon at about four, our group's administrative assistant was looking for someone to go down to the third floor and grab a ream of copy paper. I volunteered.

After getting off the elevator, I turned right and went through the security door. Strolling down the hallway, sticking my head in every room and around every corner, I was just taking it all in and seeing what's what. People's behavior never ceases to amaze me; some would look at me and then quickly turn to someone else with that "Who is that guy?" look, hoping for some kind of assurance. Others would merely see me, give a nod, or maybe even say "Hey." Regardless of which reaction, the assumption was always the same: "He's here, so it must be okay for him to be here." (Again, the best place to hide is sometimes right out in the open.)

Having made the rounds, I worked my way back to the copy room. Stacked along the wall I found my sought-after prize. Office supplies are generally worth more than their weight in gold in government buildings. As I reached for it, I noticed a DEA building directory taped to the wall near a phone.

Checking the clock and hoping that she might still be at her desk, I grabbed a pen and scanned the directory. There it was. Her name and desk number. I scribbled the information down, grabbed the paper, and took a step toward the door. Suddenly I was surprised by someone who was just walking in; neither of us had been paying much attention and we almost collided. I recognized her instantly—Keri.

"Hey," she said. "What are you doing here?"

"Oh, um, not stealing paper if that's what you think," I replied.

Glancing down at the large box of paper I was holding in my arms, she looked back up, cocked her head slightly to the right, crossed arms, and put on a slightly playful smirk.

"I'm appropriating, not stealing," I explained.

"Uh-hum."

"We're all one big government." My bullshit now almost too much for even me to handle. "So we can't steal from ourselves."

"Okay," she said, losing her smirk, "but that paper isn't for you guys."

Sensing an alarm bell would start ringing at any second now, I felt somewhat short on time. "I'm glad I ran into you," I said, "I read that there is some kind of social tonight at the yacht club in our neighborhood. Do you ever go to those things?" The yacht club was a small building that housed two little paddleboats and two tiny sailboats and it sat on the shore of a rather large retention pond as you drove into our neighborhood.

"No, I don't," she answered.

Knowing that this could go only one of two ways, yes or no, I called an audible and asked, "Well, how about going out for a couple of drinks or something tonight?"

I've never understood the many games played during courtship. Why is it a big deal to simply ask someone out? Worst they could do is say "No." And how bad is that—not very. Bad is having your cover blown as you're standing in a heroin den in southeast D.C., bad is getting shot, or bad is getting poked by a dirty needle—for the third time—when you're arresting some junkie. Bad, like most things, is relative. Someone not wanting to go out with you may be disappointing, but it's not bad. "No problem, just thought I'd ask." And you move on. By this point in my life, I had been married twice, divorced twice, and had two kids to raise. I should have been much more afraid of someone saying *yes*.

Keri would later tell me that that's why she accepted my invitation: because I wasn't afraid and had just asked her, right on the spot. She said she could appreciate that and found it attractive.

We exchanged numbers, and she gave directions to her house so that I could pick her up at 6.30 P.M.

"Sounds like a plan," I said. "See you then."

That night, we went to the Sandbar in Glendale. We drank a few beers and shared an order of nachos. While we were there I told her about my getting her number from the directory and how I had planned on calling her as soon as I got back to my desk, but fate must have intervened otherwise. She told me how every other woman in the finance office had warned her to never go out with an agent, but for some reason she thought it okay to risk it.

We spent a lot of time sharing stories that night. She told me how she had two young daughters and how her husband had abruptly ended their marriage. We had a lot in common.

After all that was going on at work, spending time with Keri over the next weeks was a great escape.

Since we spent nearly every evening together, and our children were spending the summer with their other parent, Keri basically moved in for the summer. We went to a couple of barbecues together that other guys from work hosted at their houses and she began to get a better idea of what was going on with me at work by listening to some of them talk about it.

One such time, a lot of us were at Joe's house, including Casa, Alt, and Gary Styers. Styers was one of the GRIT guys brought in from the Lubbock, Texas, office to help out with Fast and Furious. He was stocky and gruff; I liked him. He was a great guy, and a damn good agent.

I don't remember who said it first, or how exactly it even came up, but when we were talking about Fast and Furious that day, somebody's crystal ball had been spot-on: "We'll be lucky to get out of this without a congressional inquiry." Politics, Washington, and Congress were way off in a vastly distant realm. Inhabited by politicians and bigwigs, staffers and lobbyists, we knew it as the root of every stupid decision and policy that came down the pike. It was more of a commentary on what we deemed as the obvious repercussions of something so stupid rather than a prediction of things to come . . . or so I thought.

We knew we were watching a train wreck about to happen. Forced to be a part of it, none of us really knew what to do or how to stop it. Some of us had tried but were publicly berated for doing so, all the while being told how involved ATF headquarters and DOJ were and how great they thought it was. Who were we to question such authority? Or more important—how?

At one point that summer, our then acting ATF director, Ken Melson, traveled out to Phoenix for, in that all too overly used phrase, a "town hall" meeting with us.

Melson and select upper echelons were making the rounds to all the divisions and our number in Phoenix had come up. The order had been handed down that the town hall was mandatory.

Nearly two hours of being force-fed nugget after nugget of mind-numbing bullshit, the meeting was basically a self-affirming admiration of, by, and for the brass, all in an overt display of incompetence and government ass-kissing. "Hey, aren't we great at headquarters?" "Why yes—yes you are great at headquarters. Aren't we great here in Phoenix?" "Why yes—yes you are great out here in Phoenix." "Look how lucky you are in getting to work for such great leaders." Mercifully, Melson finally concluded the town hall by asking, "Who's ready for lunch?"

I raised my hand to affirm that yes, I was indeed ready for lunch.

"Oh—wait, wait, we have a question in the back," Melson said. "Everyone sit down; we have one last question. You there in the back." His finger was pointing straight at me. "Stand up."

I leaned forward and began to rise. I was in the spotlight at this point, so I thought, *Hey, might as well take advantage of the opportunity.* The broken Kanuter valve was in full effect. Casa, Medina, and a few other agents I had gotten to know by this point were seated near or around me. "Don't do it, Dodson . . . Don't do it," I heard whispered from somewhere nearby. Deciding, for once, it seemed, to play it safe, I heeded the advice. "Sir, everyone is ready for lunch; my question can wait."

"No, no—go ahead," Melson replied.

"Don't do it," I heard again.

"Okay, well . . ." Thinking quickly on my feet, I remembered Melson touting the new rental car program that the bureau had worked out for our task force officers. ATF provided each officer with a rental vehicle that they could return and switch out for a new one, anytime and for no reason. I had always argued against agents being issued the same contracted vehicles that GSA purchased. They were unmarked and without logos, but it didn't matter. Bad guys know that cops drive Impalas, Crown Vics, Trailblazers, etc. Having a non-police-looking rental car that you could switch out whenever it got burnt would be a godsend.

But, since it was an idea that actually made sense, agents weren't allowed to take advantage of the rental car program. I formulated my question: "You mentioned earlier about the rental car program for the task force officers. For those of us that regularly do surveillance and have our cars burned pretty often, it would be great for us to be able to trade out our cars like the TFOs can do. Any chance that the program can be extended to agents?"

I remember feeling . . . almost dirty after that. Although I asked what I thought was a good question, I felt like crap. I was guilty and gutless, because when forced to ask the acting director a direct question, rather than ask what I wanted to or what I should have asked, like "Why are you allowing Phoenix to walk fifteen hundred guns straight into the hands of the Mexican drug cartels?" or "How many bodies are we going to stack up along the border before you jackasses finally decide to shut this thing down?" I traded doing the right thing for not getting in trouble. Or, so I thought.

"Who is that? Who asked that question?" Bill Newell shouted as he stood up, his Lurch-like frame towering over all the agents seated there in the large open room.

"Dodson," I heard someone answer to him.

"Who?"

"He's in Group 7 . . . Dodson," I heard someone say again.

Newell continued: "So, a guy with one of the new cars, a brand-new car, wants to complain about cars, huh? Other agents have to drive old, beat-up wrecks and he's not happy and wants to complain about his new car. Well, we'll see what we can do about that."

Clearly, the point of my question had been missed entirely. I wasn't complaining about my car. My experience had been that it was more effective, and safer, to not always be identified as the police. My question was geared toward safety and effectiveness.

Melson was still standing at the podium. Like everyone else who was there, he had heard it all—and never said a word.

Later, on the drive home, that feeling of *everything I do here turns to shit* started creeping up on me again. I had serious doubts as to why I had come out here. Clearly I didn't fit in. Asking questions made me stick out like a sore thumb, and that only kept getting my head bashed in. I was almost at the point of not even knowing what the right thing to do was anymore.

Keri would listen to me lament so many times and do her best to offer advice. I remember sitting down to breakfast one morning before we went to work. Feeling like the weight of the world was on my shoulders, I looked at her and said, "I've been doing this job for more than eighteen years now. This is the first time I have ever dreaded going to work. Ever. And I had always said that if this day ever came, it was time to do something else."

I could see in her eyes that she really felt bad for the situation I was in. She answered me in a sympathetic and caring tone: "For you to go that long and love your job that much is a huge blessing. Most people don't get that. Be patient. It won't stay like this forever."

As summer went on, we spent hours and hours talking about my situation and how best to deal with it. She suggested that I keep trying with Dave. "The best way to get someone to listen to you is to listen to them first. Go have another meeting with him . . . keep trying," she said.

I agreed and tried again. A week or so later, I went into Dave's office and he and I actually had a rather civil conversation. Dave had been upbeat and we talked about what kind of cases we wanted to work in the future and what direction we thought the group should take. I remember walking out with a little bit of hope. Maybe we could figure this out, learn how to work together.

It didn't take long to have my hope vanquished. I got word that within hours of our meeting, he had told another supervisor that I was a "soup sandwich," hard to work with, and he was looking for a way to get me out of his group.

I went home to Keri and told her yet again about the latest in my long list of defeats. She kissed my head and used the phrase that would dominate the next two years of my life: "Be patient." She added, "Losing a battle doesn't mean you've lost the war."

Patience may be a virtue, but it certainly had never been one of mine. Even though I wanted to take matters into my own hands, fly off the handle, or hang a boot in somebody's ass, I yielded to her advice.

Things went really great between us over the summer and we started discussing what to do when the kids returned from summer vacation. She was about at her rope's end taking care of a house and two kids alone with no family around. I knew how she felt. Two kids at home was taking its toll on me as well. Since we were both in precarious situations, we saw the advantages a partnership could bring and so we decided to join forces. A better partner I couldn't have asked for or ever imagined. She would end up saving me many times.

Keri rented out her house and she and her two girls moved in with us—me, my son, my daughter, and my dog. We both realized the gravity of what we were doing and because of that, committed to really keeping our communication open between us. Our relationship had just entered the "sink or swim" zone.

About the same time Keri was moving in, I got a message from an agent who worked over in Group II. "I hear you're going to be with us full-time working the storefront case." A storefront case is an investigation where ATF clandestinely opens a store, staffs it with undercover agents, wires it to surreptitiously record audio and video, and then invites criminal activity into it. Storefront cases can be designed to target a specific crime or many different ones at the same time: narcotics, stolen property, stolen or illegal firearms, gangs, what have you.

"News to me," I said. "Let me check with Dave."

I emailed him and asked why Group II thought I was going to be working with them on their storefront case. Dave replied that it was true. I would now be reporting to them and one of their agents would be reporting to Dave to work on Fast and Furious. "Prick!" I said out loud as I read his email.

I didn't mind helping or working with another group at all, be they ATF or not. Many times I volunteered or was tasked to help out another ATF Group, DEA, FBI, ICE, whoever. Dave would later claim that as an excuse for having sent me to work on the storefront.

My assignment on the storefront case consisted of manning a small surveillance room that monitored the undercover activities and happenings in the store. It was slightly larger than a closet and dark due to having no windows of any kind. My days and evenings were spent locked inside watching closed-circuit monitors and writing reports.

After more than a month into my troglodytic captivity, Dave summoned me to the Strike Force office for a meeting. I arrived and took my usual position in front of his desk. Dave began telling me how the Group II supervisor was happy with how things were working out with me over there, and he was pleased with my replacement. Thinking me buttered up enough and pointing out how everyone else involved thought it would be great, Dave asked if I wanted to make the transfer permanent.

Casa had been openly politicking to be transferred to another group for months only to be told over and over again that it wasn't possible. The reason given was that he had PCS'd (permanent change of station) to Phoenix under the Southwest Border Initiative to be a part of Group VII. The money for his move had come from the border initiative and could only be spent on related matters. I had come to Phoenix the same way, under the same funding programs, and yet Dave was trying to sell me a permanent transfer to another group.

These moves aren't cheap. The government pays tens of thousands of dollars, sometimes well above $100,000 or possibly more, on each move. They pay closing costs to sell your current residence and closing costs on your purchase of a new one. You can elect for the additional lump sum $25,000 payment or itemize the other moving cost (house-hunting trip, establishing new utilities/services, vehicle registration and licensing changes, etc.). They also pay for the shipping of your personal vehicle and for a moving company that comes in, packs, loads, ships, unloads, and unpacks all your household items. On top of that, in the event that you can't sell your existing home within an allotted time, the government will even buy it from you. Most agents refer to getting such a transfer as "winning the government lottery."

I had kept track of things and had estimated the tally of my move to Phoenix. It had to be on the low end as they go because my situation made it easy: I had already sold my house and my ex ended up with all the furniture, appliances, and most everything else that constitutes "household items." Of the crap I was left with, I had sold, donated, or thrown away the majority of it, so the movers had only a small load to pick up . . . and I had already packed most of that for them. The rest I threw in the back of my truck when I drove out with the kids and the dog. It still cost the government around $75,000.

That being said, I hadn't come to Phoenix to sit in a closet and watch other agents work. I had come to work firearms trafficking to Mexico; to confront the cartels on the front lines of America. I came to bring the fight to the bad guys for once instead of just having to clean up their mess when it was over. I had been chosen to do it, the government had spent a lot of taxpayer money to bring me out here to do it, and so that's what I was going to do.

So when Dave asked if I wanted to make the switch to Group II permanent, I told him "No thanks." I explained to him that as soon as my assignment to Group II was over, I was going to start landing on every suspected straw purchaser and trafficker that wasn't "hands-off" because they were involved in the Fast and Furious case. Dave seemed surprised by my answer. He stumbled for something to say. I excused myself since I was due back at the storefront and walked out.

Eight days later, George Gillett called me down to his office at division headquarters. He wanted to chat about something. Having gone through these chats with him before, I knew it couldn't be good.

Dave was there in Gillett's office when I arrived, sitting in one of the chairs in front of Gillett's desk. "Oh, I didn't know you were coming," Voth said, as I plopped down in the other chair. His acting was not even on par with what I'd seen during my third grader's class presentation of "Guess Which President I Am?"

"You wanted to see me, sir?" I asked Gillett.

Pleasantries aside, Gillett began to make his offer. "I have a very special assignment that needs someone with your background and experience. And I wanted to talk to you about it." I knew he was full of shit. Gillett had no idea what my background was or what experience I had. "It's with the JTTF [Joint Terrorism Task Force] and you'd be working on a new type of partnership with the FBI and a brand-new role for ATF."

"Wow!" Dave said turning toward me. "That sounds cool!" His next lines from the script: "George had called me over here, too, and I didn't know what this was going to be about." His acting had not gotten any better. Gillett took his turn again, saying how this was a "great opportunity" and how I was a "perfect fit" for it. Dave nodded in agreement with every word that came out of his mouth. Gillett told me that I would be working on the "classified side" in their human intelligence (HUMINT) squad, all top-secret, all high-speed, low-drag, secret-squirrel shit.

"Awesome," Dave kept saying to himself—but just loud enough for me to hear.

Sitting there, I couldn't understand their need for all the performance art: a surprise meeting, in the dark of night, real cloak-and-dagger kind of stuff.

They both must really want me gone, I thought. Here I was, having already turned down the offer to go to Group II, and now this. I'd been offered two transfers inside of eight days while Casa was all but pulling teeth to get out of Group VII and couldn't. As Gillett went on, I picked up on certain things he said that made things a little more clear. The Group II offer had been a quick fix for them and they assumed that I would jump at it. When I didn't, they had to go to plan B. As he dangled the JTTF carrot in front of me with one hand, he made sure that I knew he held a very big stick in the other. The stick was a transfer to some shithole assignment that I couldn't take my kids to, constant travel away from home, working as a one-man satellite office from the trunk of my car, or worse—chained to a desk down in Naco or somewhere like that. Whatever the stick may have been, it was clear to me that I wanted no part of it. So I accepted.

"Good choice," he said. "All right, then, no more case work. Don't pull any ATF case numbers; close out or get rid of what cases you already have. If you run into anything that needs to be worked, just pass it off to us [ATF] or whoever has jurisdiction."

Gillett was clear that with my new "classified" position, the fewer people who knew about it the better. I was told not to tell anyone and that I should never come to or be seen around the division office. I was to deal with Gillett directly; he was now my immediate supervisor and only handler, and if I needed something, I would deal directly with him at some off-site location.

"Roger that," I said, then walked out of his office and left the building.

A few days later, I found out that Larry had been summoned to a similar meeting and that he was getting transferred out of the group, effective the same day that I was. The difference: Alt was going to be the new senior operations officer (SOO). The SOO has a dog of an assignment, handling fleet maintenance, communications issues, and division statistics. Worse still, the grunt agent SOO has to survive in the ivory tower with all the bosses. I don't know of anyone who has ever volunteered to be an SOO, nor do I know any reason why one would. Alt and I had been the two most vocal in our opposition to what was going on with Fast and Furious. In one fell swoop, we were gone.

We were both to report to our new duties on October 1. Even though they had tried to paint this wonderful picture of us being transferred, we all knew it was for speaking out against Fast and Furious. My new assignment landed me at the FBI, away from all things ATF. Alt landed chained to a desk on the ninth floor, where the brass could keep a close eye on him.

At this point I felt there was nothing more I could do. I had tried so many times and so many different ways and had met with nothing but failure and consequence. I talked with Keri about it and we both agreed that maybe it was just for the best.

My new assignment wasn't a bad gig. I would have no ATF paperwork, no NFORCE, and best of all no Fast and Furious. I was also working for people I could actually get along with. I chose to embrace this new assignment and do it the very best that I could. Maybe now I could just move forward with my life. I allowed that thinking to lull me into a sense of comfort and new beginning. I recognized it as it was happening. My internal thoughts were that because "I tried" I could justify my new position of "I'm not involved." I knew guns were still being trafficked under the watchful eyes of the ATF, but now, as I sat over at JTTF licking my wounds so far away from it, I could declare it no longer my battle to fight.

But my new stance didn't sit well. I was haunted by that saying, "All that evil needs to succeed is for good men to do nothing."

And I'd wonder, *Am I doing nothing?*

A heated argument began to rage in my head. Feeling bribed by my new assignment, my silence now bought and paid for, the arguing continued: *I did more than most everybody else!* was countered by *And now I do nothing as it still goes on.* As many rationalizations as I could muster, I couldn't escape that one voice: *Knowing that it continues and doing nothing to stop it, I'm as much part of the problem as they are.*

The Joint Terrorism Task Force has a relatively simple mission—to combat terrorism. Achieving that mission, however, is not so simple.

The thought of being on a team to combat terrorism, working to prevent horrific acts like 9/11, appealed to me. It wasn't what I thought I'd be doing in Phoenix, but life is always throwing you something unexpected. Might as well roll with it.

It took me a few weeks at the FBI to get all my training done, credentials, and security clearances pushed over. Finally, after all the loads of bullshit, I was ready to do some work.

I started by reviewing the ATF multiple sales report system, which keeps track of who buys more than one handgun during a single transaction, and looking for discrepancies and odd patterns of gun purchases in Arizona. There was one that stuck out to me. A Nigerian-born man who was a permanent resident in the United States had purchased fifteen Jimenez pistols. There were multiple reports on him. It was hard to argue that he bought fifteen of the same guns because he was an avid collector—of Jimenez pistols, no less.

I didn't have enough at this time to arrest him, but there was no harm in talking to him. Interviewing a suspect is a worthy investigative tactic. Before I came to Phoenix and had to do things the "Phoenix way," we did it a lot, and it worked—a lot.

I asked another guy on my squad to go with me. He had something to do close by to where I was going and planned on meeting me there. When I arrived, the door was open and a man was leaving the apartment. I decided to approach him rather than simply have to watch him leave because my backup hadn't arrived yet.

He was thin, in his late forties, and had a thick Nigerian accent. I introduced myself, said I was an ATF agent, and asked if I could talk to him. He was unfazed. We walked back up to the apartment and welcomed me in. After confirming that he was indeed the man that I had come to talk to, I asked him about the Jimenez pistols.

He told me that he pistols were for his collection, which he said he kept in a storage unit—in Nigeria.

"Okay, so you're buying all these pistols and shipping them to Nigeria?" I asked.

"Yes," he responded.

"Are they here now, or are they in Nigeria already?" I followed up.

"No, they're right here," he said, pointing down the hall at stacks and stacks of boxes lined up along the wall.

I got a call from my buddy at JTTF. He was pulling into the apartment complex. I told him where I was, that everything was fine, and to just hang out close by and keep watch. I didn't see any reason to burn him with this guy, or whoever might be watching, if I didn't have to.

Back to the boxes, I looked down at the imprinted logo of a Nigerian shipping company that was emblazoned on the sides of them. An address was scribbled on the side of each—but it wasn't an address for a storage unit company. They were all addressed to a person. I pressed him: "Whose name is this?"

"My brother," he said.

"I thought you were shipping them to your storage unit?"

"My brother will put them in it for me," he shot back.

We went back and forth like this for a while. He'd lie—I'd call bullshit on him—he'd modify his lie—I'd call bullshit again. Only after confronted with absolute proof of any point in contention would he then retract his lie, often doing a complete 180 of the last thing that came out of his mouth, looking me square in the eyes, and saying: "Yes, yes, that is what I've been saying the entire time."

He didn't show a hint of nervousness as he brought me over to the boxes and started opening them. Inside each were bundles of clothes: jeans, shirts, and dresses, as well as towels, all tightly rolled and taped. Inside some of these rolls were the guns, but not only the original fifteen pistols I knew about. There were another twelve that I didn't know about and twenty-two tactical shotguns, all wrapped up tightly inside. The way they were packed alone was tantamount to trafficking.

"They're being shipped tomorrow," he volunteered.

"No," I said. "No, they're not."

This was International Firearms Trafficking 101. My job at FBI was to cultivate potential sources. My plan had been to get this guy to tell me about a Nigerian arms-trafficking ring, not to step both feet right into the middle of one. Any other agency stumbles across something like this and they call ATF—so that's what I did. Unfortunately, Group VII was responsible for all international firearms trafficking cases, and thus the call had to go to them.

I had no reservations about calling Dave that night. I thought he'd be happy to get the case already wrapped up with a pretty little bow while I would disappear into the night back to FBI. Then he and the ninth floor could have a press conference as they played slap and tickle and pranced around for the cameras, pointing how they were so great for bringing down a Nigerian arms-trafficking ring. Hell, they could even call it a Nigerian cartel if they wanted to.

"Dave, it's Dodson. I've got something here for you," I said.

"Go ahead?"

Standing in front of the Nigerian man in his apartment, I gave Dave the CliffsNotes-type rundown and the address.

"Okay, we're on the way," he said.

Hope and Lane showed up a few minutes later. I had the Nigerian guy stand outside his apartment as I went and met them a few feet away in the parking lot. Walking over, I notified my JTTF cover man that he could bug out and then saw him drive away.

It was good to see Lane again. Since my transfer, the two of us hadn't golfed much and it had been a while since we chatted. "Hey, John," he greeted me warmly.

The good feeling that seeing Lane had brought me dissipated immediately as Hope walked up and began to speak in the parking lot. First thing out of her mouth was "I spoke to Dave on the way over here. And if this doesn't have anything to do with Mexico, I told him we're not dealin' with it."

"Does Dave know you're calling the shots?" I asked. I already knew the answer—of course he knew. He backed her up every time. No single person ran Group VII; it was a circle-jerk of collective authority piped in by Newell to fill the pet-project basin of Gillett before it then swirled around the bowl of Dave, Hope, and Tonya. It was a giant commode so full of inappropriate shit that it desperately needed a good plunging.

Dave showed up shortly thereafter.

"Hey," I said, "you ready for the rundown?"

He looked at me blankly. "I don't know what you're doing out here or what you have going on but we're just here to cover you," Dave told me. "We want nothing to do with this. This is yours . . ." He was channeling Hope now. "We're not working it."

"What do you mean it's mine and you're not working it?" I asked him. "You were there at the meeting with Gillett in September when he transferred me to FBI, when he told me that I wasn't allowed to work cases. I'm not even assigned to a group anymore, Dave," I continued. "I can't even pull a case number."

His eyes narrowed.

"I don't have access to a vault, no place to store evidence. Hell, I'm not even supposed to go to the office. You heard that yourself!"

"Well, I'll take your evidence for you tonight and keep it in the office or store it temporarily, but you have to get it tomorrow," he said. "This is yours, we're not dealing with it," he reiterated.

Pissed-off, I had already made the decision that, if this was mine and they weren't dealing with it, then they didn't have to go home— but they had to get the hell out of here.

Lane's voice interjected. "ICE would love to have this case," he said. "Can I take it?"

Exhaling slowly and staring at Dave, I used that breath to say: "Glad to hear somebody wants to work international firearms trafficking."

Dave agreed to let Lane take it, but solely as an ICE investigation, which forced Lane to have to seek authority from his ICE supervisor.

Lane called his boss at ICE and asked if he could take the case on behalf of the agency. ICE and ATF had been through a few disagreements lately, and Dave had been a part, if not the cause, of those. ATF Phoenix was known for not playing well with others and not sharing credit, so Lane's boss was naturally skeptical when Lane told him ATF wanted no credit for the case. He was so unconvinced that he asked Lane to confirm it with Dave while he was still on the phone.

Lane leaned in, holding the line up. "You're okay with ICE taking this case, counting the seizures, an international firearms trafficking case—ATF wants nothing to do with it, right?" Lane asked Dave, his boss, there listening on the phone.

"That's right, we want nothing to do with it," Dave responded, loud enough so that it could be heard on the other end of the line.

"Got that, boss? Yes, sir. We're on it," Lane said before he hung up.

With everyone in agreement, I helped Lane work the recovery. By this point, all the guns—the pistols and the shotguns—were unwrapped and laid out on the kitchen table and the floor in front of us. The jeans, T-shirts, and towels that concealed them in the boxes were strewn throughout the apartment. Dave and Hope only barely glanced at all the weapons, seemingly uninterested. All the while, though only five feet apart, they were giggling as they went back and forth texting the other sarcastic remarks.

The Nigerian man sat in his living room somewhat intrigued by the drama unfolding in front of him. It was ICE's decision whether to arrest him at that point; we had plenty of probable cause for it, but it was their case, their call. They chose not to. So, before we left, Lane took a statement from the man and then we hauled the evidence out of the apartment and down to the parking lot.

All of the guns wouldn't fit into Lane's car. So Dave told Lane that he could put them in his Ford Explorer and he would hold them there overnight until Lane could pick them up the next morning.

Before we left, Lane got with me alone and thanked me for letting him take the case.

"Letting you? You're helping me, brother. It's I who am thanking you," I told him.

Lane thanked me again, saying that I had no idea the position that Dave had repeatedly put him in with his ICE bosses. Scoring this case was going to go a long way in helping Lane with relationships at his agency.

I had barely hit the highway before my BlackBerry buzzed. I pulled it out and glanced at the screen—Dave. "Asshole!" I said pushing the little green phone button with my thumb. "Yeah?"

Dave said he had just talked to the ASAC, Needles, and he thought that this made for a great case. *Well, maybe Needles isn't so stupid after all,* I thought to myself.

Dave continued, now saying that he was taking the case back from Lane and that he was generating a Group VII case number and counting the guns as a seizure for ATF. Dave hadn't told Needles how he refused the case, and then upon learning that Needles not only expected ATF to work it but even thought it was a great case, Dave had to get it back. Stabbing Lane in the back didn't give him a second's hesitation.

When I called him and told Lane, he was at his wits' end. "This is not good . . . not good for me at all. My bosses are going to flip," he said, the concern obvious in his voice. "I promised them this was worked out, that it was going to be an ICE case. Now exactly what he worried would happen is happening: Dave is screwing him over again and I'm the one who is going to get fucked."

While this type of thing would normally be nothing more than a bureaucratic small-ball argument, Lane's ICE bosses had been through this chain-yanking so many times before—as evidenced by his boss's concerns on the phone earlier that night. This might be the straw that broke the camel's back, Lane ending up spending the rest of his career doing nothing but immigration checks from his new desk at the Yuma Point of Entry or somewhere like that.

I told Lane I would handle it.

When I got to my office in the FBI building the next morning, I emailed Needles. I said I needed to talk to him right away and he told me to head down to his office. It was 9 A.M. and Dave was already blowing up my cell phone and email about the Nigerian case. He had already drawn and issued it an ATF Group VII case number and was busting my balls about getting the guns into the vault and booked into NFORCE.

I got to the division office, went straight up to the ninth floor, and knocked on Needles's door. Needles was different than most of the management at ATF Phoenix. A few years older than the others, in his late forties, his brown hair had mostly grayed by this point in his life. He appeared disheveled, most of the time looking like he had just emerged from the losing end of a tussle. His suits were the inexpensive kind, not pressed and often wrinkled. I had liked that about him, thinking maybe he had actually done the job before getting promoted rather than making getting promoted his one and only job. Needles also didn't seem to me to be as malicious or vindictive as both Newell and Gillett were, nor did he seem to have the same vaulted aspirations they did of one day ruling from on high within the ivory palace of headquarters.

My complaint with Needles, though, was his failure to lead. Rumor was he wanted to shut the F&F investigation down as soon as he took over as the Group VII ASAC, but he didn't. I could tell at the meeting that day that he knew he should deny the Fernandez proposal, but he didn't.

Failing to lead, refusing or being too scared to act, always deciding to not make the decision: these are systemic problems in our government. Like so many others in service of the government, he was too concerned with protecting what he had than to risk losing it by actually doing the job, doing what was right or simply needed to be done. I was learning that "Go along to get along" was the mantra at every level of the government.

"I understand Dave briefed you on the Nigerian case and you think it's a good case," I said to him.

"Yes," Needles confirmed.

"Did Dave brief you on how he had refused it, said he wanted nothing to do with it before he talked to you last night?" I asked him. "Did he tell you how Hope had ordered that Group VII wasn't going to work it because it had no nexus to Mexico in it and he supported her on that?

"Did Dave brief you on how he was prepared to let that case die last night right then and there because he knew that I was under orders from Gillett to not work cases, that I couldn't draw a case number, and that I didn't even have access to a vault to secure the evidence in?"

Needles's full face was now showing a crimson tint.

"Did he brief you on how he would have rather simply let those guns go, let 'em walk to Nigeria, before he was going to lift a finger on that case? And, at any time when he was speaking with you, did he bother to mention that he had already given that case to Lane to be worked strictly as an ICE case because ATF wanted nothing to do with it?"

Needles's face was now glowing red.

"Dave washed his hands of it and when Lane asked if he could take it, Dave gave it to him. He promised this case to ICE. And believe me, ICE had serious reservations at first because they were worried they were going to get screwed by Dave again. But then Dave assured Lane that that wouldn't happen, with his boss listening right there on the phone. Lane's ass is grass if you let Dave renege and take that case back. It's not fair to Lane, it's not fair to ICE, and it makes us look like shit."

Clearly, all of this was news to Needles. When Dave had called him the night before to tell him about having been called over there, and then when Needles thought it only logical that ATF work an international firearms trafficking case, especially such a good case, Dave changed his story.

With his anger visible on his face and detectable in his voice, Needles rocked forward in his chair a little and said: "Fine, let ICE keep the case."

Thinking that finally, for once, something was going to work out the way that it should . . .

"But Dodson, this . . . this is all your fault!" Needles yelled. Now aiming his finger at me, looking down the barrel of it I could see his shiny red nose in line behind his knuckles. "Because your ass should have never been out there by yourself anyway," he concluded. "Now get out of my office!"

I left shaking my head. I had just got to my car when Gillett called. I had spoken to him about the case the night before, just gave him the facts, and now he wanted to speak to me. Back up the elevator to the ninth floor, I was thinking *Do they have a schedule for chewing my ass? "I've got the nine thirty. Who wants the ten o'clock?"*

When I got to Gillett's office, I walked in and sat down. I didn't play dumb by asking, "You wanted to see me?" or even "Yeah, boss?" I knew why I had been called there—pull the trigger already.

Never disappointing, Gillett tore into me. "You never should have been out there," he said. "And we checked—you never did an ops plan—that's a violation of ATF orders."

An "ops plan" is a specific play-by-play layout of what we as agents plan to do whenever taking enforcement action out in the field. Now it seemed we were required to do one and have it approved by fourteen different people whenever we left our desks, went to the bathroom, or put our socks on in the morning.

Stunned, I shot back: "No, no, no, Hold on a sec. Yeah, I work for ATF, you pay my salary, but you farmed my ass to work for the FBI. My being there was for my FBI assignment, and they don't require me to write an ops plan for a simple knock-and-talk. I was in complete accordance with the rules and regulations of the agency that you yourself sent me to and told me not to come back from. My FBI supervisor was informed and kept abreast of everything and was fine with it."

Visibly irate, Gillett said, "We're through then." And he pointed to the door.

I went home that night and filled Keri in on everything that happened. Another day—another mark in the "L" column.

I promised myself I would do my best to stay away from all those people. I was tired of trying with them. Hopefully, JTTF would become my way to not have to deal with them. For the next few weeks, I just worked with the FBI people. Life was starting to become somewhat normal as Christmas was quickly approaching.

The past year had been difficult, but life with Keri was going well, and I had new hope for my job. I should have known better.

− 7 −

REVELATIONS
AND REGRETS

December 13, 2010, had started out much like any other Monday since my transfer to the JTTF. Our alarm was set for just before 6 A.M., rousing Keri and I awake. I stumbled through the dark to grab a cup of coffee and turned on the television. Keri and I cherished this part of the morning. It was the calm before the storm when we had to awaken the kids at six thirty to really begin the morning routine.

After coffee and a bowl of cereal, it was a quick shower and then out the door. As I walked toward my g-ride parked on the curb in front of the house, I couldn't help but laugh at the irony: the first brand-new car, or even relatively new car, that the bureau had ever given me was now a hideous eyesore due to a freak hailstorm that had run through a small portion of the Valley of the Sun a few weeks before. So rare was this, many Phoenix natives had never before even seen hail, much less a storm that had left the desert ground and sodded lawns covered in a white blanket of nearly fist-sized balls of solid ice. The epicenter of this extremely rare meteorological event was directly over me as I was stopped for the traffic light on Thunderbird Road at Fifty-First Avenue. The storm's pounding left my g-ride riddled with countless dimples as if you had unleashed an entire kindergarten class armed with ball-peen hammers upon it. Seeing it there every morning since and thinking about how I had to explain the damage caused to my official government vehicle as being caused by a desert ice storm made me chuckle every time.

I jumped in and started my commute. My usually silent morning drive was interrupted, however, by the ringing of my bureau cell phone. Calling me was Travis, my partner from my former field office back in Virginia. He was a true oddity among the ranks of federal law enforcement officers: highly intelligent, charismatic, hardworking, and with never a thought, act, or notion of elitism. Travis cringed at the moniker of "agent" and seemed to take genuine offense whenever labeled "special agent." He was thin and unassuming, with a wit so sharp that many never realized he even had a sense of humor, much less that they were often bearing the brunt of it. Wrapping up his doctoral degree, and armed with a vocabulary that often forced me to "confer with Uncle Noah" (in other words, *Webster's Dictionary*), Travis might seem far better prepared to be lecturing at a podium somewhere than kicking in doors on a search warrant. However, that perception would be wrong. He was alert, tactically sound, and able to drive nails with a .40 caliber under any conditions. I'd go through a door with him any day—and had done so already, many times.

Surprised as I was—Travis hates talking on the phone as much as I do—I answered. Lacking all the normal pleasantries that you might expect to hear during a conversation between two friends that have been through so much together, what came blurting at me from out of the phone was "Have you read the *Post* this morning?"

"Not yet. It's three hours earlier here, remember? I haven't even made it to the office yet."

"Make sure you do," he said, and then hung up the phone.

Soon after, I pulled into the parking lot at work. It was a single-story, nondescript brick building, with several others similar to it in the same north Phoenix office park, and a passerby would have no reason to suspect that housed within was the hub of the FBI's Domestic Counterterrorism efforts for the entire region. Even the blacked-out windows drew no attention, as this was Phoenix, and they are all but mandatory to keep out the brutal desert rays. The entire area in front of the building and facing the road consisted of parking lot. The only thing visibly setting this building apart from those around it was an opaque security fence encompassing both sides and the entire back. The fence was high enough that you couldn't look over it, but not so high as to raise any suspicion. However, inside the fence was a different world.

I pulled through the lot and drove up to the large steel rolling gate on the north end. Rusted and discolored, it and its twin on the south end were the only ways in or out of the back lot. I quickly reached down the collar of my shirt and fumbled to retrieve my access badge hanging from the lanyard around my neck. Not much bigger than a driver's license and bearing an equally poor photo of me, it was the first thing that the FBI had issued me after my being assigned to the JTTF.

I leaned out of the window and held my badge up to the access reader. The familiar beep was followed by the small red light changing to green and the gate began to lumber open. Inside the secure area, it was a much different scene; filled with bland four-door sedans and SUVs. If not for the hail damage, my car could have easily been lost in the rows of fleet government cars when I parked it.

I walked up to the building and again waved my badge at the

access reader. The same familiar beep, only this time followed by an ascending set of tones and a scrambled number-pad appearing on a small digital screen before me. I typed my numerical code and then heard the loud clank of the lock releasing on the door.

Once inside, I began the trek to my workstation, all the while in view of no less than two closed-circuit cameras, down a short hall, past the SCIF, and through another security door. The SCIF, or Special Compartmentalized Information Facility, is a highly secure area, usually within a secure facility, that has very limited access. No cell phones or other outside electronic devices are allowed inside; there are no windows, it is soundproof, transmitted waves cannot exit from it or penetrate into it due to a Faraday cage–like design in its construction, and it has other electronic countermeasures. In short, it's the cone of silence.

Clearing the second security door, I entered the work bay and arrived at my cubicle. I then performed the normal routine of powering up my computers, first my ATF laptop, then my FBI "low-side" (for regular, unclassified information) computer, and finally, turning and sliding to the other side of the cube, my FBI "high-side" (for classified information). I had to seek special authorization from FBI to allow me to even bring my ATF laptop into the JTTF building. When ultimately approved, the security technician insisted that I disable the Wi-Fi and Bluetooth antennas and that I keep it on the same side of the cube as my "low-side" terminal only. She explained that FBI regulations do not allow any other electronic devices within three feet of any "high-side" terminal. I couldn't help but wonder how this three-foot rule could effectively prevent a breach of the "high-side" system, but who am I to question the FBI? I logged in with my laptop and opened Internet Explorer. I quickly punched in "WashingtonPost.com."

Travis wasn't specific about what I should be looking for, so I didn't know at first. But since it was important enough for him to pick up the phone and call me, I knew it would jump out at me when I saw it.

I scanned up and down the site. Headline about some legislation the knuckleheads up on Capitol Hill were proposing, another piece about the recent midterm elections. Then, there it was: "The Hidden Life of Guns; As Mexico drug violence runs rampant, U.S. guns tied to crime south of border." The article, written by Sari Horwitz and James Grimaldi, was all too familiar a subject. That had to be what Travis was referring to.

I dove into it, frantically consuming every word. Within seconds I stopped, my mouth agape. "A year-long investigation by *The Washington Post* has cracked that secrecy and uncovered the names of the top 12 U.S. dealers of guns traced to Mexico in the past two years," Horwitz and Grimaldi wrote. The article blamed southwestern states for the majority of gun violence in Mexico. "Eight of the top 12 dealers are in Texas, three are in Arizona, and one is in California. . . . In Texas, two of the four Houston area Carter's Country stores are on the list, along with four gun retailers in the Rio Grande Valley at the southern tip of the state. There are 3,800 gun retailers in Texas, 300 in Houston alone."

I stuck my head out of my cubicle and looked around. I stole glances over my shoulder. Something wasn't right. "Drug cartels have aggressively turned to the United States because Mexico severely restricts gun ownership," the *Post* said. "Following gunrunning paths that have been in place for 50 years, firearms cross the border and end up in the hands of criminals as well as ordinary citizens seeking protection."

I wanted to stand up and scream "Bullshit!" I wheeled around again in my chair. Everybody else in the FBI building was still going about their regular business, filling coffee cups, making morning phone calls, and checking their emails.

"What is different now, authorities say, is the number of high-powered rifles heading south—AR-15s, AK-47s, armor-piercing .50-caliber weapons—and the savagery of the violence," Horwitz and Grimaldi continued.

Midway down page two, my horror was confirmed. "To examine the gun flow from the United States to Mexico, *The Post* reviewed hundreds of court documents and federal reports and interviewed Mexican officials and dozens of current and former U.S. law enforcement officials," the authors wrote. "ATF in 2006 launched Project Gunrunner—a program that now involves more than 220 agents who make criminal cases against gun traffickers and about 165 inspectors who check gun dealers for compliance with federal regulations. The agency has conducted about 1,000 inspections in the border region, leading to the seizure of more than 400 firearms." I was one of those more than 220 federal agents—I knew better.

"U.S. law enforcement has traditionally focused on seizing drugs moving north from Mexico, not guns moving south. In 2008, only 70 guns were seized at U.S. border crossings," the article continued. "The cornerstone of the $60 million program is gun tracing—tracking weapons to the dealers who originally sold them. It has long been considered a powerful tool for combating trafficking."

They're stacking the deck.

I kept scrolling through. On page five, Horwitz and Grimaldi named one of the gun dealers that, through Operation Fast and Furious, we told to keep selling to straw purchasers.

"No charges were brought against any of the gun dealers involved, and there was no indication the dealers did anything wrong," the *Post* reporters wrote. "One of the dealers, J&G Sales in Prescott, ranks third on the top-12 list, with about 130 of its guns traced from Mexico over the past two years."

How could they say there is "no indication the dealers did anything wrong"? Of course they didn't do anything wrong. They thought they were helping us. J&G and Lone Wolf were both a part of our investigation—we *told* them to continue with their sales.

J&G's owner defended himself, saying he was unaware those straw-purchased weapons ended up making it to Mexico. "I would stand by every transaction we make at the time we make it," J&G's owner told the *Post*. "But I'm disappointed to hear that number. It saddens me. It should not happen."

The *Post* again suggested that the gun dealers shared responsibility for this. "The lack of charges against dealers is not unusual, in part because it's difficult to prove a straw purchase took place," Horwitz and Grimaldi wrote.

The next paragraph gave it all away. Bill Newell—who was well aware all along that *we were telling the dealers to make these sales to straw purchasers,* and that they weren't doing it of their own accord—blamed the dealers, or at least hinted at it enough that that was his intent. "If you're a gun dealer and you see a 21- or 22-year-old young lady walk in and plop down $15,000 in cash to buy 20 AK-47s, you might want to ask yourself what she needs them for," Newell said. "If she says, 'Christmas presents,' technically the dealer doesn't have to ask for more."

But, as Newell didn't say, the dealers had refused just such sales and then called ATF Phoenix to report the suspicious activity. It was only after we had told them to go through with it that they made such sales.

Page four of another article accompanying that first big one blamed Lone Wolf Trading Company and its owner, Andre

Howard—who went out of his way to cooperate with us—in a way similar to how the first one blamed J&G. "Lone Wolf Trading Co. in Glendale, Ariz., a suburb of Phoenix, is ranked eighth on the list with about 1,515 firearms traced," Horwitz and Grimaldi wrote. "Lone Wolf sits in a strip mall, next to Spa Tahiti. Inside, model airplanes hang from the ceiling and the heads of animals adorn the walls. A sign behind the cash register advertised AK-47s for $499."

"Lone Wolf has jumped from No. 61 on the 2004 list," the article continued. "Last year, 12 people were indicted on charges of making false statements in order to buy 17 AK-47-type rifles headed to Mexico. The guns were purchased from seven stores, including Lone Wolf.

"Owner Andre Howard could not be reached for comment. ATF officials said they have no indication that Lone Wolf is doing anything wrong or illegal."

Another one of Hope's cases, no less.

Sitting there in my FBI cube, I couldn't believe what I had just read. A lot of things clicked into place. More thoughts raced through my head. Worries were swimming through my conscious. *Those numbers are only so high because these gun stores are helping us,* I thought. *I know the people quoted in that article attacking the guns stores—and I know they're briefed on this case. And I know that they know J&G and Lone Wolf were only selling to straw purchasers because we told them to.* At the same time, I countered those thoughts with others. *They couldn't organize a conspiracy like this, could they?* To quote a government lawyer friend of mine, "I've been with the government long enough to know—we can't even organize a bake sale much less a conspiracy!"

Even so, how can I let this happen? It was clear that Newell and other ATF leadership were going to frame the gun dealers for what went wrong. It was still only a matter of time before a Border Patrol agent or local cop was killed with Operation Fast and Furious weapons. What they said in the press wouldn't change that. Or was that what they were waiting for? I didn't know what to think, what to do, or who to talk to.

I mulled that question over in my head for the rest of December 13 and throughout the next day. Should I warn somebody else in the agency? Should I call Internal Affairs? How about the inspector general? Should I call the reporters for the *Washington Post* and try to talk to them?

I emailed a link to the article to Keri, who couldn't believe it, either. Together we talked about what to do, but soon the situation changed.

Two days later, Keri and I were repeating the same morning ritual.

As we sat in front of the TV, this morning's breaking news was "The Border Patrol has confirmed an agent was shot and killed overnight north of Rio Rico. His identity has not yet been released." It stopped me cold, in mid-sip of my coffee.

Keri and I looked at each other. This wasn't the first time our morning routine had played out like this. Many times before, when similar violence had been reported on or near the border, our minds had gone to the same place. We had asked each other the same question so often that we now communicated in silence: "Could this be it? Is this the one?" I remember one incident when a U.S. consulate employee had been gunned down in Juarez. Keri and I had feared the worse then also, and we weren't alone. Assholes all around Phoenix ATF slammed shut that day; everyone was on pins and needles. At one point, I even heard it said: "I hope they never solve that, or at least I hope they don't recover any guns."

Events were still unfolding and there wasn't a lot of information. We continued our morning, got dressed and ready, got the kids off to school, I headed out to my car, and started off to work. This morning, coincidentally, I was actually headed to Tucson for a completely unrelated case that was "high-side" JTTF stuff. After about a two-hour drive, I was still a few minutes outside of Tucson when my Black-Berry buzzed. I much preferred the days when email had to wait until I was actually sitting in front of my computer, but alas, I did what we all do but shouldn't. I took control of the steering wheel with my knee and proceeded to clear out the still-incoming notifications, my eyes darting between the road and the two-inch screen.

George Gillett had emailed the entire division. The FBI was primary on working the Border Patrol agent's murder—U.S. Customs and Border Protection's Border Patrol and ICE were on scene, our ATF guys from the Tucson office were assisting, and they were still looking for suspects in the desert.

Truth be told, I had never heard of Rio Rico before this morning and had no clue where it was. I had assumed it was much closer to the actual border, some far-off corner of no-man's-land. It wasn't until reading Gillett's email that I thought it within response distance. I quickly pulled over, grabbed my personal cell, and Google-mapped "Rio Rico." Although it was roughly an hour south of Tucson, relatively close to the border, and more than likely still in no-man's-land, I figured it was close enough for our Tucson guys to go. I was now in Tucson, so it was close enough for me to go.

My career had already seen far too many "officer down" or "signal 13" calls—one would have been too many. It was never as if I wanted to go to something like that, but to me there isn't a choice. Someone needs help, you go. A cop gets killed, everybody goes.

I emailed Gillett back from where I had pulled over on the side of the road. "I'm in Tucson today. Do they need any help?"

Gillett responded back probably not but said I could reach out to the Tucson ATF supervisor and make the offer.

I did. I tried calling and emailed him. But those guys were out in

Peck Canyon, so far in the middle of nowhere you'd be lucky to reach them by sat phone.

Frustrated, I went about finishing my JTTF assignment. At one point, I saw a couple of Border Patrol vehicles parked in an Arby's parking lot. I whipped in the lot and walked inside. Packed in a corner booth, I saw a group of young Border Patrol agents, all in uniform, with one clutching a radio out in front of him atop the table. They were all staring at it, fixed in on it, as if that could somehow make it come to life and squawk out some nugget of information that might give them an idea of what was going on out in Peck Canyon.

I thought about asking them if I could help, but decided against it. If they were sitting in Arby's because their help wasn't needed, there probably wasn't much that I could do. Finishing what I had to do, I reluctantly drove back to Phoenix. Still feeling the need to do something, I felt guilty. I felt like I should be helping.

The next morning, I was on my way to work at the JTTF building when I got the call. It was Larry Alt. He was calling me from his small office on the ninth floor of the Phoenix Division to which he had been banished. He was tasked with auditing NFORCE case files and scheduling fleet maintenance. Putting Alt in the division office as the senior ops officer was one of Phoenix ATF's biggest mistakes and not just because he was overqualified for the position, not just because they lost a great asset out in the field, but because he was smarter than any of the brass that was up there on the ninth floor with him.

When Alt had learned the news, he reached out to me. He knew I'd want to know. "Two guns recovered at the scene of the BPA murder are Fast and Furious guns."

My heart leapt up into my throat.

Alt went on to say that the ninth floor was in full lockdown mode; everybody had been in closed-door meetings since the previous afternoon and they were all freaking out. Crisis management at its worst.

Our conversation was short. Neither of us wanted him to get busted for telling me, and we both knew that he would. I arrived at the JTTF building, key-fobbed and security-coded my way inside, then sat down at my desk. After knowing for so long that this would someday happen, I had barely begun to process it when my phone rang again. This time it was George Gillett.

When I was banished, Gillett was the one who told me to stay away from the ATF office. Now he wanted to see me there right away. He didn't say why, but I had a pretty good feeling. I headed straight over and was pulling into the parking garage inside of fifteen minutes.

I rode the elevator straight from the lobby to the ninth floor. Through the mailroom security door, left down the hall, I stopped just outside Gillett's office. "Come in, John," he said. "Have a seat."

Newell was standing behind Gillett's desk. I didn't want to barge in on the two head honchos, but they beckoned me forward. Suddenly, and strangely for the first time, I found myself in the midst of a warm welcome among them. Clearly they had been having an in-depth conversation.

Gillett's office was sparsely furnished except for his desk, a bookcase, and a few chairs. All of it was typical government, inmate-manufactured UNICOR crap. Bosses like Gillett enjoy a slightly better quality of crap than we street agents get. The exception to the unremarkable government motif was his own little touch of personal flair—the "I love me wall," a virtual requirement for all supervisors on the federal payroll. On that wall were Gillett's many plaques, awards, praises, accolades, pictures with faked smiles, and attaboys from the ATF and a host of other agencies.

I walked in and sat down. As I did so, Newell announced his exit and began to leave. He lumbered around the chair I was seated in and lurched up behind me.

He rubbed my shoulders and gave me several more than obvious pats on the back. For a guy who is used to getting kicked in the balls every time he set foot on the ninth floor, I found this unusual, and most of all, uncomfortable. Especially since Newell and I had never even been formally introduced and I had never personally spoken to the man.

"How's it going, John?" Newell asked.

"Fine, sir," I replied.

"How are things over at the FBI? You doing all right? You need anything?"

The fact that he had called me by my first name was odd. The only time he had put a name to my face was the day he berated me at the town hall meeting. Now, however, his tone was very different.

"No sir, I'm fine," I replied. After feeling that I had been buttered up good enough, he asked Gillett if he wanted him to close the door on his way out.

Gillett leaned back in his chair and said, "You can close it."

Now, with Newell gone, and just he and I behind a closed door, it was Gillett's turn: "How are things going over at the FBI?"

I don't remember if I offered anything more than a grunt.

"Anything going on?" Gillett continued. "Anything you want to talk about?"

"Nope," I told him, "not on this end. Anything you want to talk about?"

"All right, then, good talk," he said. He stood, reached his hand out, and added, "Thanks for coming in." That was it. I shook his hand, opened the door, and walked out; muttering to myself as I walked down the hall back toward the mailroom, "Sons of bitches."

They're wondering if I know, I thought. For Newell and Gillett to call me up to the ninth floor so we could all have a nice little bro chat the day after a Border Patrol agent was murdered? Really? This whole meeting was to find out if I knew already about the link between the weapons and the murder ... if I was going to be a "problem" for them or not. They assumed if I knew, I would say something or they could pull it out of me.

I hadn't said anything, for a number of reasons. First, I hadn't yet fully comprehended what just happened. Second, trusting them or revealing anything to them didn't seem like a smart thing to do. Last, and most important, I owed them nothing. But my silence seemed to relieve them. Maybe if I didn't know, if no one had told me, they still had a chance to hide it.

I left Division and headed back to the FBI office. Life was moving in slow motion like it does when your senses are heightened to everything around you. I was hyperobservant to everything, looking over my shoulder, driving a different route to see if I was being followed, not saying anything to anyone that I didn't trust implicitly, and that was just about everyone.

As I sat at my FBI desk, emotions started to flood me. One realization after another would come crashing down on me. Little did I know that this was just the beginning of an eye-opening journey. I was just starting to see things in ways that I've never seen them before: things about my fellow agents, my agency, my country, and even things about myself. It's one of those times in your life that you regret not trusting yourself, not trusting your gut.

I had been right all along. All those times that they told me I didn't know what I was talking about or that the benefits outweighed the risks or when they treated me like I was second rate, I was the one who was right. And it wasn't a feeling of "I'm better than you" or even a feeling of vindication. It was anger, guilt, shame, and regret.

Anger at a group of people who carried out this madness with their arrogance and incompetence. Guilt that I was ever a part of any of it. Shame that my agency was capable of such stupidity. Regret that I hadn't done more sooner. And then sadness . . . sad that a warrior I had never met had given his life, and there was a family out there that might never know the true circumstances surrounding their loved one's death.

I thought it before, but now it seemed unavoidable that they were going to have to own it. Headquarters, the ninth floor, Group VII, all of them would now have to explain their insane strategy, what we had been doing—letting all those guns walk. I didn't know to whom, but I knew that now they were going to have to explain it. They would have to try to rationalize it to someone else like they had so many times to me. Try to force-feed it to others with that same "we know better than you" bullshit. I had an inkling that simply justifying things as "the Phoenix way" wouldn't go over too well in a public forum.

I never thought I'd be asked any questions about it, or have any-thing to do with it. It seemed so obvious to me that it would just erupt on its own. Besides, no one ever asks the grunts. I was just a lowly GS-13. Never had it seriously crossed my mind that I'd have to utter a word about Fast and Furious or gun walking.

Regardless, it was all about to be out in the open now. Again, they were going to have to own it. My thought at the time was to quietly go about my business while they were berated, chastised, and perhaps even punished for implementing a strategy of such utter lunacy. And then, when the time was just right, I would, alas, deliver that all too well deserved "I told you so." But, as I had learned many years ago, no battle plan ever survives first contact with the enemy.

That same day, while working in our intranet-based reporting system, NFORCE, I learned that my access to the Fast and Furious case had been abruptly taken away. I had been assigned on that case for a year now, and it had become such a familiar sight on my case log screen. Furthermore, I had authored ROIs (Reports of Investigation) on that case, was listed in an untold number of others as a participant and material witness to countless overt criminal acts, and was even documented on the "6(e) List," referring to Rule 6(e) of the Federal Rules of Criminal Procedure. Being on the "6(e) List" means that you have access to secret information derived from a grand jury and have been advised of the secrecy requirement. This advisement makes you eligible for punishment and prosecution if you breach it.

Now my access was denied? I had been out of Group VII for more than two months by this point, so my transfer to JTTF didn't pass the smell test as a viable excuse to remove me from the case. They also did it without even notifying me.

My suspicion rising, I began checking a few other things. All agents with access to NFORCE can query and read any Significant Incident Report (SIR) sent by any office or field division up the chain to headquarters. It's mandated that a SIR be done following any "significant incident," which unofficially means anything that might make the news, whether good or bad. Thinking there would be one for our Tucson office assisting with the murder investigation, which there was, I also found one for Group VII.

On January 16, 2010, Jaime AVILA purchased three (3) AK-47 variant rifles from a Phoenix area FFL. On December 15, 2010, after the shooting death of a U.S. Border Patrol agent in Southern Arizona law enforcement officers/agents conducted a search of the area. Two (2) of the AK-47 variant rifles purchased by AVILA on 01/16/2010 were recovered in the area during this search.

On December 15, 2010, ATF agents located AVILA and subsequently interviewed and arrested him on charges stemming from this January 16, 2010, firearm purchase. In summary AVILA admitted to ATF agents that he straw purchased these firearms for an unidentified Hispanic male.

AVILA was held overnight and ATF agents have prepared a criminal complaint for Jaime AVILA on firearm charges relating to the straw purchase of these three (3) AK-47 variant rifles on 01/16/2010 and are presenting it to a Federal Magistrate today (12/16/10).

Twenty-four hours after a Border Patrol agent was gunned down in Peck Canyon, and two weapons from the Fast and Furious investigation were recovered at the scene, Group VII finally went out and arrested Jaime Avila. But the SIR doesn't mention how Avila had blipped our radar and had been identified as a straw purchaser in Fast and Furious back in November 2009. It did not say how we had surveilled him many times as he purchased firearms from local gun shops. How we had tracked his many purchases, or listed him in our databases. There was nothing about how we knew, in real time, whenever a weapon he had purchased was recovered at violent crime somewhere along the border. The only things we hadn't ever done: interdict him, arrest him, interview him, or anything else that might hinder his firearms trafficking, or worse, at least by ATF Phoenix standards, to stop it.

I was still reeling over what information I had been able to track down and put together thus far when yet another discovery knocked the wind out of me. Sometime between when the SIR report was sent out in the dark hours of December 16 and when the federal court for the District of Arizona opened a few hours later, the plan had changed.

Avila had bought three AK-47 variant rifles in January 2010 from the Lone Wolf gun store in Phoenix. Two of those guns were found at the murder scene. ATF agents working the Fast and Furious investigation arrested Jaime Avila twenty-four hours later. But they did not arrest him for what the SIR report stated. They arrested and charged him for lying on a firearms transaction record (Form 4473) stemming from an incident in June 2010, when he had purchased three pistols from the Scottsdale Gun Club.

In other words, they arrested Avila on charges having nothing to do with the purchase of the AK-variant rifles recovered from Peck Canyon. They were trying to hide the connection.

Holy shit! I thought. *They're going to cover it up.*

– 8 –

DO SOMETHING

Driving home that evening, deep in thought, I tried to digest everything I had learned that day. Brian Terry. That was the name of the slain Border Patrol agent. That was a name I knew I would never be able to forget.

Forty years old and with prior service in the Marine Corps and as a police officer, Brian Terry had been with Border Patrol for three and half years. Terry was known to his friends and family as "Superman"; his courage and perseverance were legendary. As a member of the elite U.S. Border Patrol Tactical Unit know by its acronym BORTAC, Terry and his three fellow agents were in Peck Canyon that December night attempting to arrest a rip crew that had been operating in the area.

I pulled into my driveway at about six thirty. I walked in, went past the living room, and turned the corner into the kitchen. Keri was standing in front of the sink, busy with dinner and kids. The smell in the air signaled that our meal was close to being ready.

She turned and greeted me with the usual kiss and "Hey, babe." Then she looked at my face. Since we had been together, it seemed like there was a new work story to tell on almost a weekly basis. They were hardly ever good. She had grown accustomed to that certain look on my face.

"Uh-oh, what happened today?" she asked in an all-too-familiar tone.

"Remember the Border Patrol agent that was killed? We watched it on the news," I reminded her in a soft tone as I stepped a little closer.

"Yeah," she answered, "I remember."

"Two of the guns they recovered from the scene were from Fast and Furious."

She immediately stopped what she was doing. We were standing face-to-face and just stared at each other in silence. It was a lot to take in.

The kids had been making their way to the dinner table and noticed us. One of them asked, "What's wrong? Did something happen?"

We broke off our stare and Keri answered, "Nothing, just work stuff."

They seemed satisfied with that answer and didn't press further. We all sat down for dinner together and tried to engage the kids in normal dinnertime chatter. But every few minutes we would just look at each other. I think we were both wondering, *What do we do now?*

After dinner, while we were cleaning up, I filled in Keri on the rest of the details and how the brass in Phoenix were trying to cover it up. We started throwing out ideas about what to do next and the possible consequences of each idea.

There was a part of me that just wanted to run out with guns blazing and shout the truth to everyone. *Do something,* I'd been telling myself. Right, wrong, or indifferent, just do something. Doing anything was better than doing nothing.

Action of any kind makes you unpredictable, an unknown and unaccounted-for variable, and a much harder target. The notion holds true for both sides; if attacked, do something—if attacking, be cautious of those who do. Lieutenant Colonel Robert Blair "Paddy" Mayne, a decorated World War II hero and founding member of the British Special Air Service, once said, "When you enter a room full of armed men, shoot the first person who makes a move, hostile or otherwise. He has started to think and is therefore dangerous."

My experience at countless crime scenes had taught me that those who had fled, fought back, or merely just got out of the way had a much higher survival rate than those who just did nothing. If making a move means you're thinking, and thinking makes you dangerous to those attacking you, then dangerous I wanted to be.

But Keri advised me to be patient, to "just wait and take things one step at a time."

"I know waiting may feel like you are doing nothing," she added, "but sometimes waiting is a very valuable tactic. This is not what you're used to, John. This is a whole different ball game and you have to learn to play it before you start swinging."

I was so frustrated and angry. But she was right. That single moment of "now or never" wasn't upon me yet and I needed to know *what to do* before I just did anything.

Time passed so slowly. I was completely unaccustomed to this alien and foreign concept known as waiting. No longer able to subdue my instincts, I thought about the *Washington Post* article that I had read two days before Terry's murder and decided to contact the reporters who wrote it. Not to tell them anything, just to get them looking for something.

I created an anonymous Gmail account and emailed Sari Horwitz and James Grimaldi. "You're so close," I wrote, "just dig a little deeper." They might be—as I thought reporters were supposed to be—dogged pursuers of the truth, real Woodward and Bernstein types. If they thought that there was more to it, maybe they would ask the questions and find out the truth: that the reason guns were showing up in such unprecedented numbers south of the border was that we had opened the floodgates on "the iron river" and allowed them to pour down there.

Grimaldi and Horwitz never got back to me.

Some days later I learned that, in response to the *Post* article, the local Fox News affiliate in Houston, Texas, had reported that gun retailer Carter's Country was claiming that ATF had made them sell to straw purchasers. " 'We were working for the ATF,' " Carter's Country attorney Dick DeGuerin told the local television station. What DeGuerin was saying in that Houston interview was an exact description of what we had been doing in Phoenix.

"Thank you," I said to myself. "This guy is on it." To me, this was a bombshell. I figured it was to everyone else, too. Not wanting the connection to Brian Terry's murder overlooked, I called the television station and asked to speak to the reporter. All I was going to say was 'You should talk to some of the gun shops in Phoenix.'" Surprisingly, they transferred me straight to his desk.

"I saw your report on the Carter's Country thing," I said, still not identifying myself to him.

"Yeah," the reporter breathed into the other end of the phone.

"Are you planning on doing a follow-up on that?" I asked.

"Nah," he rejected. "We've moved on. My editors aren't interested in doing the story anymore."

"But . . ."

"Excuse me, but I got to go." And he hung up the phone.

Also during this same time, I began to wonder what ATF was telling the FBI. The FBI's Tucson Group was the lead agency on the murder investigation. If it were me, I'd want to know everything I could about a case I was working. I went to see my boss at the FBI. Ron was a good guy all around. Late forties, sporting a thick mustache and graying hair, he was easy to talk to. He would muddle his way through the bureaucracy, citing the lunacy of it as he did, but resolved in that for every nine bullshit tasks that came down the pike, the tenth one would be worthwhile and mean something. Not always knowing which ones were which, he was sure to do a good job with them all.

I asked Ron what ATF had shared about the guns in the Brian Terry murder investigation. I told him what I knew about the Fast and Furious investigation and the suspect Jaime Avila. I asked him if ATF had said how Avila had been a suspect in F&F since 2009, that we knew his associates, that we had surveilled him, that we had his phone records, had done intercepts that he might be on, that we observed and documented his firearm purchases, or that we had logged all the traces that came back to him? Ron said that he didn't know, but he would find out. He picked up his desk phone and I walked back to my cube.

A few minutes later, Ron walked up to my desk. Leaning on the wall and rolling something through the cup of his right hand, he looked over both shoulders, checking the area behind him, and said, "No, they were not aware of that information."

I turned my eyes up at him, paused, then returned them to the calendar and said, "Okay. You have now been made aware."

I had scheduled a trip home to Virginia for two weeks at Christmastime. Keri stayed in Phoenix with her kids, and I traveled back with mine. My parents' house is in a fairly remote area in Virginia, no Internet and not a whole lot to do. I helped them with some things around the house and on their small farm. For a short time I was able to escape from the madness of it all.

I was constantly mulling things over in my mind, trying to figure out the best course of action. I knew I had to be careful. I had to talk to someone and explain the whole story. If I just simply made a complaint, chances were that someone in my direct line of supervision would be contacted. If Newell, Gillett, or even Dave got on the phone to explain, then they would assure whomever that I was just a disgruntled agent and a soup sandwich, all the while plotting my demise. If that were to happen, then the truth would never get out. Somehow I had to figure out how to get around my chain of command.

Keri and I had both thought that contacting my old partner from Harrisonburg, Travis, was a good idea. He knew lots of people at ATF and I could trust him. I gave him a call. He said he was going to get a message to someone at headquarters. He couldn't tell me who it was, but it was someone he knew who could get a message to the Office of Professional Responsibility, ATF's version of Internal Affairs, and let them know what was going on.

I flew back to Phoenix to spend New Year's Eve with Keri. We both decided to move forward trying to contact someone who would know what to do. I spent the first couple of weeks of January trying to get in touch with someone while I waited to hear back from Travis.

I decided to try to contact our chief counsel's office. At first I contacted someone I had spoken with previously on unrelated business. I didn't tell her what it was for, just that I had an ethics issue and needed some advice. She referred me to the "attorney of the day" voice mail. I left a message with my name and phone number, but no one ever called me back. A week or so later, I emailed the chief of the ethics department, who referred me to the same voice mail.

I then remembered one of those online training classes that all agents are required to take every year on how to report waste, fraud, and abuse in government. When I was taking the class, I thought it was another baloney pro forma requirement. But in it they said it's our duty to report waste, fraud, and abuse to our chain of command or the Office of the Inspector General.

Since I knew reporting it up my chain of command would get me nowhere other than the stockade, I pulled up the Department of Justice inspector general website on my computer. I called the anonymous hotline number posted on it. There wasn't a real person on the other end of the line, just a long recorded message that directed callers to fill out an online form and send it in.

I was hesitant at first to submit the form online. I didn't want it documented that *I was the one* reporting it. I wanted the whistle blown—but I didn't want to be the one blowing it.

I couldn't handle the thought of the truth surrounding Terry's murder never getting out. Since ATF wasn't about to own it, somebody needed to make them own it. I tried to submit the OIG form via email. Twice, actually. It was kicked back to me both times, labeled "undeliverable."

I then tried to look up another number for the inspector general, a number where I could actually get somebody on the phone. I knew from my uncomfortably chummy meeting with Gillett and Newell that they were suspicious of me already, so I didn't want to use the Justice Department intranet and find a number. I had to use open-source searching. I found that they had an office in Tucson and I called it. Voice mail, so I left a message. Then I decided the best way to get in touch with them was just to go there myself. I wrote down the address and drove all the way to Tucson to try to talk with someone face-to-face.

But it was a wrong address, a missing office, and another dead end for me. No one ever called me back from that voice mail message, either.

My next idea was to try to talk directly with the deputy director, who was Billy Hoover at that time. I had worked a case with his brother-in-law, Dale, who was a detective at a small town police department near Harrisonburg. Billy at least knew my name, and maybe, if I could get a message to him, I could talk with him directly instead of risking him contacting my bosses in Phoenix after I emailed him. When I couldn't reach Dale, I called another detective friend of mine in Virginia and asked him if he could. But, as I found out, Dale had retired and he couldn't. Another dead end.

Each day was more infuriating than the last. Keri would ask me whenever I'd get home from work, "Did anything happen today?" She knew how I was struggling with waiting. We'd walk through what we had already done and what options we had left—if any. The days seemed like years. I felt guilty. I wanted to help. But nobody was listening and everything I was trying made it more and more difficult to get the truth to someone.

During one of these frustrating days in early January, there was a news article posted on our ATF intranet site. Headquarters post any news articles on there that has anything to do with ATF. The article was written by a guy named David Codrea and referenced a website called CleanupATF.org. The report alleged that Phoenix ATF had walked guns and some of those guns had been linked to the shooting of a Border Patrol agent. CleanupATF.org is a blog of sorts, created by some former and current agents calling for reform at the agency. Headquarters dismisses it as the rantings of disgruntled wing nuts, and Acting Director Melson even went so far as to block the sight from being accessed by agency computers. I had heard about this site, been on it only twice before when somebody had specifically told me to check something out, and I had never posted on it.

I found it surreal that this article was on our ATF home page. Whoever edited the page wasn't reading the articles that it linked to. Regardless, I was excited by the fact that there was someone out there speaking up. Equally so that it wasn't me—self-preservation still having the best of me.

I emailed the article to Keri and she began to dig into it a little deeper. She told me how Codrea, who wrote for Examiner.com, and a guy named Mike Vanderboegh, who had a blog called Sipsey Street Irregulars, were reporting on the story. Some of the information was coming from agents who were posting on CleanupATF.org. It was a relief to me that these guys had sources, and that I wasn't one of them. Whoever was talking to them was giving them accurate information, although it didn't seem like firsthand stuff.

As I was still trying everything that I could think of within sanctioned avenues, Keri was keeping an eye on the blogs; they were the only source of information. At one point, rumors began to surface that a Senate staffer was speaking directly to some ATF whistleblowers.

Panic ran through me; fear was swimming in my head . . . First, I could tell their sources weren't directly in the know and so probably could only provide hearsay and couldn't prove anything, either. I imagined the interviews to go something like "Well, I heard that . . ." or "I know a guy that knows a guy that heard something . . ." and then the staffer saying, "Okay, then . . . thanks, everybody, for wasting my time."

Over before it began. And even if they were able to spark interest, any senator or staffer looking into this would make two basic phone calls: one to Bill Newell and another to somebody in ATF headquarters, who would then call Bill Newell. Newell would lie to them both. Nobody would be the wiser.

If there ever was an official investigation, ATF was going to think that I had tipped off the senator and/or the reporters, even though I didn't. They would automatically assume *I was the one* who crashed their little gun-walking party and spoiled their fun of using Mexicans as piñatas and AKs as bats before they could eat up the candies of all the awards and promotions for having done so.

Realizing that there wouldn't be any second chances, that this was one of those moments, *Do something* rang out inside my brain. I emailed Codrea from the covert Gmail account and told him that if anyone was looking into this, to please have them contact me. No name, no number, just the return email address.

Doggedly pursuing the story (yes, that was a mild ding on the other reporters), Codrea emailed me back, provided his contact information, and invited me to be one of his sources. I declined.

Sometime in the second half of January 2010, I had gone to a conference in Las Vegas as part of my FBI duties. As I was driving back, Codrea reported that a staffer had interviewed one or two ATF sources already. Upon learning this, I pulled over on the side of the road outside Henderson, Nevada, and then whipped my car into a nearby gravel lot. I jumped out of the car, other vehicles whizzing by in each direction. The lot belonged to a storage facility—units filled with who knows what and all secured behind a chain-link fence. I looked out in the other direction and could see Lake Mead off in the distance. Nobody was around.

My decision to pull over had two causes: I'd learned the hard way that cell service drops off completely at the state line between Nevada and Arizona; and, for what I was about to do, I had to get out of the government car in case it had been wired up.

I wandered around the lot searching for a cell signal. After finding that shred of signal I needed to make the call, I punched in the number that Codrea had given me.

"Hello," he answered.

The gravity and importance of the message I was conveying to him was clear in the sound of my voice. "If somebody is looking into this . . . tell them to talk to me. You have my email, they *have* to talk to me."

"Okay, got it," Codrea responded.

I hung up and finished the rest of the five-hour drive home.

Phoenix ATF was a rambunctious place in late January 2011. They were planning a raid on the Operation Fast and Furious suspects' homes, at which point they'd arrest the straw purchasers and others connected to the investigation. The same raid could have been done in January 2010, with the only difference having been two hundred guns walked as opposed to two thousand. The decision to finally do it now was brought on entirely by the murder of Brian Terry.

Group VII was hardly the only ATF entity employed for the big takedown. Almost every able-bodied ATF agent in the division was put to work. ATF agents were pulled from other groups and assignments to help, brought up from Tucson, in from other field divisions; even DEA and ICE agents were called in to assist. For obvious reasons, I was the only ATF agent in Phoenix who wasn't assigned on that roundup.

Before dawn on January 25, doors across Phoenix and Arizona were busted in. It happened all at the same time. That's standard procedure for a big takedown. If you do it while most of the suspects are sleeping, they can't warn others in their networks.

While I was working out of the FBI JTTF building at this time,

Keri still worked at the DEA building that housed the Strike Force and Group VII. When Keri arrived at work that morning, she walked into a big show. ATF, DEA, and other federal agents were milling about everywhere.

"Did you help out with that big ATF roundup?" Keri asked one of the DEA agents that morning.

"Yeah," the agent responded. "That was so overkill. It was ridiculous."

Clearly ATF wanted to make this a big public to-do, to make sure all agencies knew what a "big case" they had been working on.

Somewhere around nineteen suspects were arrested and charged—including Jaime Avila. With Avila, they actually dismissed the original indictment handed down when he was arrested twenty-four hours after Brian Terry's murder and reindicted him as part of this group before the press conference.

Later that morning, Newell held a press conference at the division office. They were announcing the arrests and the indictments of the suspects from the Fast and Furious case.

At the press conference, the usual "display weapons" were laid out. These were weapons that had been in our vault at Division for who knows how long. They were not seized weapons from the raid that day, or even from the case. They were completely out of the legal system from age-old cases already adjudicated. It was just all part of the show. The weapons were big, and on the blue ATF tablecloth the guns seemed important. The camera-wielding reporters ate it up, never looking hard enough to realize they were filming the same weapons over and over and over again.

It was well known in the office that Newell had been trying to get the U.S. attorney general, the deputy attorney general for the Criminal Division, or at least some other high-ranking Department of Justice bigwig to show up for the press conference. Newell had been planning the press conference, destined to be big, since shortly after the case had started. But for whatever reason, whether because of the link to Terry's murder or not, the only political figure there was Arizona's U.S. attorney Dennis Burke. There was also other brass from other agencies like DEA and IRS. They were all a part of the Strike Force, too, and even though ATF was sure to do this case on their own, everyone wanted to show how successful the Strike Force had been.

Newell and Burke made the announcement, only there was no mention of the case as Operation Fast and Furious in front of the reporters. They had renamed it and billed it as the "Jaime Avila" case—interesting in that Avila was only a low-level straw purchaser, not even the main target of the whole investigation. He was, however, the link to the Brian Terry murder. They were trying to make it look like all of this was a result of their investigation spurred by the murder.

It wasn't. Truth is, the case had lagged since the wires were shut down in August. The straws continued to make purchases, the FFLs were still being told to make the sales, Group VII was still putting the guns in the Suspect Gun Database, and the traces were still coming in. Gun after gun found at crime after crime all traced back to this case and these suspects, but they did nothing to stop it, nothing to even slow it down. The only reason this takedown was even happening was Brian Terry's murder. This way they could be portrayed as having taken action in response to the murder rather than because of it. Knowing that rumor was getting out about the connection to Fast and Furious, they could reframe that connection entirely differently— even to benefit them. The best lies are 90 percent truth and the best place to hide is right out in the open. So they paraded around in front of the cameras, laid staged weapons out on tables, and orchestrated it all to look like they had gone out and shut down this ring of gun traffickers after following leads developed from the investigation of the murder of Brian Terry.

Toward the end of the ATF dog-and-pony show, a local reporter who had apparently heard the rumors shocked Newell when he asked him if this case involved ATF "walking guns" to Mexico.

"Hell, no," Newell said brusquely, and walked out of the room.

All day I was disgusted, sick to my stomach after hearing about the raid and the press conference. Discouraged and feeling beaten, I thought they were going to pull it off—their cover-up of the gun walking and the many deaths that had resulted from it was going to succeed. "Sons of bitches," I said to myself and then again out loud, many times that day.

But later that afternoon, sitting at my JTTF office, my cell phone pinged with a new email alert. The subject line read "Our Contact Info." I tapped on it. It read:

> My name is Rob Donovan. I work for Senator [Charles] Grassley and I was provided this email address. If you know why I contacted you, then here is our contact information:
>
> If you have documents for us:
>
> whistleblower@judiciary-rep.senate.gov or fax to 202-224-3799
>
> Or, if you would like us to call you, please provide a telephone number.
>
> Thanks,
>
> Rob

My fingers couldn't move fast enough. I emailed Donovan back, giving every number for every phone that I had the means to answer. I can't recall which one, but one of them rang shortly after.

"Hello?"

"Hello, this is Rob Donovan and I'm here with Brian Downey."

"Hello," said a different voice.

"And we're with Senator's Grassley's office . . ."

I had never heard of Donovan or Downey. *Senator who?* I thought. His preamble still going, I was already searching the Web for the names.

I was soon confident that they were who they said they were. But at first it was awkward. They started by asking, "So, what do you want to tell us? Do you have knowledge about something that you'd like to share?"

Continuing our dance of first-date jitters, I replied, "Is there something you want to ask me?" I was a bit hesitant to just give up any potentially sensitive or confidential law enforcement information. "Do you guys have any questions for me?"

We continued a nearly identical back-and-forth for a few minutes. *Holy shit!* I thought. *I'm as good as dead.* If this whole thing was dependent upon these two junior-high weenies who were both collectively afraid to unsnap a bra and were there only because of some bizarre new internship program or maybe just left unsupervised near a telephone on "take your kid to work day" there at the Hart Senate Office Building in Washington, D.C., then this whole thing was going down in flames.

Realizing the perpetual circle jerk that I now found myself in, I broke the pattern. "This is stupid. We're not in middle school anymore so grab your pens and try to keep up."

I took a deep breath and walked them through everything: Who

I was, what my experience had been, and how long I had been in Phoenix. I told them how we had walked guns, how Brian Terry was murdered with them, and how the press conference that day was part of the ongoing attempt to cover it up. I brought up the Significant Incident Report on Avila's arrest the day after Terry was murdered, and how it purposefully left out crucial information on Operation Fast and Furious. I told them about the *Washington Post* article. I told them about the gun shops and how we had instructed them to do the sales, I told them about all the traces and about the Suspect Gun Database, and, finally, I told them how it all added up to be a fixed ball game, rigged to ensure a win for ATF and a loss for the gun dealers, all the dead people in Mexico, and Brian Terry—just to name a few.

The majority of the conversation was me helping them wrap their heads around what was going on. It was hard to understand. It isn't much easier to understand even years later, with all of the benefit that hindsight provides. I had difficulty explaining it to other agents and cop friends back in Virginia. The brain just doesn't seem to want to go there. "To combat gun trafficking, we allowed and facilitated guns to be trafficked, sometimes doing so ourselves."

After they had heard my story, the table was now turned. They questioned who it was they were talking to on the other end of the line. Was I some wing nut, my brain damaged by the hot desert sun, running around in my tinfoil hat wearing nothing but boxer shorts with red suspenders and a pair of green galoshes with the toes cut out? I didn't blame them; it had to sound that way.

"Can you prove any of this?" they asked. "Do you have any documents that can prove it?"

"Yes, sir, I can, and yes, sir, I do."

Releasing documents tightly held by a government organization is a big deal. I knew the ramifications of doing it. Most of the documents relating to this case, and any other case, are held under the classification "law enforcement sensitive." I asked about it and they informed me that the whistleblower laws covered such releases.

I wasn't so sure. What I *was* sure of was that there two official ways I could legally share the documents.

The first is if someone appeared on what's called the "6E list," mentioned earlier. Under the Federal Rules of Criminal Procedure, until a case is cleared—fully adjudicated—information derived during a grand jury session is considered secret. It can only be shared with those whose names appear on the 6E list. Those who are on the 6E list include people like other agents or analysts who might be necessary to help with a certain part of a case or a topic they specialize in. Anyone whose name is on the list is legally obliged to keep that information secret. Congressional investigators are generally not on the 6E list. So that wasn't an option.

Besides, ATF leadership had a narrow reading of the 6E rule and a grossly inaccurate interpretation of it. To them it was all-encompassing. In their wonderland, if a grand jury had ever been utilized for even a single aspect of a case (subpoena for phone records, banks accounts, etc.) then everything else in that case could be classified secret under the 6E rule. Although this was completely wrong, they'd use it to lock people in ATF headquarters out of cases and keep things secretive when they didn't need to be. So I knew that the minute I released any Operation Fast and Furious documents to anyone not on the 6E list they'd come after me claiming I violated that part of the law, even though I hadn't.

The other way I could legally share law enforcement sensitive documents with someone was if I could justify that such a decision to share them was for a legitimate law enforcement purpose. Since Congress had oversight, I deemed this a legitimate law enforcement purpose and emailed them what documents I had.

I couldn't have been more wrong about Donovan and Downey.

Not only were they both very intelligent and very sharp, but they seemed to get it, and it seemed to fire them up. I could sense not only a genuine concern from them, but also that they were appalled by the sheer stupidity of it. They easily recognized what the tragic outcome would be. They began talking about what they were going to do. Their confidence and decisiveness were overwhelming.

All that tension that had been building inside me started to pour out. These two men now knew what I knew, but unlike me, they were in a position to do something about it, and best yet—they were going to do just that. I trembled holding the phone; the sudden release was a shock to my entire system.

I was under no illusions, however, that it was all sunshine and lollipops from here on out. Releasing those documents would only put a target on my back and a price on my head. There was no undoing this now. ATF leadership folks would likely try to gut me with a butter knife using the 6E list rule. The retaliation I already endured was about to get a hell of a lot worse.

I hurried home and told Keri about my call with Donovan and Downey. She shared my sense of relief, but was still worried.

"Can you get in trouble for releasing any of that?" she asked me that night.

"No. They're a competent authority because of their oversight responsibilities," I answered. "I'm only releasing 'sensitive' information, not anything classified and nothing derived from a grand jury. However, that may not stop ATF from trying to accuse me of releasing something illegally and coming after me for it."

Keri gave me a hug and said in a calm voice, "Babe, regardless of what they try to do to you, if you know you aren't doing anything illegal, and you know deep inside it's the right thing to do, I support you no matter what they do."

Support? I thought to myself. *I hope that includes bail money!*

– 9 –

CATEGORICAL DENIAL

I contemplated my conversation with Downey and Donovan, the two congressional investigators who now seemed like the only ones in the world besides Keri who understood what I had been witness to and played a part in. They had both impressed me, but in somewhat different ways. Downey seemed like one of those guys who knew the system well enough, its workings and its flaws, that he could navigate his way through it and use both to his advantage. All the while, he was not afraid to try something that others might call risky, or to blaze a path to new ground.

Donovan was a different animal. Though equally as smart and competent, he seemed a little less like a "cowboy." For the most part, he understood what I was saying first and sometimes helped me explain it in a way that was easier to comprehend. There was something about him that I just couldn't put a finger on, though—but I knew it was there. His ability to translate my vernacular, to speak "cop," was truly a godsend.

As you can imagine, my explanation, of how in order to stop gun trafficking to the Mexican cartels, the ATF began an investigation that facilitated gun trafficking to the cartels, was hard to understand at first. Even more unbelievable was the fact that when the guns found at crime scenes were traced back to us, after they had been used to murder countless people, we touted that as a sign of the success of our investigation.

I told Downey and Donovan from the very beginning, "Ask me anything that you'd like. But there is one question that I just cannot answer for you: 'Why?' I simply don't know." What ATF Phoenix had done defied all logic and common sense. I had trouble understanding that even in the minds of those like Newell, Dave, and Hope there was a rationale.

On January 26, 2010, I again heard from Donovan and Downey. They wanted another call. This time, we were joined by a third man, Jason Foster. Foster, smart and lawyerly, was the lead investigative counsel on Grassley's staff. I assumed that after Downey and Donovan had briefed him, he wanted to hear the unbelievable story straight from the horse's mouth and evaluate it for himself. We went over the whole thing again from beginning to end. Foster was genuinely offended when I told him about the "If you're going to make an omelet, you've got to scramble some eggs" comment.

Regardless, the phrase—and the cavalier attitude that went along with it—described well the prevailing mind-set among that portion of Group VII—Dave, Hope, and Tonya—of the Phoenix ATF chain of command, and of those at headquarters who were familiar with the case. The full-time involvement of the Department of Homeland Security in the F&F investigation with ICE agents meant that they either shared that sentiment or at the very least condoned it. More disturbing was the fact that it was their "eggs" that were going to be "scrambled." Foster was floored. By the time our conversation ended, he was all in.

During that call, they also asked if I had any additional documentation that offered proof in whole or of specific aspects. I did. Sending documents classified as "law enforcement sensitive" to congressional investigators isn't exactly like attaching your term paper in an email to a college professor. It's a complicated process fraught with legal pitfalls, monitored computer systems, and stamps and banners all reading "Not for Release." Even though I knew I wasn't breaking the law, I was still hoping to have F&F exposed without it being overtly known that I was the one to do it. I wanted to cover my ass.

I already had a Gmail account set up for my dealings as a whistleblower, so I created another anonymous account with another smaller provider. I never shared anything from my FBI "high-side" computer—the tower on my desk that was for classified documents and information. So, I'd pull up ATF documents on my ATF laptop, print them to an Adobe PDF file, and email them as attachments to my FBI "low-side" computer. Then I'd use my FBI computer to change the metadata of the file, save it as a different PDF, and then email it to the first ghost account, which I had set to auto-forward and double-scrub it and email it to the second. Finally, accessing the Gmail account solely through my personal Droid phone, I'd send the documents to the whistle-blower email address. Then I'd call Grassley's guys and confirm receipt.

You may think it odd, but the strongest security wall in that sequence was routing through my FBI computer. Already under suspicion by ATF, I assumed they might be monitoring my computer, internal accounts, keystrokes, and emails. If they were, and they observed me sending a document that they didn't want to get out to my FBI account on my FBI computer, when they tried to track it from there FBI would shut them down on the spot. There was no way that the FBI was going to allow their screwed-up little brother to monitor anything on any of its systems or any of its computers. It just wasn't going to happen. At the very best, FBI would start monitoring me on their systems and when they picked up the email traffic, examined it, and learned it had nothing to with FBI, they wouldn't care. Sending me to JTTF was the worst thing ATF could have done to try to keep me quiet. Although under the thumb of Big Brother ATF, I was also in the pocket of Bigger Brother FBI.

I don't know how many times I went through this exhausting process. It seemed too many to count. For every piece of evidence I'd hand over to the Hill, they'd ask for something more. "Got it," they'd say, "but do you have *this*?" or "How about *that*?"

I still had access to Operation Fast and Furious case file documents that I had saved on my hard drive, but I no longer had access to the ones in NFORCE or the "S-Drive," a shared intranet server with thousands of spreadsheets and other documents. Twenty-four hours after Brian Terry's murder, Casa, Alt, and I were cut out of them both—access denied.

Sometimes I had what they wanted. Sometimes I didn't, and I'd have to go through a backdoor channel or make a new channel to try to get it. If they wanted a certain piece of information and I didn't have access to the certain document that contained it, I'd often have to piece it together from other documents that I did have access to. One plus two equals three, but so does one plus one plus one. Government redundancy means every department and section having its own form to fill out that lists and counts the same information, all for the purpose of padding the numbers or skewing the stats so each can justify its own position or show why it needs more funding. And I was working the Bureau of Redundancy Bureau against itself.

I wasn't blowing the whistle and casting a disapproving finger at any one person or group of people—I was owning my part of it as well. Yes, I thought it was stupid, absurd, moronic, and, ultimately, deadly. Yes, I could say who had told me what and who had done this or that. But I never said, "There they are. Go get them." My blowing the whistle was "We did this. This is how we did it." And "This is what happened as a result of doing it."

My motivation for doing so was equally plain. "We owe people the truth. We owe it to the victims' families; we owe it to the Terry family. We don't get to lie about it. We don't get to cover it up. That's not who we are—that's not what we do."

I remember going through the local criminal justice academy when I started as a deputy with the Orange County, Virginia, Sheriff's Office. For our ethics class, the academy had brought in a captain from some city police department to be the guest lecturer. He explained: "Ethics is hard to define. Imagine that you're driving out in the middle of nowhere. It's the middle of the night and you come upon a crossroad with a lone traffic light. It's red for you and you stop. Looking left and right down the crossing road, you can see for miles and there are no cars coming. As a matter of fact, there are no other cars or people anywhere around . . . you're all alone. What do you do? Run the red light or wait for it to turn green?"

"Ethics means what you do, what decisions you make when no one else is looking," he concluded.

Holy shit, I thought to myself, turning to look at my fellow Orange County deputy Jim, who had been hired on the same day and was going through the academy with me. *We're screwed!* I knew damn well that he and I both were blowing through that red light.

Thinking about it now, however, I would ask a different question: "When everyone else around you is doing something that you know to be wrong, telling you that it's okay and wanting you to do it with them, knowing that doing so means you keeping your career and that not doing so means you losing it; when everyone is around and all eyes are on you . . . what do you do then?" That's what ethics means.

Over a two-day period, having proved ATF gun walking to Grassley's investigators, I cleared the second hurdle. (After my bounced emails and unreturned voice mails, I count just getting them on the phone as the first.) Confident in what evidence they had, they went to their principal himself, Senator Charles Grassley, and briefed him. At that point, they decided to take action.

As the Iowa senator's staffers readied their first inquiry on the matter to acting ATF director Ken Melson, on January 27, 2011, I faced hurdle number three. I had to tell ATF that I had spoken with Grassley's office about the case.

I felt I had an obligation under ATF rules to disclose to them my contact with the staffers. Foster and his crew argued differently, citing that all citizens have the right to speak with Congress. They assured me that maintaining my anonymity was but the first level of whistle-blower protection and that they and Grassley himself took that very seriously and would not violate it. I believed them.

However, I felt a duty. I knew I was doing the right thing and I had no reason to hide it. And again, I would own what I had done.

They asked me if I had an attorney.

"What do I need an attorney for?" I asked.

"You need one," Foster said, then explained. "Look, these normally don't turn out well for the whistleblowers. I'd be lying if I told you any different. There might be adverse personnel actions or they might just come after you in some other way to try to discredit, disparage, or smear you. Attack the accuser and take away his credibility—I've seen it happen so many times."

"I can get an attorney."

"Good. Get somebody. We'll be in touch."

I was a member of the Federal Law Enforcement Officers Association. It's more of a lobby group than a union; most federal agents pay $160 per year for membership. Part of the membership package is free legal representation. I would later remember that old adage, You get what you pay for.

I contacted my direct line supervisor, Marge Zicha, and notified her of my contact with Senate staffers. I told her that it was a developing situation and that I would keep her, and thus ATF, informed every step of the way. She emailed me back; I had a meeting with her and Gillett down at Division.

The meeting was set for around 2 P.M. that Friday, January 28. Before I went, I met Casa, Alt, Joe, and another Group VII agent, Mark Sonnendecker, for lunch at Cooper's Town, Alice Cooper's restaurant in downtown Phoenix.

Seconds after we sat down, I blurted out everything. "Look, investigators from Senator Grassley's office contacted me," I announced. "They asked me about Operation Fast and Furious, gun walking, and how it all tied in to Terry's murder."

I'm not sure what I was expecting: "Hell yeah! I can't wait to talk to them!" would have been nice. But they didn't react much; they all just went about with lunch. Finally I added, "Grassley's investigators want to know if anybody else will talk to them."

Medina remained silent. I understood the predicament he was in—he was a new agent and didn't want to rock the boat too hard or else he'd lose his job. Alt and Casa each piped up. "Tell them to serve us with a subpoena," each said. "We'll talk then."

Sonnendecker, whom I hadn't yet gotten to know very well, asked me, "So, who called who?"

"What?" I asked back.

"Did you call them or did they call you?"

"They called me," I responded. Which was true. When I replied to Donovan's email with my cell phone number, they were the first ones who called. "What damn difference does it make?" I responded, his questions feeling like crosshairs zeroing in on me.

He pressed further. "Well, what number did they call you on?"

"Say again?"

"Did they call you on your work phone or did they call you on your personal cell?"

"I don't remember, Mark," I answered. "But it was definitely one of the two."

Feeling like I had to get out of there, find some cover, something, I told them my next move. "I'm heading over to Division to meet with Gillett and Marge." I put my money down and left.

Crossing the street to where I had parked, I tried processing what had just happened. I had trusted these guys. We had had so many conversations about the insanity of all this; I thought they'd be right there with me. The whole thing gave me an uneasy feeling.

I made the short drive over to Division. After parking, I rode the elevator up to the ninth floor. Something was going on; there was a palpable sense of urgency all over the office. All the doors were closed, but with people darting in and out of them, from one room to another and then quickly closing doors again. I looked for Scooby and Shaggy to come running out of one and some monster out of the other. I hadn't known it at the time, but it wasn't hard to figure out: Grassley's letter had hit Melson's desk and the calls to Phoenix were already coming in. The letter was stinging:

It is my understanding that the ATF is continually conducting operations along the southwestern United States border to thwart illegal firearm trafficking. I am specifically writing you concerning an ATF operation called "Project Gunrunner." There are serious concerns that the ATF may have become careless, if not negligent, in implementing the Gunrunner strategy.

Members of the Judiciary Committee have received numerous allegations that the ATF sanctioned the sale of hundreds of assault weapons to suspected straw purchasers, who then allegedly transported these weapons throughout the southwestern border area and into Mexico. According to the allegations, one of these individuals purchased three assault rifles with cash in Glendale, Arizona on January 16, 2010. Two of the weapons were then allegedly used in a firefight on December 14, 2010 against U.S. Customs and Border Protection (CBP) agents, killing CBP Agent Brian Terry. These extremely serious allegations were accompanied by detailed documentation which appears to lend credibility to the claims and partially corroborates them.

I made it down the hall to Gillett's office, knocked on the door, and walked inside. He was sitting at his desk, Marge in a chair in front of him; both were waiting for me, and neither stood up. Marge was holding a brand-new notepad freshly picked from the shelf in the supply room. Bouncing the point of her pen on it, she was unable to control her eagerness to take notes. I sat down in one of the chairs that I'd unfortunately grown all too accustomed to during my time in Phoenix.

Grassley's letter had ruined my plans to deliver the ol' "I wanted you to hear it from me first" speech. Forced to think on the fly, I decided to forgo the pleasantries. I began: "I was contacted by investigators from Capitol Hill, and they were asking me questions about Operation Fast and Furious, Project Gun Runner, and the Southwest Border Initiative."

Gillett's tone had a sense of urgency. He seemed rocked, clinging from his normally arrogant perch. "Did you call them or did they call you?" Gillett asked.

"They called me," I responded. If that was not the answer he wanted, well—he should have phrased his question differently.

Marge was feverishly taking notes.

"Did they call you on your work phone or your personal phone?" he asked next.

"I don't remember," I said, responding truthfully.

I was more than a little suspicious now; those first two questions were the same first two questions that Mark had asked me at lunch a few minutes earlier.

"What did they say?" Gillett asked next, referring to the congressional investigators' questions.

The letter having already hit and my suspicions raised, I felt like they had gotten a jump on me and that I was trapped behind the eight-ball. I wasn't going to lie to him, but I decided to volunteer as little as possible until I could get a better grasp on the situation.

"They asked me about Project Gunrunner," I responded coolly, my eyes locked on his. "They asked me about the Southwest Border Initiative, and they asked me about Operation Fast and Furious."

"And what did you tell them?" he followed up.

"I told them that I couldn't answer their questions about Gunrunner and other stuff like that because they are funding initiatives that I know nothing about. All that stuff was echelons above Dodson. I told them that they would need to ask somebody else." I spoke as calm as ever. "They asked if I had an attorney, I said 'No,' and they told me to get one. I told them I would and he'd be in touch. After, thinking that I had an obligation to tell ATF about it, I emailed Marge, and now, here I am telling you."

As I continued explaining all this to Gillett, Marge's pen was moving at light speed. "As soon as I hear back from my attorney and figure all this out, I'll let you know. And, like I told Marge, I'll keep you abreast of the situation, every step of the way."

I hadn't uttered a word that was untrue. Was I hoping that he thought I had lawyered up? Hell yes.

"Okay," Gillett said. "This is what I want you to do. I'm ordering you to go, right now, and write me a memo about the whole thing. I want it to include who called you, what phone they called you on, how it all came down, and exactly what was said. Write exactly what they asked you and exactly what you told them."

"Ten-roger," I said, and I got up and walked out.

I hopped in my car and drove back over to my FBI office. I was still unsuccessfully trying to reach my Federal Law Enforcement Officers Association attorney, Larry Berger. As I sat down to write the memo, a thought popped into my head. I quickly called Marge and said that I needed another meeting with Gillett right away.

"Come on down," she said.

When I got back to Gillett's office, the scene was déjà vu all over again. He was at his desk and Marge was in the same chair, bouncing her pen.

"Okay, I went to write your memo," I replied, "but I need to ask you about something first. You told me to write down 'exactly' what happened, 'exactly' what they asked me, and 'exactly' what I said."

"Yes," Gillett responded.

"Well, I figured since you didn't ask me what those details were before, you might want to know them before I actually put 'em down in writing?"

Here I was, out of time, out of options, unable to reach counsel, and ordered to stroke out an official memo that would not only be damning to him, his boss, and his friends, but the Phoenix Division, a good bit of headquarters people, and to ATF as a whole. I was giving him a chance to rescind that order before the rock he thought he had me under came crashing down on the hard place that I had just laid at his feet.

"All right," he said. "Tell me."

"They asked me about Operation Fast and Furious. I told them that we were walking guns, two thousand or more that I knew of. I told them how we had coerced the FFLs into helping us and pressured them to go through with the sales when they didn't want to go through with them. I told him how two guns found at the scene of Agent Terry's murder were F&F guns and purchased by Jaime Avila. I told them that we had Avila identified back in 2009 and had been watching him ever since—we knew him, his friends, his associates, and who he met with. I told them we knew every gun he had purchased and every purchase he made, most of the time in real time. I told them how I had complained and warned about what we were doing, that we were going to get people killed—specifically a Border Patrol agent—and that I had only caught shit for it and was transferred out. Then I told them that the case was only shut down after Agent Terry was killed and that now you guys were trying to hide the connection and cover the whole thing up."

Gillett was stunned. Usually cocky and arrogant, I could see his cool escaping him fast.

"Now, I ask you, do you want me to put that in a memo? On official government letterhead?"

Gillett was red in the face when he answered. "No! Now I'm ordering you to sit, right now, and you're going to write me a memo saying how you came in here and lied to me the first time and how now you're coming in here again with a different story!"

"Whoa, whoa, whoa." I slowed Gillett down. "I didn't lie to you. Everything I said before was the truth. I told you what they asked me about and I said I couldn't answer most of it. And then I told you

about wanting to talk to my legal rep. You didn't ask me for any details or to elaborate.

"You only asked for that when you ordered me to write a memo,"
I continued. "A 'detailed' memo. Now, I'm here asking you, are you
sure you want to do that? Because the detail is something that you
might not want to see written down."

"I'm ordering you to write that memo right now," Gillett said.
"Detailing how you lied to me."

"I'm not writing a memo confessing some bullshit lie to you," I
said. "I didn't lie. I will write a memo about what happened, but now I
want to consult with my attorney first."

Screaming and pointing now, Gillett replied, "Oh yes you are.
And now you're refusing to obey a direct order and you're gonna put
that in there, too. Lying and refusing to obey an order. You're going to
sit down and write it for me right now."

"Why? So you can gut me with it?" I screamed back. "I didn't lie
and I'm not refusing your order. I'm just wanting to consult with my
attorney first."

"Right now!" Gillett tripled down. "You're not leaving here until I
get that memo. You're going to sit down right there at that table and
write it and you're not leaving until you do."

It was a Friday, late afternoon, and most everybody else had already shuffled out of Division except for the ninth-floor people who
were trying to put out the fires that Grassley's letter had started.

"No, sir, I'm not."

"God damn it!" Gillett came from around his desk and screamed
into my face. "You're insubordinate! Don't disobey my order! You're
not leaving here until you write that memo!"

"Look, I'm not writing your memo until I talk to my lawyer." I
stood my ground. "And if you tell me I can't leave, fine. But I guar-
antee you one damn thing." I was squaring up with him, my finger

pointing straight at his. "Your ass is going to have to sit here and babysit mine all fucking night, all fucking weekend long or until I can get a hold of Berger. Because if you don't, the first second you leave, my ass is out the door right behind yours." My voice in a cadence now, thumping in time, I continued, "I ain't writing your goddamn memo until I talk to my lawyer."

Finally, Gillett relented. "Get out of my office. Get out of here!" he bellowed. "I want you back in here first thing Monday morning and you better have that memo with you and you better have your stuff together."

On my way home, Grassley's guys called me and asked me how it went.

"Oh," I replied. "It could have gone better."

They weren't too surprised at the visceral reaction from my boss. Grassley's letter to Melson had caused a frenzy in ATF, and apparently at the Department of Justice as well, I'd later find out. I had expected that now that all the bigwigs were forced to look into this before responding to Grassley, the admission of wrongdoing might not come right away, but it would come. My part was done. I just wasn't sure if my job was going to survive it, though.

When I finally got home, Keri was in the laundry room. I walked in and began filling her in on the details. As we were standing there talking, Gillett called my work phone. I didn't answer it. Then my personal cell phone, then my home phone all began to ring. It was Gillett. I still didn't answer, but he left a voice mail on one, telling me to call him.

Keri said, "John, you should call him. Remember, you haven't done anything wrong."

I took my phone, stepped outside, and called him back. He answered, sounding polite yet stern. His inflection signified the gravity of what he was saying. "I've got the director on the other line. He wants to know what you have done."

I answered him: "Sir, I'm trying to get in touch with Berger. I just want to talk to him first."

It bothered me. I had never lawyered up before or hidden behind anything. I felt like that was what I was doing and I didn't like it.

Gillett started screaming at me over the phone. "Damn it! Did you hear me—the director wants to know what you told them. Did you turn over any documents?"

"Sir," I said, "I just want some advice first. But you can tell the director to call me himself if he'd like. I'll speak to him."

The phone went dead. It was a short conversation, and I was glad about that. I tried calling the attorney again, but there was still no answer.

I found out later that the brass up at headquarters had been burning up the phone lines. One of them had even told Gillett that they needed to send someone out to my house to find out what I had turned over to Grassley's office. They were not at all interested in whether what I was saying was true or not, or if I had a legitimate reason to talk to Congress; they only cared about what I had divulged. They and the U.S. attorney in Phoenix were already thinking about prosecuting me under their expansive interpretation of the 6(e) rule and were trying to build their case to do so.

Berger finally called me back later that night and told me it was okay to go ahead and write the memo. I spent the rest of the weekend trying to get prepared for being fired on Monday morning when I hit Gillett's office. I had taken his "get your stuff together" comment quite literally. I cleaned out my g-ride of any personal items and put all my gear and equipment in the trunk. Anything that belonged to ATF was all packed up and ready to be turned in to them.

Thoughts raced through my head. *What about my family? If I don't have a job, what will happen to them? What about Keri? We haven't even known each other for a year. Is she sure she wants to do with this me?*

Keri and I talked a lot that weekend, and she assured me she was by my side. We both felt pretty certain that I would be fired, and it was a strong possibility I would be arrested. I had heard them threaten other folks with the 6(e) rule many times, and I knew they would use it as their trump card. They could never convict me on it, but arresting me and throwing me in jail until I could finally get a trial was all too possible.

Keri and I had both grown up in the rural South, and our parents didn't have much. We are both very proud of our families and where we are from. When I told her that come Monday, I might not have a job, she just looked at me and said, "That's okay. We grew up poor, we can go back. It's more important to do the right thing. Besides, ATF is just your employer; they are not God. They may sign your paycheck, but God is our Provider and our Defender. I trust Him."

Even though we were going through so much, and there were times we got frustrated with the situation and with each other, I fell more in love with Keri every day.

"Best-case scenario," I told her, "I get fired and need a ride home. Worst case—here." I handed Keri what I called my personal "Oh shit" list—names and numbers, listed on a piece of paper, in the order in which she needed to call them. If they arrested me, I could simply call her, setting off a chain of notifications and hopefully amass enough of a cavalry to come and get my ass out of jail. Among the numbers on the list: Alt's and Casa's, all of Grassley's investigators, Berger, my old Loudon County detective partner Kenny, Travis, my brother, and a few others.

Since I didn't have it memorized because it was programmed in my phone, I wrote Keri's number down on my hand. I had the memo drafted and was ready to go. I rode into my FBI office and printed it out on ATF letterhead. As it was falling down off the printer, the spool still spinning, my work phone rang; it was Gillett.

"I'm leaving JTTF now," I answered. "I just had to swing by here and print it."

"Never mind," he said. "Don't worry about it and no need coming down here."

I was confused and somewhat relieved. Relieved that maybe I was being spared somehow and then terrified by wondering what even more of a terrible fate they must have in store for me.

"But I have the memo written and I'm ready to answer all your questions. I'm walking out the door right now."

"Don't worry about it," he said. "And, as a matter of fact, there's no need for you and I to ever talk about this again." Click. He hung up.

I had no clue why Gillett had done that. It didn't make any sense to me. What had happened? What could they be up to? Then, *ping*. An email came in from Donovan at Grassley's office: "Here, take this with you to your meeting this morning," he wrote, referencing the email's attachment. It was a second letter from Grassley to Melson berating ATF for their conduct.

After Gillett's going high-order on me the previous Friday when I told him about how I had talked with Congress, Grassley sent *another* letter to Melson admonishing him for Gillett's behavior on behalf of the agency:

> I understand that Assistant Special Agent in Charge (ASAC) George Gillette [*sic*] of the ATF's Phoenix office questioned one of the individual agents who answered my staff's questions about Project Gunrunner. ASAC Gillette allegedly accused the agent of misconduct related to his contacts with the Senate Judiciary Committee. This is exactly the wrong sort of reaction for the ATF.

Rather than focusing on retaliating against whistle-blowers, the ATF's sole focus should be on finding and disclosing the truth as soon as possible.

Whistle-blowers are some of the most patriotic people I know—men and women who labor, often anonymously, to let Congress and the American people know when the Government isn't working so we can fix it. As such, it would be prudent for you to remind ATF management about the value of protected disclosures to Congress and/or Inspectors General in accordance with the whistleblower protection laws. Absent such a clear communication from you, ATF management might be able to intimidate whistleblowers to prevent them from providing information to Congress.

Grassley even suggested that Gillett's actions that night, and by extension those of the ATF leadership, could have constituted a crime—because they appeared to be an effort to obstruct his congressional investigation.

A U.S. senator looking out for me? He didn't have to do that. I certainly didn't ask for it, but I damn sure appreciated it. I guess the letter got to Gillett through the ATF chain faster than it got to me and that's why he called off the meeting and the memo.

I remembered some of my earliest training: "Cover versus concealment—concealment only hides you, cover stops bullets!" And I had just found some cover.

I can't overstate how relieved Keri and I were that day. We had really believed that Monday was going to end in chaos, but instead, I finally felt like I had one in the win column. I hadn't felt that way in a while.

I found out a few days after that Gary Styers had also been contacted by Grassley's office and spoke to them. Even though he had not been there for as long as I had, he backed up what I had said. He stated that Hope and Dave widely disregarded anyone else's opinions or advice and stated that agents were ordered off surveillances during the case. He notified his supervisors of his contact with the Hill and then when asked to write a memo by his superiors, and probably handling the situation somewhat better than I had, he did so and detailed his statements to Grassley's office about the case. It was a huge relief and I respected and appreciated Styers very much for doing so. I still do.

As later documents would prove, that memo from Styers was sent to ATF headquarters on February 3. Our assistant director at the time would also later tell congressional investigators that he forwarded it to main Justice that same day. In short, by the close of business on February 3, 2011, ATF headquarters and the Justice Department were both aware of what I had reported to the senator and that pivotal parts of what I had said had been substantiated by another agent, from another field division, who didn't have a dog in the fight. So, even if they believed the line of shit being fed to them that I was disgruntled or had an axe to grind, how could they account for Styers and his February 3 memo?

The rest of the week I spent on the phone with the senator's staffers and talking with Keri about how ATF might respond to Grassley's letter. We thought they would answer and take the "we're checking into it" route. We believed there was too much solid evidence there to ignore and that an all-out denial wasn't even possible. Regardless, we knew nothing was going to happen fast.

February 4, the day after receiving Styers's memo, became a day of reckoning for me. Grassley's office received their first response from their first letter. Interestingly enough, the letter came from the

Department of Justice even though Grassley's letter was addressed and sent to Acting Director Melson at ATF. ATF had lawyered up. As I read it, I simply couldn't believe it.

> At the outset, the allegation described in your January 27 letter—that ATF "sanctioned" or otherwise knowingly allowed the sale of assault weapons to a straw purchaser who then transported them into Mexico—is false. ATF makes every effort to interdict weapons that have been purchased illegally and prevent their transportation to Mexico. Indeed, an important goal of Project Gunrunner is to stop the flow of weapons from the United States to drug cartels in Mexico. Since its inception in 2006, Project Gunrunner investigations have seized in excess of 10,000 firearms and 1.1 million rounds of ammunition destined for Mexico. Hundreds of individuals have been convicted of criminal offenses arising from these investigations and many others are on-going. ATF remains committed to investigating and dismantling firearms trafficking organizations, and will continue to pursue those cases vigorously with all available investigative resources.
>
> In this vein, the suggestion that Project Gunrunner focuses simply on straw purchasers is incorrect. The defendants named in the indictments referenced in your January 27 letter include leaders of a sophisticated gun trafficking organization. One of the goals of the investigation that led to those indictments is to dismantle the entire trafficking organization, not merely to arrest straw purchasers.
>
> I also want to assure you that ATF has made no attempt to retaliate against any of its agents regarding this matter. We recognize the importance of protecting employees from retaliation relating to their disclosures of waste, fraud, and abuse. ATF employees receive

annual training on their rights under the Whistle-blower Protection Act and those with knowledge of waste, fraud, or abuse are encouraged to communicate directly with the Department's Office of Inspector General. These protections do not negate the Department's legitimate interest in protecting confidential information about pending criminal investigations.

We also want to protect investigations and the law enforcement personnel who directly conduct them from inappropriate political influence. For this reason, we respectfully request that committee staff not contact law enforcement personnel seeking information about pending criminal investigations, including the investigation into the death of Customs and Border Patrol Agent Brian Terry. Like you, we are deeply concerned by his murder and we are actively investigating the matter. Please direct any inquiry into his killing to this office.

The Department would be pleased to provide a briefing to Committee staff about Project Gunrunner and ATF's efforts to work with its law enforcement partners to build cases that will disrupt and dismantle criminal organizations. That briefing would not address the on-going criminal investigation referenced in your letter. As you know, the Department has a longstanding policy against the disclosure of non-public information about pending criminal investigations, which protects the independence and effectiveness of our law enforcement efforts as well as the privacy and due process interests of individuals who may or may not ever be charged with criminal offenses.

The letter was signed by Assistant Attorney General Ronald Weich. *Who the hell is he?* I thought. *And why is he writing and sending such a bullshit letter?*

Having anyone at ATF headquarters, much less the Justice Department, come back to Grassley with a denial hadn't even been a
possibility for me. I knew what had happened, I knew what I said
was the truth, I knew that none of it was false. I expected some
bullshit about needing time to look into it. I could have even believed some legalese political nonsense that was convoluted and so
confusing that you really didn't know what they were trying to say.
But to deny the allegations and declare them false meant only one
thing: that my statements were a lie. I had seen a lot of screwed up
things in my career, a lot of mistakes, a lot of stretching the truth,
but I had never seen a blatant lie from a law enforcement agency—
much less the highest one in the land. That's not what we do, that's
not who we are, and it's for damn sure not who we are supposed
to be.

Furthermore, why would Justice respond on their behalf and
put their fingerprints all over this hot mess? Surely they'd want to
maintain plausible deniability. On the other hand it had to be true
that Justice Department officials knew what the ATF was doing. The
wiretap affidavits had to be approved at Office of Enforcement Operations, which requires approval high up in the department.

Grassley's guys were surprised by it, too. They had the documents,
they had the proof. They couldn't understand how or why the department could just flatly deny it.

The questions were racing in my head. Why did ATF lawyer up?
Why did the department take the reins on this so quickly? How do
you deny allegations without even attempting to talk with anyone
who made the allegations? Who were they talking to? Nobody was
calling my phone. Styers had sent his memo in the day before, so it
wasn't just me making these allegations. If the Justice Department
was handling this now, it was clear to me they were not interested

in actually looking for the truth; they just wanted the problem to go away.

The only reason that I could come up with is that Justice was not only trying to help cover ATF's ass: they were covering their own as well. It seemed the cover-up went much higher than I ever believed it could have.

– 10 –

LEAP INTO
THE BOUNDLESS

With the Justice Department's denial, tension began finding its way into our home. Keri and I didn't really fight, but between my having to lie in a pitch-black room with earplugs until the headaches subsided and her having to deal with all the household stuff, it wasn't always happy times. We pressed on, however, trying our best not to let the outside stress of the situation consume our lives.

I was content to let the congressional investigation take its own course, as long and stressful as it might be. Talking directly to the press wasn't something I was inclined to do. Grassley's staff had explained to me the importance that the press could play in a matter such as this. Often, pressure from the media can be the only thing to shake something loose. Keri and I discussed it and agreed: going to the press didn't seem like a good move for us. Besides the fact that I knew there was no quicker way to get myself fired, it simply wasn't me. I had spent nearly my whole life hiding from attention, moving only in the shadows or on the periphery, going completed unnoticed whenever possible.

I was hoping that the press would pick it up on their own; that was what I supposed investigative reporting was all about. With what documents were already out there, having been attached to Senator Grassley's letters, and the background his staff could provide—a first-year journalism student could have brought the whole story to the fore. However, Jason Foster and his team in Washington explained that they were having a difficult time getting a good reporter involved. They all wanted a source, an interview, a face to put on the story. No one wanted to do the story without it. "Most reporters are simply lazy," they concluded.

So, in the midst of our frustrations, as the giant wheels of bureaucracy slowly began grinding me down, all we could do was bide our time and hope. I don't think we knew what we were waiting for, exactly: some insight or direction, maybe even salvation? Regardless, we had faith and figured whatever it was we were supposed to do next would come to us eventually . . . and secretly I prayed that we would recognize it.

In the meantime, Keri checked the blogs regularly and was gaining information. There were rumors of how the ATF attaché in Mexico had raised concerns about the case and how there had been heated discussions about it at headquarters. This gave us some hope that the few of us in Group VII were not the only ones who had seen where this whole thing was headed.

Grassley's staff began working even harder. I spoke with them on the phone daily, going over documents that they would receive or just answering general questions about law enforcement techniques, what I thought this meant, had I heard about this or did I know about that.

In the beginning I spoke with Downey and Donovan the most, though Foster became more involved as things progressed. They became a new set of friends for me. No one from ATF was really talking to me; I was too toxic—completely radioactive.

There were many late nights when we talked about everything that had happened and brainstormed over what steps to take next and placed bets as to what would happen with this whole situation. Keri was my anchor, but they were my sail and rudder. They kept me informed, gave me insight into why certain things were happening, and took time to explain it to me.

Foster gave me the number for Jay Lerner at the Justice Department's Office of the Inspector General (OIG). I had told him the trouble I had getting in touch with him, and Foster said it was a good idea to file a complaint. I called Lerner and emailed him the form that I tried to submit those two times before. It took a week or so before I was able to confirm receipt.

Shortly after that, two guys from the Colorado office of the IG came to Phoenix to interview me. I was nervous because I had been warned that the inspector general's office might try to turn everything around on me. I spent about three hours telling them the whole story. It seemed like they could hardly believe what I was saying. At the end of the interview, I looked at them and said, "I've told you everything I know; now you guys tell me, is there anything else I could have done?"

"No," they said. "Sounds like you did everything you could."

When Grassley got the February 4 letter back from Justice, denying that anything resembling Fast and Furious ever took place, he requested that the department and ATF give his staff an in-person briefing about it. His staff wanted to be able to ask questions of the Justice Department lawyers and ATF brass in person about the allegations of gun walking—and their vehement denial that it had ever happened. In an immediate sign that this was going to get political, Justice refused to do the briefing unless Senate Democratic staffers were there too, since Grassley is a Republican, a minority in the Senate.

I didn't give a rat's ass about anybody's political affiliation; I just wanted the truth to get out. However, I was seeing how if one political party asks a probing question of the other, swords and shields are fast at the ready. The substantive matter of the question is irrelevant, because if it came from the other side one must defend against it at all cost. No one cares if the information is true or if it's a legitimate question that needs to be asked—everyone just starts taking jabs against whoever asked it.

Having Ron Weich, a deputy attorney general, answer on behalf of ATF with their February 4 letter to Grassley was the first punch. I realized that the department was right smack in the middle of the whole ordeal. This put it all right at the feet of the attorney general, and regardless of what party holds power in the executive branch, it is now but one person removed, only one degree of separation, from the president of the United States himself.

Rather than seek out the truth, ask the questions, or look into it in any way, ATF and DOJ's reaction was to fight back—regardless that they weren't even under attack.

Back at work, the retaliation hadn't stopped. It had only become more subtle.

Alt would provide some information here and there about what was going on in the division office. However, the couple of people who were talking to me tried to keep their communication to a minimum. One day, I had a training requirement, so I asked Alt about it. As the SOO, he was handling the schedule for it. He and I exchanged a couple of emails of witty banter until ultimately he said I needed to contact my supervisor directly. I forwarded Alt's email to my administrative supervisor (since I reported strictly to Gillett operationally and he decided not to be bothered with the mundane administrative aspects, I now had two direct supervisors), and she promptly forwarded it to Gillett.

Not pleased that Alt had even provided me with a "Sorry, can't help you," George called him to his office immediately. Gillett was so anxious and fired up he waited outside his door and met Alt in the hallway. Brief but loud, George barked at Alt for having exchanged emails with me and ended with his finger pointing and thumping to the cadence of this conclusion: "Communication with Dodson is detrimental to any ATF career." Several people saw and heard the whole thing. Word spread through the division like twenty-five-cent drafts at happy hour—Gillett had issued a standing order that no one who valued their job whatsoever should have anything to do with me.

Around the same time, Marge called me. She informed me that I would be required to attend a class in Artesia, New Mexico, for five days. The class was "Emergency Spanish for Law Enforcement Officers." Seeing that I was now working on a terrorism task force for the FBI, I didn't seem like the best candidate for this school. Not to mention the fact that, in comparison to most of the agents I had been working with in Phoenix, my Spanish was top-shelf. Wouldn't it make more sense to send someone who needed it? Someone who was actually going after Spanish speaking suspects?

Since I was a single dad and had my kids at home, leaving for five days was an inconvenience, to say the least. My FBI boss was none too happy about it, either, ATF leaving him a man down for that week. I decided to ask Marge to reconsider and cited the FBI and kid issues. Marge, who had also been there that day when Gillett exploded on me for blowing the whistle, answered, "Don't try your luck." She added, "That letter from Grassley didn't do you any good."

Knowing my situation, knowing that overnight child care would be difficult if not impossible for me, and with less than a week before I had to leave, I thought they wanted me to say "I can't go" so they could then fire me for refusing an order, refusing training, or something of the like. What they didn't know was that I had a secret weapon. They didn't know I had Keri. She held down the fort while I headed to Artesia. It was one of many times I was glad we hadn't advertised our relationship very much.

There were about twenty students in the class. All but four were uniformed cops from other federal agencies—National Park Service, Federal Protective Service, and Tribal Police. The class was likely beneficial for them, as it was geared for street cops pushing a cruiser around out on a patrol.

Of the remaining four students, there was me, some new guy from our Tucson office, and two suits from ATF headquarters in Washington. They were high-ranking HQ types who hadn't worked in the field in years, if ever, and there was no reason for them to be in this emergency field Spanish for street cops class. The teacher even remarked at one point that he was glad ATF was so interested in the course but that it really wasn't geared toward what we do.

The two headquarters guys stood out like a sore thumb. On the first day, when the teacher had everyone introduce themselves and explain what they did in law enforcement, everybody else said their name and whatever agency they worked for. When it was these guys' turn, they said their names and gave long official descriptions; one was the "program manager in charge of the Southwest Border Initiative for ATF based out of Washington, D.C.," and the other had some similarly bureaucratic title.

The teacher asked them in front of the class: "You're not doing any street work down on the border?"

"No," they responded.

"You know this is emergency Spanish for law enforcement right?" the teacher followed up.

"Yes," they said.

I don't know about you, but if I'm some manager at headquarters and I got enough pull to send me and a buddy to some weeklong Spanish class, first thing: I'm going to make sure I can justify it as applicable to my job. Second thing: I'm signing up for the one in Miami, or San Diego, or Vegas ... anyplace other than Artesia, New Mexico—in February no less. I couldn't help but think that they were sent there to keep tabs on me somehow. Of course, I don't know if that's true or not—God knows our government is fully capable of wasting tax dollars on things that make no sense—but to me, because of everything that had been happening, it just seemed odd and too coincidental.

While I was in Artesia, Grassley's staffers called me to report on their briefing from ATF and the Justice Department that had finally taken place. I had been anxiously waiting for it. By this point, I figured ATF and Justice surely had had enough time to look into it and realize I was telling the truth. Certainly, they were sending people who knew what they were talking about to do the briefing, and the worst possible outcome, in my mind, was that they would say how they were now aware of some things and needed more time to look into them.

The guy that Justice sent to Capitol Hill for the briefing was Deputy Assistant Attorney General Jason Weinstein. ATF sent a few people, one of them James McDermond, who was one of our assistant directors. McDermond was retired Secret Service.

Weinstein and McDermond gave Grassley's staff what they told me was the "eighty-thousand-foot briefing." They explained Project Gunrunner and walked through the Southwest Border Initiative.

They coughed up some statistics and said they'd created these kinds of groups around the country to deal with the problem. It sounded patronizing as hell.

Grassley's staffers pushed for answers to the basic questions laid out in the senator's January 27 letter: Were guns allowed to walk?

Weinstein and McDermond were cagey in their answers. "We already answered that for you in the February fourth letter from Weich," Weinstein told them. "ATF never walked any guns. That's absolutely right. We stand by the letter."

Grassley's team followed up: "Well then, why are these whistle-blowers saying this?" and "What about the documents?"

McDermond jumped in. "Well, these guys are just field agents, GS-13s, out there in the field; they can't wrap their heads around these vast international conspiracy cases," he said. "They don't understand this kind of stuff. They don't understand how we work the really big cases."

McDermond didn't know anything about working cases, the field, or conspiracies—international or otherwise. He was Secret Service his entire career, never worked a single day as an ATF agent, and had never been to the field, in any capacity, while employed by ATF.

When I heard that, I came unglued. Not only were they all calling me a liar, but now I was also a dumbass. The powers that be were insulting my credibility and my intelligence all in an effort to perpetuate their bullshit and lies.

"I can't wrap my brain around his complex conspiracy, huh?"

I was screaming into the phone at the staffers while I was walking across the parade field at the federal training complex in Artesia. It was still cold in February, a bone-chilling wind cutting straight through my coat and watchcap, a slight snow flying sideways through the air. "You tell McDermond that I'll put my investigative experience up against his, case by case, any day of the week and twice on

Sundays. 'Complex' my ass. The only complex part of this case is how they've managed to fuck it so damn bad and the only conspiracy he's ever seen is this one, that has him coming in there and lying his ass off to you guys."

As serious as it was, the staffers were still understandably humored by my rant; holding back their laughter they told me, "Calm down, calm down. They just went all in on the February fourth letter and neither of these guys are at enough of a pay grade to back away from it."

"That's no excuse for them saying that I'm too stupid to understand this bullshit and it doesn't pardon either of them."

I had never met McDermond. I had never talked to him. He never tried to contact me before that briefing, after, or anytime since. Yet, this man who had no idea what he was talking about had the gall to go into a U.S. senator's office and accuse me of not only being a *liar*, but of being a *dumb* one at that?

K eri called on a Thursday morning while I was still in New Mexico and told me that a reporter by the name of Sharyl Attkisson with CBS News had posted on CleanupATF.org looking for information on the Fast and Furious story. Attkisson posted her phone number and asked anyone with information to please give her a call.

We both hoped that someone would take her up on her offer. There were so many people who knew what was going on, who could give her what she needed for the story.

When I got back to Phoenix that following weekend, Keri and I couldn't talk about it. It's not that we didn't want to—we were just so physically and emotionally spent that we couldn't take it anymore. I had just spent a week living in a military barracks in New Mexico learning how to say things in Spanish that I'd never need or use; Keri was beat from going to work and having to take care of all our kids for the whole week. To top it off, I was still reeling from the swift kick in the balls from the briefing back in Washington. We were both just hoping it would all go away somehow.

We hung out all weekend at home. I was beginning what would be a long sentence in isolation. My phones tapped, my emails being read, seemingly a surveillance team on me at every turn—home was becoming both my fortress and my prison. As we were sitting and just trying to relax on a Sunday afternoon, Keri's cell phone rang.

I was on the couch in the living room—she was in the kitchen. She didn't recognize the number on the caller ID but answered it anyway.

"Hello," I heard her say. "I don't know, he's right here. Let me ask him."

Keri came out of the kitchen and handed me the phone. I took Keri's phone and said, "Hello?"

"Hello," I heard a female voice respond. "This is Sharyl Attkisson with CBS News."

Terrified, I jumped straight up, papers on my lap hitting the floor in front of me.

By this point, Grassley's team had told me they were working with Attkisson and her producer on a story. The only thing they weren't sure of was whether it was going to be a *60 Minutes* piece or a *CBS Evening News* piece, but either way the whole country was soon going to be exposed to Operation Fast and Furious. They had already said that if I had thought about doing the press and was agreeable to it, they'd set me up with her. I had declined.

The line was quiet for a few seconds. Maybe she expected me to say something first.

"Hello?" I heard the feminine voice repeat. "Look, I know you're one of two people: you're either Larry Alt or John Dodson," she said. My heart raced.

Holy shit! I thought, *A reporter knows my name.* Attkisson knowing my name had sucked all the air out of the room and I felt like I was in a vacuum. I made a dash for the backyard and the safety of the open air.

For some reason, probably still thinking about McDermond, I couldn't simply just hang up the phone. I paced around the yard as Sharyl began telling me about the story that she was preparing to do and how important she thought it was. Between Grassley's office and other agents she had already spoken to, it was clear she was putting all the pieces together. I grunted out an "Okay" or two.

Hearing her pitch, I wanted to help her, and not only because she was convincing and I believed her to be sincere. Since they lied in their February 4 letter and then played the "He can't wrap his brain around it" card at the briefing, I wanted her to bust this thing wide open and cram it down their throats. Finally realizing that she could never confirm who it was she was actually speaking to, I began to talk a little more.

I didn't tell her anything; I didn't give her any new information. She walked me through the outline of her reporting and, with barely more than a "yes ma'am" or "no ma'am," I confirmed for her that the information she had received was accurate; the people who were talking to her were telling the truth, and that was it.

Attkisson then asked me if I'd go on the record—go on camera to do an interview to talk about what happened.

"No, thank you. Not me," I responded.

"We can disguise your voice and silhouette your picture to keep you anonymous," she pressed.

"Absolutely not," I replied. "Ms. Attkisson: I assure you of this, if ever the time comes that I have to sit down and do an interview with you or anyone else, I won't hide my face or disguise my voice. If I have something to say, something to tell the American people, then I will tell them. I will not hide."

Keri and I had already discussed this point and were both instantly in agreement that if it came to it, that's how it would be. I would do this with my head held high.

Attkisson said she had a story coming up later that week. "Watch my story, please," she said. "You'll see that I'm trying to do this justice. Watch and make your decision then."

Ending the call, I walked back into the house and up to Keri. "Something you want to tell me about?"

"I didn't know she would call me back, John," she said. "I didn't even give her my number."

Keri went on to explain how she had called Attkisson when I was in Artesia. Keri asked her what she was looking into, what she needed to get the job done, and what questions she had. Keri said that Attkisson had a long list of questions. Toward the end of the phone call, Keri told her: "I know the guy you need to talk to so you can get these answers. I know he's contemplating talking to the media but he is really trying to avoid it."

"And that was it," Keri told me. "I didn't tell her anything, never answered any questions, nothing. I never even mentioned anybody's name. Not yours, not mine, nobody's."

Keri was the only other person with skin in the game at this point. The stress of it all got to her as well. Not having been around it as long, she felt just as deeply as I did the utter disappointment in our government and those who were running it, although she had a different perspective. Most important, what happened to me affected her and her children as well. As an amalgamated family, our well-being, our finances, our safety, and our security—it all was in play. And Keri didn't work for ATF; she wasn't under any restrictions and she could talk to whomever she damned well pleased.

As we waited for the story to come out, I had hopes that this report would really start to shake things up. Sharyl had enough documentation and had talked to several people in the know—whoever they were. There was a part of me that was praying that I'd turn on the TV and there might be Alt and Casa or any one of a bunch of others standing up there telling the truth. But then again, I feared seeing that, too. What would it say about me if someone else did it . . . and I had not?

Keri and I talked at length again about going public: all the pros, the cons, and the unknowns that we would be faced with if I took this leap. We finished the conversation with her saying, "When you can look me in the eyes and say you're at peace with it, then we'll both know that's what you have to do."

When the report finally came out, it was a good story. Attkisson did a great job with what she had to work with, but still it upset me greatly. Grassley's office had explained to me the importance of putting a face on it and how, lacking that, they might never get the truth.

I watched as Attkisson went out on a limb with a story that she could back up with neither face nor name, and yet still had the conviction and sense of duty to put forward. I was in awe of her; I was disheartened by us agents. Nobody went on the record. Nobody stood up. Not one of us. She had a couple of silhouetted figures—they weren't even real silhouettes of people, they were stock photo silhouettes. None of us had the balls to just stand up and say it. Something so unbelievably wrong, so incredibly threatening to public safety, and no one had the guts.

My thoughts went to Brian Terry's family: surely they would see this, a story describing how our agency's stupidity had directly led to the death of their son and that still there wasn't an agent among us, not one cop who would stand up and say it. I was disgusted; not only with ATF and the Department of Justice, but with my profession, my peers, my colleagues, and myself.

I heard from a few colleagues back in Virginia who were following what was going on—mainly because they knew me. When they saw those silhouetted figures on the screen, some ribbed me and said they thought that was me. It wasn't, I told them.

It made me think. I wondered whether this was a matter of courage, and whether I really had any. If I really thought the right thing was for this story to be known, for the Terry family to get the answers that they deserved, for the American people to know that their government had lied to them and to Congress, and for the Mexican people to know that they were paying for it with their very lives. If I truly believed that this fatal, murderous scheme that we were executing needed to be stopped, how could I just wait and hope for someone else to pull the trigger? I was now convinced that what we had been waiting for was right there in front of me, glowing like a large neon sign, a giant blinking green arrow pointing the way and large block lettering that blinked and buzzed as it illuminated. If I believed it was the right thing to do, then it had to be done.

And I had to be the one to do it.

I emailed Foster, Downey, and Donovan in Grassley's office right after the story ended. They had already talked about setting me up with Attkisson and a guy named John Solomon, who worked at the Center for Public Integrity. They explained that Solomon was once the editor of the *Washington Times* and that a joint print and television piece would be the most effective.

I told them to set up the interview with Attkisson.

They each called me back that same night. "Hold on, John," they responded. "Are you sure you want to do this? Think about what you're doing. We can't protect you from what happens because of this. Once you do this, there's no going back. There's no hiding."

I understood what they were telling me. I understood that there would be great consequences to what I was about to do. I was ready to take whatever was dealt to me. Whatever would happen—losing my career, being publicly smeared, or even lied about to the point I was thrown in jail—it was not going to be worse than having to look at myself in the mirror each morning and know that I lacked the courage to do what I knew to be the right thing.

"You've got a whole group of federal agents involved in this," I told them. "ATF and the Department of Justice are lying about it. Brian Terry and God only knows how many others have been killed and will be killed with the guns we walked. And none of us have the balls to stand up and say something about it?

"You set this shit up, you set it up now, or I'll call Attkisson and set it up myself."

"John," Foster said, "I'm not going to lie to you—I want you to do it. It needs to be done, but I would never ask you to do it, because I know how bad the consequences are probably going to be. Listen to me for a second; think about what you're doing. The next play will be to kill the messenger and the first move is to destroy your credibility; they will smear you and they will try to disgrace you. And because you went to the media first, they will do it all very publicly."

One of my favorite movies is *Tombstone*. Johnny Ringo has it out for Wyatt Earp, but Earp has a friend closer than a brother in Doc Holliday. Holliday approaches Ringo one day for a fight, to stand in the gap for his friend Earp, and Ringo tells him, "My fight's not with you." Holliday answers with a quote that on this day in my life seemed most appropriate.

"I'm your Huckleberry," I told them. "Set it up."

I didn't start this war and I sure as hell wasn't the cause of it. But now that I was in it, I'd rather go down charging the pillbox than be sniped while sitting on my ass in the hedgerow. Here I come.

From the minute that I made the decision to do the interview, a wave of relief came over me. Sometimes when the decision is made, either by you or for you, regardless of whether it is the best or worst, the simple fact that it is finally made brings comfort.

Sometime later that night, Downey called me from his cell phone after leaving his office there on the third floor of the Hart Senate Office Building. Thinking I knew why he was calling me, I answered the phone with "Don't even try to talk me out of it."

"Fuck that shit!" he said. "You gotta do it."

Downey and I suffered from some of the same character traits—we both had no problems shooting from the hip and calling things as we saw them. Even though the situations were different, as dictated by our chosen professions, the results were the equivalent—sometimes we had missed, sometimes we had hit, and sometimes we had even managed to shoot ourselves in our own foot. But none of that apparently ever gave either of us a moment's hesitation when the time came to do it again. This was one of those times—for us both.

"Dude, you know that Sharyl isn't going to get another story on the air without somebody sitting down with her and that story tonight won't even be a flash in the pan tomorrow here inside the Beltway," Downey said. I could hear his breathing as he was fast walking from the Hart Building, darting through traffic on Second Street or Massachusetts Avenue, on his way to the Union Station Metro stop.

"You're smart enough to know that if this story dies, you die with it. Once the attention is off it and everyone's attention is distracted by some other bullshit, then they're free to fuck you however they want and nobody can say a damn thing to them."

"I told you that I was doing it," I reiterated. "My decision is made. No need for the pep talk."

"Good," he said, the horn of the car that had just barely missed him still blowing in the background. "I just wanted to be sure that that other shit didn't talk you out of it or something. I'm going into the Metro. I'll call you tomorrow."

"Okay."

Grassley's office set it up. Attkisson was flying into Phoenix on Sunday and we would do the interview that afternoon.

When I got to the FBI office on the Friday morning before the interview, I couldn't do anything but pace the back parking lot where I had parked my g-ride. I couldn't face the people inside, all going about their normal lives, making plans for the weekend, getting ready for cookouts, parties, and dates, or setting stuff up for next week at work. My life was going to change forever in less than forty-eight hours. It felt wrong somehow being in there, seeing and talking to them, and them not knowing what I was about to do. It was akin to betraying them, our profession, what we did or who we are.

I was having trouble coming to grips with it. I couldn't talk to any of them about it. They were all blissfully unaware of what was about to happen. When I did that interview and it aired on the news, it was over for me. Millions of Americans, coast to coast, would know what had happened and that I had blown the whistle on it. And then—I'd be destroyed. They would be back in to work as usual, maybe look at my hastily cleaned-out cubicle and think, *That's where he used to sit,* and then go about their lives as usual.

As this floated through my head, I remembered seeing television interviews that ATF agents Jay Dobyns and Vince Cefalu had each given in the past. They were the only two agents I'd seen on the news who weren't retired and what they had said wasn't very flattering for ATF. Cefalu had been fighting retribution and retaliation from having blown the whistle on an operation worked out of the San Francisco office. Dobyns detailed his involvement in an outlaw motorcycle gang case where the agency and the U.S. attorney's office had left him out to dry.

So I looked them up in our agency directory, Dobyns first because I knew he had been working in the Phoenix Division somewhere. His name came up and I was surprised to see he was assigned to the Tucson office; I had never heard him mentioned or seen him around anywhere, such as at the all-hands "town-hall" meeting we had with Melson that summer. Not knowing what to say, I emailed something like "We've never met. But I could really use your advice on something, could you give me a call please?" Then hit SEND.

Minutes seemed like hours as I paced there in the parking lot. Thirty minutes was about all I could stand. I feverishly worked the rollerball on my BlackBerry until I found Cefalu—San Francisco Field Division. I knew that he was somehow involved with the CleanupATF.org website that had first publicly mentioned gun-walking by the Phoenix Field Division, but I didn't know how exactly. Since Keri had kept a quiet eye on it, however, I did know it had been posted: someone in the Phoenix Division had blown the whistle but because the lockdown was so tight, nobody outside Phoenix and headquarters really knew who it was. Desperation being one hell of a motivator, this email was more to the point: "I'm the whistleblower in Phoenix. Can I ask your advice on something?" SEND.

Seconds later my phone starting ringing from a 209 area code. "Hello," I asked cautiously.

"God damn, boy . . ." I heard a raspy, hardened voice yelling from the other end. "You have caused a motherfucking shit storm bigger than anything this agency has seen in years—maybe goddamn ever."

I didn't know what to say to that. Was that a good thing to him or not?

"I can't believe the honest-to-god Phoenix motherfucking whis-tleblower just reached out to ol' Vince for advice. As much shit as you've stirred up, gotten all of HQ's panties in a big fucking knot and even got fucking DOJ tripping over ATF's turds now. No one figured you needed any fucking help, boy. So, what can ol' Vince do for ya?"

And so we talked. I didn't get into all the specifics with him, but I did ask how he had managed to go to the media, be interviewed on TV, and not get fired over it. Every agent knows that there is no quicker way to lose your job than speaking out to the media. So I asked, "Is there some secret switch I need to flick before I do it?"

"Fuck those candy-ass motherfuckers," he answered. "They won't fire you, not for that anyways. Go do the goddamn interview. Those assholes know that Grassley would be up their asses so goddamn fast that their heads would spin." Then, and you may have thought this impossible, Vince became even more eloquent: "They're all a bunch of motherfucking, over-fucking-paid, expensive-fucking-suit-wearing bunch of motherfucking pussies."

Vince was still fighting the fight, not only in his case, but in help-ing many others along the way. He had been with ATF for more than twenty-five years and had friends and enemies alike at every level of the chain of command.

The F-bombs aside, Vince gave me some great info that he heard from his sources at headquarters, or those in Phoenix, or simply had garnered through his personal experience. Vince told me that ATF or Justice, maybe even both, was definitely up on my phones, monitor-ing all my emails, and tracking my every move. He knew the smear machine was already warmed up and waiting to be unleashed on me and that they already put together enough of a paper trail to hang me with. He told me to watch my back and that I could trust no one. They were all ready to set me up, but he didn't know for what or how they were going to do it exactly.

Depressing as that information was, still, it felt good talking to Vince. Misery loves company, I suppose. Knowing that there was one person in ATF out there who didn't hate me and would still talk to me was huge, and it helped me a lot. Soon that number would double.

Having spoken with Vince, I was still pacing the parking lot contemplating what he had told me and thinking about what lay ahead when my cell phone rang again. It was Jay Dobyns. Like Vince, Jay too had been engaged in a long, drawn-out fight with ATF and the Justice Department, and also like Vince, Jay had more than his share of scars from it.

We spoke for a little bit. He was insightful and helpful and he too offered advice. He told me that the whistle-blower protection laws might help me, but then again they might not, and that it was great that I had the air cover that I did from Grassley's office. However, he explained, the brass at ATF and Justice, and especially Newell and Gillett, were capable of doing anything, regardless of the rules, and I wasn't safe whether I did the interview or not.

After getting off the phone, I remember thinking how much I had appreciated Jay and Vince talking to me. Their calling me "brother," just in the flow of normal speaking, actually meant the world to me at the time—and I thank them.

Sunday morning arrived in a hurry. As I raked a wet hand across the mirror, completely fogged over from the steam that had escaped the shower, I looked into the blurred reflection of those familiar blue eyes.

So many people's lives are changed forever in an instant—a nanosecond event that sends them spiraling off into another direction, one they never anticipated or even could have predicted. Whatever the cause—a tragic accident, a sudden death, or meeting that perfect "someone" for the very first time—their life is forever changed, altered by the surprising events of that unforeseen moment. This would be mine. But not only did I know it was coming, I had demanded it so.

As I stood there, I knew I was saying good-bye, that there could be no going back after this, that things were about to change forever. The man whose reflection stared back at me would be no more.

My whole life had been spent trying to stay under the radar, or low profile. Always turning away from cameras or disappearing into crowds. No Facebook. No Myspace. No Twitter. Undercover work had taught me the safety of going unnoticed. I had a part in sending some very violent people to prison for a very long time and many of their parting words were vile threats toward me, and worse—my family. I did everything I could to shield my personal life from my professional one to protect my family: cleaning my name from property and tax records, unpublished phone numbers, PO boxes, and vehicle registrations.

My children couldn't even have their pictures in their elementary school yearbooks for fear of the association being made. My daughter didn't even know what I did for a living until she was in the sixth grade. She once told her teacher when asked about it, "I don't know but I hear him talk on the phone about buying drugs and there are cops at our house a lot of times." Try explaining that at the next parent-teacher conference as you sit there with a hoop in your ear, a braided goatee, and a ponytail.

So now, after all those years of being so careful, I was supposed to be getting ready to be interviewed and Sharyl Attkisson was on a plane bound for Phoenix.

I just stood there, staring.

Keri walked into the bathroom. A Sunday morning in early March, we had skipped church because of what lay ahead.

"You okay?" she asked.

How does one answer that? Physically, I felt fine, but was I "okay"? I watched as the steam crawled down the glass, opening up the reflection underneath, my arms and chest now coming into view. Though still blurry, I began to make out the scars. I thought about all the pain I had endured, all the blood that I had shed: the fights, and the bites, and the cuts, and the stabs. I remembered the car chases and the wrecks, the broken glass and the twisted metal. I recalled the broken bones, the broken ribs, and the casts, the splints, the stiches, and the screws. Every scar on that reflection, every crick or chronic ache, they had all been to pay my dues. My body had been levied to pay the stipend.

Nearly two decades on the job that I had risked my life for, sacrificed my body for, missed all those holidays and birthdays for, and arguably lost two marriages over—and today, it would be no more.

"I'm fine," I told her. Somehow that sounded safer—and more truthful—than "okay." I couldn't say that I was "okay." I knew that I wasn't.

I had always felt that I wasn't defined by my profession—I was who I was, not what I did. Watching it stare back at me through that mirror, however, and knowing that it was headed off to a different realm behind that glass, nevermore to be seen again, I questioned that. Was I who I was without doing what I do?

For nearly eighteen years, I had never been to a movie theater, restaurant, bank, or grocery store without a gun hidden on me and my badge in my pocket. My greatest fear was being caught in a situation where I could have helped, could have made a difference, could have done something, but didn't because I hadn't bothered with the inconvenience of carrying those things with me that day. This morning, though, I was looking at a life of never doing that again.

When I first spoke to Grassley's office and told ATF about it, I knew that my bosses would be pissed, but I also had thought that common sense and justice would prevail at some level. Somewhere, ascending beyond Phoenix, or higher than ATF itself if need be, somewhere somebody would step in and recognize that what I was saying was true and then everything would be fine. But that didn't happen—rather than be my saviors, those upper echelons were backing ATF's horse and had now become my persecutors.

What I was about to do came with no illusions of salvation. I knew that it would only intensify their campaign against me, speed it up, and ensure that I wasn't merely dealt with, but that I was destroyed first, discredited, smeared—all in a very brutal and very public way.

I thought about my family, my children, Keri and her daughters. What would happen to all of them? How would their lives change after I had lost my job, with no income, my career over, and disgraced to the point of being unable to find a new one?

Before, I hadn't believed the bureau as capable of something as stupid as F&F. I hadn't believed ATF capable of throwing those gun dealers who were helping us under the bus in that *Washington Post* article. And I surely never thought them capable of lying to a United States senator about it, all of it. But now, with the Justice Department standing in staunch defense of ATF, and with so many powerful people involved, people who had staked their reputations on what I knew to be a lie, what ends would they go to have me silenced? What might they be capable of? Would they try to charge me, arrest me on some trumped-up charges? Or something worse?

Keri says that we always have a choice, in every facet of our lives and with everything we do. I argue the opposite. It's merely a difference in perspective. She concedes that there are choices she knows she could never make—I argue that those are not choices, then.

I had decided many years ago to set my standard as a simple one: to be the man that my children believed me to be. As someone they loved unconditionally, were proud of, trusted, looked to for their safety and security, ran to when they cried, and trusted more than anything in the world—how could I ever explain to them that I hadn't done the right thing when I knew that I should have? So, what choice did I have?

I looked down in the reflection at the tattoo on my arm. Although I had gotten it many years ago, it was more appropriate now than it had ever been before. A simple Latin phrase, used in antiquity to mark the prisoners and Christians alike who were to be used as sport in the Roman Colosseum. Simply translated it means "Condemned to the Games." A self-fulfilling prophecy?

I got dressed. I was supposed to meet Sharyl Attkisson at a hotel in an industrial section of Phoenix out near the airport and I had told her that it would take me about forty minutes to get there. She was going to let me know when to start heading that way.

Sharyl emailed me at about at 2 P.M.

I grabbed my jacket and kissed Keri good-bye. She grabbed me and said, "Look at me."

"I'm at peace," I told her. She could see it on my face.

I turned and headed for the door. Looking over my shoulder at her, I smiled and announced, "Leap into the boundless—and make it your home," as I walked out the door.

I hopped in my truck, checking under it first for any tracking devices, and headed down the hill. I had left my work phone at the house. Having already been told that ATF was listening to it, I could only assume that they were tracking my movements with it as well. I did take my personal phone with me, in case something happened or I needed to map directions to the hotel.

As I rolled down to the bottom of the hill, I was passing by the Goodyear Baseball Stadium, where the Cleveland Indians hold their spring training. I called Jay again.

"I'm on my way," I said.

"Cool," he responded.

It was a solemn conversation. The mood was tense, but calm.

Jay had "been there" and was well aware of the ramifications of what I was about to do. He knew there wouldn't be only professional consequences but personal ones as well, and he understood them. He knew all too well how a decision like this affected somebody as a whole; their whole life, whole family.

That day, that conversation, what Jay said to me was some of the best advice that I had ever received.

"Brother, when I went to the media, that first time, my only regret was not putting it all out there," he said. "I wish I hadn't've pulled that punch." Those words reverberated in my head.

I got off the phone with Jay, took the battery out, and threw it in the center console. I reached I-10, turned right onto the on-ramp, and headed east.

I knew what Jay was saying. He had thought that by minimizing the blow, ATF would appreciate it, recognize that he wasn't their enemy and then in turn do the right thing by him—pull a punch of their own. That didn't happen, though; he has spent the years since in an almost constant battle with ATF, having to defend himself time and time again. Knowing now that his act of leniency was met only by overwhelming force, he regretted not taking that full swing.

Had Jay not said that, I probably would have made the same mistake. I recalled a legal principle known as "killing the king." In short, it states: if you're going to try to kill the king—you had better kill him. The meaning is clear: if ever such an attempt were to fail, fall short, or end with mercy being granted, the king's retribution would most surely be swift, brutal, and absolute.

Casting aside the "battered agent syndrome" that had manifested in me after that first month or so of having been beat up, rode hard, and put up wet, I starting feeling like myself again. And me being me, I declared that if I was going to take a swing at the king, I was damn sure going to land it.

After doubling back some, doing some crazy Ivans, and other maneuvers to make sure I wasn't being followed, I got to the hotel. Attkisson and her producer were seated at the bar inside the hotel restaurant. I had only seen her on the newscast a few days earlier, but I recognized her. She asked me to sit down and introduced me to her producer.

We chatted for a few minutes while they finished their meal, then she paid the bill and I followed her into the hotel lobby. To the right was a set of double doors leading into a large conference room.

The conference room was one of those that could either be rather large or broken down into smaller rooms when the dividers were pulled out of their accordion shape. As we walked in, I immediately noticed two men busily plugging in different cords and adjusting equipment. One was a cameraman and the other a sound guy. There were several lights shining on two chairs with a large black cloth backdrop that covered the walls and floor underneath the chairs.

Sharyl sat down in one chair and I in the other. I could tell she was well educated, cultured, and refined. She spoke very naturally and made me feel comfortable. I noticed after we had been sitting for a few minutes that our conversation had moved on from chitchat to things with more substance. The sound guy started wiring me up with the microphone, weaving it under my shirt and placing it in the right spot. I just continued talking with Sharyl.

I realized that Sharyl was using the same tactics and techniques on me that I had used on others so many times in the past, the same things that we are taught as cops to use when we conduct interviews. Most cases are normally made from good interviewing and asking the right questions rather than CSI stuff like forensics and DNA. Most agencies recognize this and spend lots of money trying to train officers on how to properly interview. Unfortunately, though, it's one of those things that you either have or you don't. Sharyl had it—and she was good at it.

Before I knew it, the interview had started. As soon as I realized that, I said, "Sorry, I've got to go to the bathroom. I would have said something before, but I didn't realize we had started."

As I got up to leave, I saw the concern on Sharyl's face. Had she pushed me away? Would I come back? I was walking down the hall to the bathroom when I remembered that I was still wearing the microphone. I laughed while thinking back to my days undercover. Always wired up and with someone on the surveillance team or cover team always listening, going to the bathroom was always a tension breaker. We would never turn off the mic and we would always make sure we made disgusting sounds in the bathroom as a special gift to the one that was listening. This time, though, I thought it best to turn it off.

When I walked back in the room, there was a palpable sense of relief that I hadn't changed my mind or was going to bail on the whole thing. I clicked the mic back on and we started the interview. It lasted about thirty or forty minutes.

When the interview was over, the sound guy and cameraman began unplugging various cords and packing up equipment. Sharyl was talking on the phone and they began removing my microphone. The cameraman, an Hispanic gentleman maybe in his late thirties to mid-forties, average-sized with short hair, leaned in close and spoke to me. "I just want to thank you," he said. He then told me how he and his family lived in Phoenix and he really appreciated what I had just done, what it meant to him, how important it was.

He knocked me for a loop. Here was just a regular guy. He wasn't thanking me for political gain, or a better job, or some great award.

He was thanking me because he knew that those guns and what we were doing could directly affect him and his family. At that moment, sitting there in that chair, his simple words of appreciation brought it all into perspective for me, and changed my life forever. This was truly the meaning of what it was about, doing the right thing for the right reasons, and protecting and serving others around me.

— 11 —

WHISTLE-BLOWING IS A FULL-TIME JOB

The interview did not air until Thursday, March 3, 2011. Until then I was on the phone with Grassley's office every day. Foster reminded me several times, "This never turns out well for the whistleblower." So I was resolved to my fate. I just hoped that what I had done would move the ball. It might have been easy for ATF and the Justice Department to call me a liar through an exchange of letters, but now I was forcing their hand by calling them out and telling them to do it to my face. We really didn't know where this was headed.

Keri and I tried to go through our week as usual and not dwell on it too much. We informed both of our families and they were all very supportive.

When the interview aired on the *CBS Evening News* on the east coast, I was still in my FBI office. Everyone on the east coast—all my friends, family, and former coworkers in Virginia included—saw it. I left work early, a little after 4 P.M., and raced home to see if I could watch it online before it aired in Phoenix.

CBS hadn't uploaded it to their website yet, so the next hour and a half or so was a waiting game. During that time, I got a couple of calls from friends and family back east.

My mom called as well. "Oh, my God," she said. "I can't believe that's what's going on. I can't believe that you're involved in that. Thank God you did the right thing by stepping forward." Hearing her say that meant a lot to me.

At 6:00 P.M., Keri was sitting on the family room couch in front of the television. I couldn't watch it. My throat was so tight I couldn't swallow. I could feel my heart pounding inside my chest. I walked into the living room where my back would be to the television so I could at least hear it. The best I could muster was stealing a glance every thirty seconds or so.

Anchor Katie Couric opened the news up. My story was the lead package for the news that night. Attkisson began talking and then I heard the interview.

"An Alcohol, Tobacco and Firearms senior agent assigned to this Phoenix office since 2010, Dodson's job is to stop gun trafficking across the border. Instead he says he was ordered to sit by and watch it happen," Attkisson's voice said over video images of our office and the border.

"You were intentionally letting guns go to Mexico?" she asked me.

"Yes, ma'am. The agency was. I'm boots on the ground in Phoenix, telling you we've been doing it every day since I've been here," I told her. "Here I am. Tell me I didn't do the things that I did. Tell me you didn't order me to do the things I did. Tell me it didn't happen. Now you have a name on it. You have a face to put with it. Here I am. Someone now, tell me it didn't happen."

She asked about what I would tell Terry's family if I met them.

"First of all I would tell them that I am sorry. Second of all, I would tell them that I have done everything I can ..." My voice trembled a bit, trying to hold back the emotion. I tried to finish the sentence. "... for them to get the truth.

"After this I don't know what else I can do. But I hope they get it."

The piece went on for eight minutes. When it was over, Keri told me that she thought I had done well. I emailed Foster in Grassley's office to get his reaction. Finally I heard back from him: "Not just a home run ... grand slam, out-of-the-park homer—the ball hasn't even landed yet."

I had taken my swing at the king, now we just had to wait and see if it had an effect.

Hopefully, some other media would pick up the story and add to the pressure. Maybe it would somehow make a difference and stop this insanity, call out these assholes that were lying about it. Foster said that they were already getting inquiries and interview requests from other media outlets. *Maybe, just maybe?* I thought to myself.

My work phone rang and it was my boss from the FBI. Ron had received a call about my interview from his bosses. I told him that yes, I had done an interview. He quickly asked me, "Did you mention anything about the FBI?"

I smirked a little when I answered, "I made no mention of the FBI and had no reason to." I know how it works; as long as I'm not bringing the FBI into it, the FBI didn't care one bit what I said about ATF. He was quite satisfied with our conversation. I had kept the FBI up to date every step of the way as things happened and continued to do so until much later when I was transferred out of Phoenix, and honestly, I never caught a bit of grief from anyone at the FBI.

Attkisson also called me. "Are you okay? What did you think?"

I was very impressed with her reporting. She really looked for the truth, dug deep to find it, and tried to get a voice from both sides of the argument. She was the one reporter who stepped out and didn't wait for everything to be handed to her. She had worked hard to understand the situation and report it accordingly.

I told her, "I'm fine, and you did a great job. Thank you."

She told me the next day that the story went over well. She was getting praise for it from her colleagues. She was also getting information from all sides. She had sources on the Hill, at Justice, and at ATF. She was getting word that the story had caused a spark and was beginning to shake things up a bit.

I did hear from a few people at ATF. Some I knew, many I didn't, but they all ignored the potential risk and emailed from their ATF accounts to mine, thanking me for doing the right thing by stepping forward. Those few emails meant so much to me. I had been isolated for so long. For those people I didn't know well or didn't know at all to reach out to me like they had, it meant the world to me and I appreciated it immensely . . . and I still do.

Pete Forcelli, a supervisor at ATF who worked on the sixth floor at Division, called me. Forcelli was a former New York City cop, and he had the accent to back it up. The agents in his group seemed to like him, so I figured he was okay. I'd seen him around, spoken to him once or twice, but I wasn't sure he even knew my name.

"Good job, brother," I heard that hard New York cop voice say. "That took stones, real stones, to do what you did. Somebody had to do it."

Shortly after the interview, I began getting inundated with calls and emails from other reporters wanting an interview. I couldn't believe how for years I had flown under the radar, but after one interview, reporters found a way to get my home number, my personal cell, my work cell, and my work email address so easily.

I didn't really want to do the first interview, so doing more was even less appealing. Not only that, but I didn't want to go out and do anything that wasn't sanctioned by Grassley's staff. I knew they were working their own investigation and I wanted to be careful to not get in the way of that or, worse, screw it up. I knew the focus had to remain on the investigation, getting the truth, and stopping this insane gun walking, and not on me. The story was the story. If I were the story then taking me out meant that the story went away, too. The issue was too important to let that happen.

There were many calls, voice mails, and emails that I left unanswered. The first one to my work email was from a producer for Univision named Maria. I found it interesting that a Spanish-language network was interested in speaking with me. I knew how important this was to the people of Mexico. But I didn't reply.

After church on the Sunday after the interview, Keri and I took the kids to a park close to the house. It was the newest one in our neighborhood and had several fields, a volleyball court, a basketball court, a tennis court, and some large slides that the kids liked. They would often see friends from school there, so Keri and I would walk around with the dog while they played. Sometimes I would even bring a golf club and a golf ball to work on my short game. That day, I was practicing chipping out of the sand from the volleyball court.

My work phone began to ring, which had become an oddity in itself, but especially so on a Sunday. I looked at the number and didn't recognize it, so I just ignored it.

A few minutes later, it rang again. I noticed it was the same number. I don't know why or what compelled me, but this time I decided to answer it.

I said hello and immediately a female voice started on the other end. She had a Spanish accent, said her name was Maria, and she begged me to not hang up the phone. She continued with her speech, telling me why she called. She was speaking so fast that I couldn't get a word in edgewise. I figured my only two choices were to either listen or hang up on her. I chose to listen.

She explained to me how she had gotten both my work email and phone number from someone she knew who was a DEA agent. She told me how much she appreciated me coming forward on CBS and how important this story was to the Latino community. Mexico was a huge portion of their viewing audience, and she and her colleagues had suspected U.S. operations like Fast and Furious had been happening over the years, but they could never prove it. My speaking out had validated their suspicions. She reiterated how important it was for the Latino community to hear my story.

Maria came across as very sincere. It reminded me of the cameraman I had just spoken to after my interview. This was hitting home for her. She had done many stories on cartel violence. She had seen lives torn apart and destroyed from the criminals' total disregard for human life. She had heard the United States talk a big game about doing what they could to curb the violence, but had seen little results, and in some cases things had only been made worse. This woman was passionately and compassionately speaking from experience. This story meant something to her and to her community.

I knew from her emotional reaction that she got it. It wasn't about politics or failed programs and she wanted to do a story to make sure everyone else understood it, too. By the end of the conversation, I hadn't agreed to an interview, but I had agreed to sit down and talk with her.

A couple of days later, she flew out to Phoenix. She was staying in a hotel downtown and asked me to meet her there. I was a little leery of the situation and didn't want to walk into a room with cameras all around, so I asked her to meet me at a driving range nearby. I told her to meet me on the far side of the building so when she pulled up and got out of the car, I could make sure there was no camera crew there with her.

I saw a van pull up and park. An attractive woman with Latina features got out of the passenger side. On the driver's side emerged a tall Hispanic guy with black hair and a thick mustache. I didn't see any cameras or equipment, so I was somewhat relieved.

Maria recognized me right away. We sat and talked for a few minutes and I could tell that she was genuine. She really wanted to make the Latino community, specifically the Mexican community, aware of this story and help them to understand it.

She wanted to set up an interview with Jorge Ramos. I had never heard of him before, but she described him as the Walter Cronkite of Spanish-language news television. She set up the interview for the following day at the local Phoenix Univision affiliate. I tried to get in touch with Foster or Downey that evening to get their take on it. I really didn't want to do any interviews without their stamp of approval. They knew this world a whole lot better than I did. But whether they went along with me doing this interview or not, I couldn't help but think how the Mexican community needed to be aware of this story. If the Mexican people became aware of this and voiced their outrage, maybe then our government would feel enough pressure to actually stop it.

Without hearing back from Grassley's office, I decided to go forward with the interview. The next day, I popped the batteries out of the cell phones, did the crazy Ivans, and headed to the address Maria had given me for Univision's Phoenix affiliate. It was a beautiful building on the south side of downtown. I walked through the glass doors and inside it was just as striking as it was on the outside. Maria was in the lobby waiting for me.

We greeted each other and she immediately whisked me through the building to a newsroom. She sat me down at a desk that had lights and cameras around it. Surrounding us, however, was a roomful of people busily trying to get their own work done. *A real newsroom*, I thought to myself.

As they began to wire me up, Maria pointed to a monitor in front of me. She told me, "You will be able to see Jorge in that monitor there. He is in Miami but you can see him as you answer the questions. There is also a camera there. Don't worry, he is very fluent in English and will conduct the interview in English."

Maria was constantly on and off the phone, but she stayed with me while the tech crew got everything adjusted. A few minutes later, the monitor came on and I saw a distinguished gentleman on the screen. He was fit, with a chiseled face and gray hair, and very well dressed.

Mr. Ramos was courteous as he introduced himself to me. His questions were concise. I answered them in turn. As the interview was beginning to close and Ramos began thanking me, I remembered Jay's advice. If I was going to put my career and life as I knew it on the line, I was going to make it count. I had something else I wanted, needed, to say. It would be up to them whether they used it, but I didn't want to leave without saying it.

I said, "Excuse me, Mr. Ramos, but I wanted to add something else. Everyone needs to understand that these guns are only going to be recovered in the *last* crime they are used in. No one will ever know how many crimes they were used in prior to that last crime. And with the amount of guns that we let out there, we will be dealing with this for decades."

I could see Maria crouched behind the camera. She held up her fist in a triumphant type of way and shook it while mouthing the word "Yes!" I could tell she was pleased that I was driving this point home.

After the interview, they unwired me, I had a short conversation with Maria, and I was out the door. I did the same routine as before, a couple of crazy Ivans and down the road a bit before I put the batteries back in my cell phones. As soon as I did, my personal phone pinged with a message from Foster so I immediately called him back.

When he answered the phone, he suggested I turn down any further interview requests. His office had been inundated with requests, and they were evaluating certain ones but disregarding others. Foster told me how the playbook on these types of situations was normally to attack the whistleblower, especially since the Justice Department had gone all in and written a letter denying the allegations. Because of that, I had to be careful. It was possible that someone from ATF or Justice would send out a reporter to interview me and use my own words to twist the story around and publicly discredit me.

I just began shaking my head and rolling my eyes. It would have been great if he would have told me this an hour ago. I then told him about the Univision interview that I had just done. He wasn't too concerned with Univision. He knew that they were not doing work on behalf of the department. Still, I took his advice to heart.

A day or so later, my work phone rang again. I could tell the number was from our division office and since I hadn't heard from anyone there since my interview, I thought this could be significant.

When I answered it, a man's voice came over and said, "Hello, Mr. Dodson, this is William La Jeunesse with Fox News. I saw your interview on CBS and really wanted to talk to you."

Surprised, I looked at the phone's screen again. I appreciated his interest in wanting to report the story, but I had no desire to do any more media. I told him, "The best advice I can give you is to call Grassley's office and speak with them."

He said he had been in touch with the senator's office, but he was in Phoenix now so it would be a great time to do an interview. I think he thought I was on some media blitz and he didn't want to miss it. I, however, was doing what I could to avoid any more exposure.

His persistence and the fact that it seemed he was calling from our division office raised my suspicions. As ridiculous as an alliance between Fox News and the Obama Justice Department sounded, I wondered if ATF brass were sending him out to complete that very mission Foster had warned me about. So I asked him, "How is it that you are calling me from my division office?"

"I'm not," he said. "I'm calling you from my cell phone."

I answered back, "My phone's caller ID said you were calling from a phone at my division office in downtown Phoenix."

He explained to me how he had called our division office and simply asked for me by name. The switchboard operator transferred his call to my phone.

I asked, "Did you tell them who you were?"

"Yes, of course. I told them I was William La Jeunesse with Fox News and I would like to speak with Special Agent John Dodson. They told me to hang on, I heard a click, and then the phone just started ringing."

It was odd. Maybe whoever answered the phone wanted me to talk to more reporters; maybe they wanted more to get out. Being in this situation had me constantly trying to evaluate who was a friend and who was an enemy.

I politely declined the interview, but La Jeunesse told me he was in Phoenix for that day and if I changed my mind to let him know.

Later, I had to go downtown to do something for the FBI. While I was down there, I decided to go by Starbucks. My work phone rang and it was another agent from Phoenix. Happily surprised by his call, I answered it. He asked me where I was and I told him that I was at the Starbucks a block and a half from the division office, waiting entirely too long for my coffee. He then hurriedly got off the phone, saying, "I gotta call you back later."

Coffee in hand, I walked outside. A man in his late forties with graying hair, a sport coat, tie, and jeans was standing there as I exited. He called me by name, immediately stuck his hand out, and said, "John, I'm William La Jeunesse with Fox News. I spoke with you on the phone."

I wasn't sure how he found me or why he wouldn't take no for an answer, but it made me question his motives even more. I tried to step around him, but he would just do a side step while talking to me. He was telling me how important this story was and how he really needed an interview with me to tell it properly. He was persistent, and normally I would have told someone to leave me alone and go to hell. But there was something about La Jeunesse that reminded me of my friend Travis back in Virginia. More than that, though, I was feeling about near kidnapped in the plaza outside of Starbucks, so I agreed to speak with him off the record and help explain things that were already public or things that I had said in my interview.

We sat down. He broke out a pen and paper. I could tell he felt like he had scored a small victory. Of course with one foot in the door, there is always another one right behind it. As we were talking, I noticed a guy behind him setting up a camera on a tripod.

I asked William, "Who is that?"

He said, "That's my cameraman. Remember? I told you we were shooting some footage around Phoenix today."

Panic ran over me. Not only did I not want more media exposure, but Foster had also said it wasn't a good idea to do any more interviews. Yet here I was, letting this guy snake me into an interview with a cameraman recording it all. I didn't know how to get out of it by this point. We were there talking and he was so damn persistent and wouldn't take no for an answer, but he didn't do it in that arrogant-asshole way. He wasn't rude, just compelling.

I gave him maybe thirty seconds of decent footage explaining how these guns were still out there and would be for years to come until they were recovered in a crime. The rest of the footage I basically sabotaged, appearing too nervous to make any of it usable.

La Jeunesse asked me why I was so nervous. After all, I had already gone public with this whole story. I explained to him how I didn't want to do any more media. I spoke my piece and I just hoped that it would all be over. Not to mention the fact that from the plaza where we were sitting, I could look up at the Bank of America building and see George Gillett's office window. I could picture him and Newell with their foreheads pressed against the glass and their hands cupped around their eyes peering down and laughing because they had set this whole thing up. It didn't look very good for John Dodson.

La Jeunesse apologized for where we were. He had no idea we were right next to my division office building. We exchanged numbers and emails and I told him that if Grassley's office sanctioned it, I would sit down with him for a more extended interview.

La Jeunesse was somehow able to make a great piece out of those thirty seconds, and fortunately, mine was but a very short segment of it. He followed it up with another report some days later where he held up a hand-drawn chart with arrows pointing south to Mexico and began to explain the dense, complicated, and totally screwed-up situation to the viewers. Keri and I were both excited that it seemed like the reporters were finally starting to "get it." William and I began to talk regularly when I needed to explain something to him or when he received some new nugget of information that he wanted to pass along. Over time, we became friends.

It all was contributing more to the inverting of my world. Those whom I'd always counted on, who I thought would have my back—other agents and my agency—were now actively out to get me. Those who I had always been told couldn't be trusted—journalists and politicos—were my only supporters. Friends had become enemies and enemies had become friends.

– 12 –

THE SMALLEST MINORITY

I was nervous that my few media appearances had put a huge target on my back. I caught wind of rumor after rumor about plots to discredit, silence, or otherwise take me out. Once I received a text message from an untraceable number that read simply "Duck!" Someone was trying to warn me about an incoming barrage.

Soon thereafter, I got an anonymous call from a man who said that he worked at a gun shop in the area. He said that several FBI agents had just been in showing a picture of me and asking if anyone there had any dealings with me. I couldn't get any more information out of him before he hung up. I was sitting at my JTTF desk at the time, then I slowly slid toward the aisle, stuck my head out of the cubicle, and looked around. *The FBI?* I thought. *That doesn't make any sense.*

Later in March, I got a message from an agent friend in the

Baltimore Field Division. Acting Director Melson's "town hall" tour had stopped there and somebody in the cheap seats had the balls to ask him about the CBS reporting. Melson responded, telling the entire Baltimore Division that I was just a "disgruntled agent" with "an axe to grind," and that I had screwed up a case so bad that the U.S. attorney in Phoenix refused to prosecute it. During my entire time in Group VII there had been only one arrest. That was by me, when I was helping DEA with a search warrant and we encountered an illegal alien in possession of a firearm. Other than that, no one in Group VII ever put handcuffs on anybody during the time I was in it. The arrest made by me was handled and prosecuted by an excellent assistant U.S. attorney named Jonell Lucca. Other than that, I had had no dealings with the U.S. attorney's office in Phoenix.

Feeling besieged without anyone in Phoenix who understood my situation, I went to see Andre Howard, owner of Lone Wolf Trading Company, the gun store that had sold most of the Fast and Furious weapons. I was hoping to find a friend; I definitely needed one. I walked in the back door and he saw me. He led me into his office and told me not to say a word until he had closed the door.

"What are you doing here?" he asked sternly. "Do you have any idea the hornet's nest that you've stirred up?"

It wasn't the warm reception that I hoped for. I began to think I shouldn't have come at all.

"Look, I just wanted to let you know that I'm not your enemy," I told him. "I said that you guys thought you were doing the right thing by helping ATF and were then getting thrown under the bus for it."

"Oh my God, man," Andre stammered out, visibly shaken with my presence. "The shit you raised. The shit you stepped in. I can't believe this. Hold on, just hold on . . ."

Andre picked up his phone and called his lawyer and put me on the phone with him. His lawyer asked me what I wanted. I simply replied that I was there to tell Andre that I'm not his enemy. "I didn't go out and try to throw the gun stores under the bus," I said. "I think they were lied to and being used."

Obviously, I wasn't getting a warm-fuzzy so I handed Andre the phone back and I started toward the door. "Hang on, hang on," Andre told me, grabbing at my sleeve.

"You can't imagine what you've done," he said. "There is shit going on that you have no idea about. Shit that we aren't allowed to talk about. Agency shit and they are knee-deep in it."

I walked out. While I was certainly intrigued by Andre's comment, I didn't feel comfortable and feared it might be some kind of trap. I knew he was close with Hope and Dave, and he was likely going to call them right after I walked out anyway. So I didn't want to give up any more information than I already had.

Having been afforded no quarter from Andre, I thought about the Scottsdale Gun Club. I remembered my first visit there and how the owner wanted something in writing. He got it. He understood; he was on to it way back then. But I wasn't about to make the mistake of walking into a gun shop again. I remembered that they had an attorney, because Hope and Dave talked about him in the office and how he had requested meetings with them and the U.S. attorney's office seeking assurances that this investigation was truly aboveboard. I gave him a call.

As soon as he heard it was me on the phone, he said that he would have to call me back and hung up. *Shit!* I thought. *He's calling ATF right now.* He called back a few minutes later and told me to come right over to his office. Suspicious and scared, I turned and headed that way.

Ironically, his office was in a complex directly adjacent to the DEA Strike Force building. I parked two blocks away and made a careful approach, hoping to make whatever surveillance or takedown team that ATF had waiting on me. Not seeing any, I made my way inside. The receptionist whisked me through the door and down the hall. Turning left and then right, we came to a closed door, and she told me to wait inside. As she opened the door, I imagined the full complement of a black-clad arrest team waiting inside to thump or perhaps even shoot me after it was determined that I had "resisted."

Alas, it was just an empty conference room. Trying to reel in my fear-fueled imagination, I sat down as she closed the door behind her. Not long after, in walked a well-dressed man, mid-forties, very professional-looking and carrying a yellow legal pad. He reached out his hand, introduced himself, and then sat down after we shook.

"Look," he began, "as you know, I represent the Scottsdale Gun Club. I just got off the phone with the owner, my client . . ."

My throat tightened up so close I could barely get air to pass through it.

". . . and they want to know what they can do to help."

"Excuse me?" I said

"They want to know first, are you okay? They know what you did, what you must be going through, and they appreciate it. They've empowered me to help you in any way that I can, with whatever it is you need. So, do you need anything? How can we help?"

I was stunned. I felt like jumping over the table and hugging him. "I don't know if you can help."

"Do you have an attorney? I can't represent you because there would be a conflict but I can find someone who can."

"I'm hoping to get an attorney through FLEOA," I said, referring to the association for federal law enforcement officers.

"I'm going to make calls and try to line up somebody just in case."

"Okay, but . . ."

"It's no trouble. Done."

As relieved as I was, I knew what I had to say. "I sincerely appreciate it. Please thank your client for me, but unfortunately, I can't accept anything. I just wanted them to know that I wasn't their enemy, and that I know they were only doing what we had asked them to."

We talked for a few minutes, about the whole thing, and I explained to him what had been happening since. As I was leaving he again expressed his client's thanks and appreciation to me. To this day, I've never met the owner of the Scottsdale Gun Club; I don't even know who he, she, or they are. I do know that I owe them an apology for that first visit, and a debt of appreciation that I could never begin to repay. It gave me a renewed sense of hope. Maybe I wasn't an island after all.

A couple of weeks later, Andre called me. After the last time we talked, I thought it best to just not answer. When I didn't, he called again . . . and again. Seven times total. Finally, he gave up on the calls and started to text me, saying that he needed to speak to me and that it was important.

My thoughts bounced from one end of the possibility spectrum to the other. *He's seen the light and wants to help. Or he's working for Hope and Dave and trying to set me up somehow.* I decided to err on the side of "it's worth the risk" and so I broke down and called him.

"I need to talk to you," he told me. "No phones, in person. Come by my house. Here's my address . . ."

I didn't want to. I wasn't sure if it was some kind of setup, but maybe he had started figuring out that what I was saying was right. He knew they were telling him to keep making these sales.

I was at the dealership getting my government car serviced. Andre wanted me to come over right away, so I planned to go straight there when the car was finished. When it was, I grabbed my "go-bag" from the trunk and hopped in the driver's seat. A go-bag is a bag filled with enough stuff to make sure that you are ready to "go" for just about anything. Mine held batteries, tape, an extra knife, a spare flashlight, trauma kit, some cash, and a bunch of other stuff. But what I was looking for now was the digital voice recorder and Velcro tape that I had in there.

As I drove to Andre's house, I grabbed the lanyard around my neck and pulled my FBI security access card out from under my shirt. I took the digital voice recorder and Velcro-taped it to the back of my card holder and slipped it back under my shirt.

Anyone who saw me could see I was wearing the badge. But nobody could see the digital voice recorder secured to the back unless I flipped it around. I knew that if this whole thing was a setup, my having a recording of the conversation could prove valuable for me and even possibly for Andre.

Hitting RECORD as I pulled up to Andre's house, I then walked to the door and knocked. He answered right away. "Get in here," he said, checking the street up and down in each direction. Walking me to his kitchen he asked, "Were you followed? Does anybody know you're here?"

"No," I replied.

Andre's house was one of the older styles in Phoenix. His full yard actually had grass, unlike many of the newer homes, which only had partial grass lawns. There were full-grown trees around everywhere, too. It could have been a neighborhood in any city in the country.

We stopped in the middle of his kitchen. "We got to talk. But first, you want a beer?" He gestured toward the counter. On it, I saw a Corona bottle, freshly removed bottle cap lying beside it, still cold since frost had formed around the neck, and small bubbles in the brew inside rising up to the top. *Setup,* I thought to myself. *I drink a beer, get pulled over as soon as I drive away from here, get arrested maybe? Maybe not? But fired definitely for driving the g-ride with beer on my breath.*

"No thanks, I'm good," I answered. "I'm in my g-ride."

"All right," he said. "Let's go out on the patio where we can talk." He moved toward the sliding glass door off the kitchen at the back of the house.

As we stepped outside, I half jested: "Are Hope and Dave hiding in the bushes?"

"No," he replied, shaking off my question.

Several wind chimes adorned the structures atop Andre's back porch. They were ringing wildly as we sat down on the patio chairs.

"You have no idea what you started," he said, picking up where he left off from when I stormed out of his store a couple weeks earlier. "You have no idea how far this goes and who's involved."

He began telling me what he knew, what he thought, what he had heard, what he suspected, and some things he was just guessing at. He talked about ATF, Dave, Hope, Tonya, the U.S. attorney's office, straw purchasers, informants, Mexican corruption, black ops, secret missions, and political predictions about which senators and which congressmen were going to do what. Then he told me he didn't know what to think when I first dropped by after that CBS News interview but he'd run everything through his head since. He said they were setting him up, that he's in a bad way, and that these guys were out to get him now as well as me. Andre told me that he and his attorneys had had two meetings with senior officials from the Phoenix offices of ATF and the U.S. attorney. At the first meeting, the officials confirmed to him that two AK-47 variants found at the Terry murder scene were purchased from his store.

At the second meeting, the government had a completely different story. They said that "the evidence would not show that those two guns at the murder scene came from his store." Andre had told them about me stopping by his store. They then asked if he would testify before a grand jury in a way that would allow them to secure an indictment against me for witness tampering.

Leaving his house, I thought about how Andre had confirmed what I already suspected: the government was trying to come up with some way to arrest and discredit me. The number of people who hated me was growing fast. I knew I would have to watch my back even more. Knowing this, it made me even more hypersensitive to anything happening around me. As a cop and federal agent who had conducted surveillance, I knew what to look for—hell, I used to teach others how to do it.

I started to notice the same vehicles on different occasions. One day parked over here, the next down the street. One day behind me in traffic, the next day in front. Feeling more and more like I was being followed, I increased my efforts to detect and defeat it. Sometimes I'd pull down dead-end streets and turn around to sit and watch what cars had come down after me. Other times, I'd zigzag across town. Instead of taking a straight path to where I was going, I'd keep turning down side streets and back onto main roads. I'd adjust my speed erratically to see who was trying to keep up with me and then slow down to see which cars would hang behind.

Once at the JTTF office, a couple of the local Phoenix police guys who were assigned there came up to me. They all knew what was going on. After they had heard about it, they came to me and asked questions; I answered. They expressed their appreciation for what I had done.

They stood at the opening to my cubicle and said, "Hey, tell your fucking shadows out there that they're taking up needed parking spots." It's true; parking was a bitch at the JTTF. Many times both the secure lot in the back and the open lot in the front didn't have an empty space anywhere.

"Say again?" I said.

"Your tag—the surveillance team riding your ass. They're all parked out there, sitting in their cars pretending to be invisible. Tell them to get the fuck out of here. We need those spots."

"Okay," I said. "I'll take 'em touring and we'll go burn some gas."

I always thought it was stupid that they were tailing me. They could GPS me by my BlackBerry—I couldn't disable that. Every time I touched the battery to it they would know exactly where I was. Or, because I had a two-way radio in my g-ride, they could have tracked me through the signal coming from that. If they wanted to pay agents full-time to burn fuel zigzagging across town following me around all day, so be it. Have fun, fellas.

One afternoon was particularly memorable. I believed I had identified a group of three vehicles tailing me: two sedans and one red pickup truck. I was in my g-ride—a seafoam-green Chrysler 300. I was issued this car after the horrific hail storm had ruined my Impala. The guys at JTTF referred to it as my "pimp wagon" and that quickly evolved into everyone just calling it "Huggy Bear." Ironically, before me, "Huggy Bear" had been Bill Newell's car. He had traded it out for his new one a few months before.

This day's tag stood out more than the others. Either the surveillance team had been brought in from out of town or a local team thought that their cars had been burnt because they were using obvious rental cars. In fact, the red pickup truck that was part of the tag that day was *the same exact red pickup truck* that I had borrowed from the GRIT guy months earlier when I was working the Fernandez case. I had picked the truck because it didn't reek like a government agent's car—and now it was following me around the city. You can't make this shit up.

I figured I'd have some extra fun. I headed out toward Surprise, Arizona, some suburbs on the outskirts of the Valley of the Sun.

Originally a retirement community, Surprise's older sections were inundated with golf carts. Everyone had one, and they were whizzing around everywhere. The red truck and the two sedans alternated back and forth between who had the lead in following me. One would bounce onto my tail, and the others would fall back. Then they'd rotate every so often with the lead turning off and falling in behind and the second now taking the lead.

Bored with Surprise, I took them out to a neighborhood even farther west—Verrado. I'd golfed several times there before. It was a planned community with an excellent course carved through it. This whole erratic path was about an hour's worth of driving through Phoenix traffic and its suburbs. Outside of Verrado, I took them across the 10 and headed through Buckeye. Trolling eastbound on MC 85, I took a right on Jack Rabbit Road and headed for Rainbow Valley.

You don't go to Rainbow Valley unless you live in Rainbow Valley. It's utterly desolate; not far in, the roads aren't paved anymore. Packed dirt and desert are lined with the occasional tread mark left by another vehicle.

As soon as the pavement was all behind us, the sedans fell back and broke off, leaving the pickup as the can-do vehicle for the job in these conditions. Hardpack dirt gave way to loose sand, similar to that of the beach. I pushed the button to take the traction control off and I stomped my foot into the firewall of the 300—smashing the accelerator pedal in between. Giant plumes of sand shot out from the back tires as the ass end drifted back and forth.

As long as I kept it moving—kept the momentum rolling—I'd be able to keep Huggy Bear from sinking into the sand and getting stuck or bottoming out. I couldn't see anything in the rearview mirror except for the tornado of dust particles whipping into the air behind me. At the next split in the road, I went left until I had angle enough to see beyond the dust cloud. No red truck. I turned my head over my shoulder to see out of the back glass, but in doing so my foot let off the accelerator. That brief reprieve was all that was needed: the rpms dropped, the tires slowed, and the loose sand seized the advantage and pulled Huggy Bear down, swallowing the massive vehicle. The 300's frame sat firmly on the sand.

I hopped out of the car and jumped on the roof to look around. My trail of dust was now beginning to dissipate and pass me by. Way out in the distance, I saw the red truck hustling away. I grabbed a couple of boards from an old corral not too far away and spent the next couple of hours digging my g-ride out of the sand, laughing the entire time.

Though my life had been turned upside down, I was receiving information that everything at division was business as usual. Newell was promoted to be ATF's attaché to Mexico. If that wasn't the ultimate case of fucked-up irony I don't know what is. I wondered who back in Washington had the macabre sense of humor to cook that up. ATF was still planning a going-away party for him. I also got word that Needles had a meeting with the members of Group VII. He told them not to worry about this at all. Fast and Furious was a great case, and all this would die down soon.

Hearing things like that was discouraging, to say the least. I knew that even though I tried, it was still only me publicly speaking up. And if it stayed only me, the lone crazy guy screaming on the corner, I would soon be squashed like a bug on the windshield of our huge government machine.

Right after my interviews, I had hopes that others would publicly step up as well. It was my "I am Spartacus!" moment. I believed that others would start standing up all around me and shouting the same thing. All I heard was . . . crickets . . . crickets . . .

Alt and Casa would still talk to me on occasion, but they were not interested in going public. Even though I understood the fear of losing your job and career, I couldn't help but think that the more of us who spoke up, the less likely it would be that we would lose our jobs. They were willing to talk to Congress, though, if Congress ever got to the place to issue subpoenas.

A couple of weeks later, Sharyl interviewed Rene Jaquez for the story. He didn't have any new information to offer, but it was a comfort to see another agent stepping up and affirming what I had said and to just help push the story along a little. A week or so after that, Darren Gil did an interview with Sharyl. He was the former ATF attaché to Mexico and the one that Bill Newell had just been appointed to replace. He was coming at this story from a whole different perspective that I knew nothing about. He said what I had suspected, that Phoenix was not informing our guys in Mexico about the case. Gil's testimony helped further validate mine.

It wasn't long after that that I heard Bill Newell's transfer to Mexico had been put on hold until the situation was resolved. *Finally,* I thought. *Maybe everything that is happening to me isn't all for naught after all.*

Even though I had lived in its suburbs for decades, I was still learning how Washington, D.C., works at this point. Truth be told, with the countless people being murdered with Fast and Furious weapons, I originally thought the Democrats would be on my side more than the Republicans were. Opinions on guns aside, with the vast majority of these deaths occurring in Mexico and Democrats seeming to be more active in Hispanic communities, I hoped that they would be my saviors as well. In my mind, when the Democrats heard about all this, they would be up in arms much more than the Republicans, and because they held power both in the Senate and the executive branch, and thereby with the attorney general himself, they would put a stop to it and then close what was now the open season on Dodson. I hadn't perceived it being a political issue at all. I welcomed the other side's involvement and, quite frankly, couldn't wait for it. I couldn't have been more wrong.

Though Senator Grassley is a powerful and well-respected senator, he was the only ranking member of the Senate Judiciary Committee. Republicans didn't control the U.S. Senate, so Grassley was not the chairman. That meant he didn't have the power to serve the administration with subpoenas to compel document releases and witness testimony.

Grassley had asked Senate Judiciary Committee chairman Senator Patrick Leahy of Vermont to hold hearings on gun walking and Operation Fast and Furious and to allow for the service of subpoenas on the matter. You'd figure Leahy might want to know how one of the nation's premier law enforcement agencies and the Department of Justice, which was directly in the committee's purview, had gotten mixed up in such a sordid affair.

"No," I was told, "it's not going to happen." I couldn't believe it, couldn't understand it at all.

On the other side of Capitol Hill, Republicans won control of the House of Representatives in the 2010 midterm elections. They now had the power to call hearings and to serve subpoenas on administration officials. There was talk about getting California Republican representative Darrell Issa—the chairman of the House Committee on Oversight and Government Reform—on board with the investigation. As chair of his committee, Issa could issue the subpoenas needed to compel testimony and get the documents. In late March or very early April, somehow it got to Issa's attention and he and his committee staff jumped into the fray.

Because Issa was now on board with the investigation, there was talk of transcribed interviews and subpoenas that could eventually lead to a congressional hearing, and Foster, still somewhat bent that I first interviewed with the Office of the Inspector General without an attorney, told me I really needed to get a lawyer who was going to be my advocate.

My first association-appointed attorney, Larry Berger, lived and worked somewhere in New York and had a busy caseload. It was hard to get him on the phone. One day, the ATF representative to the law officers' association called me and said that the union had another attorney that worked with the association and that she was located in Scottsdale. Her name was Joy Bertrand and she was in a better position to help me. So she was my new attorney. I called her right away and made an appointment.

Her office was an old brick house in downtown Phoenix. I hadn't had the benefit of legal advice, someone who was looking out for me. Grassley's people were my lone allies, but I wasn't their top priority. Protecting whistle-blowers is very important to them and to Senator Grassley, but they couldn't represent me. An attorney would be there just for me, and I desperately needed *somebody* on my side.

Joy was quite the eccentric attorney, to say the least. When I walked into her office for my first appointment her paralegal, Jameson "Jay-Jay" Johnson, greeted me. "It's Jameson, like the whiskey," he introduced himself.

Jameson handed me a business card. It was an oddity: half the size of a normal business card with his name and number printed on it and, most peculiar, a photo of him wearing small rectangular shades. Jay-Jay led me up to the second floor, where there were a couple of desks, a small bathroom to the right, and a large conference table just atop the stairs. I noticed that throughout the house were posters of Malcolm X, Martin Luther King Jr., and other civil rights leaders.

Jameson told me that Joy was running a little late. He explained how she had just recently returned from Wisconsin, where she had been protesting with the teachers' unions locked in battle with the state's governor about pay.

"Hot damn!" I thought. "Here come the Dems."

"Man, I've been checking into this shit," Jameson said as we sat at the table. "I looked up your CBS News interview. Dude, you did the right thing. You're a real hero, man, and we're so excited to be working on this. You got balls of stone."

"Hopefully you guys can help me keep 'em from getting cut off," I said.

As I finished saying that, Joy and her associate, Shannon, walked in and sat down. Joy looked like one of those people who ran marathons but was too smart to comb her hair in the morning. Her unkempt coal-black hair cluttered the top of her head. Shannon was younger, with reddish hair or maybe strawberry blonde, attractive, and just as quick.

We talked for a long while. I filled them in on the story and brought them up to speed on everything that happened since I first spoke to Congress. Each of them listening intently, taking notes, and offering opinions and commentary along the way. After we talked for a little while, I got up to go use the bathroom. Inside there were suits hanging. A toothbrush, razor, cologne, and other toiletries were littered on top of the counter. It was pretty clear Jameson lived there in the office.

When I came back and finished the story, Joy told me of how she had worked on the Hill and that she knew staffers for Senator

Leahy and for Senator Dianne Feinstein of California, another powerful Senate Democrat.

"This is an outrage," Joy said of what had happened to me. "I'll get the Democrats on our team. They need to be all over this and they will be after I talk to them."

If I had any doubts about this office being a liberal stronghold, they ended at that point.

Maybe now, having a well-connected liberal lawyer who used to work on Capitol Hill as a staffer for a Democratic member of Congress and who still had connections up there, finally we'd have some bipartisan outrage. I was looking across the table at my salvation and it was looking back at me through the faces of three "hippies." I thought to myself, *Imagine that?*

In the first week of April, Congressman Issa's investigators flew to Phoenix to conduct transcribed interviews with me and with everyone else they could. They issued subpoenas to Alt, Casa, and Forcelli. I didn't get one. We figured there wasn't much point in it now.

I met Issa's chief investigator, Steve Castor, and for the first time I got to meet the man behind the voice on all those long phone calls, at every hour of the day and night, Jason Foster from Senator Grassley's office. Foster, Donovan, and Downey had been my lifeline for the past several months—the only people I could talk to—the only people that would talk to me—my only friends in the world—and I had never met them, never seen their faces or even a picture, until this moment when I met Foster. Senator Grassley, respecting taxpayer money as he does, had only approved the money for Foster to make the trek out to Phoenix.

When I saw Foster for the first time—he had short-cropped red hair, average height, and was wearing glasses—I couldn't thank him enough for everything. Castor was taller, thin, and lanky with black hair. I had spoken to him on the phone a few times but it wasn't like it had been with Foster. I thanked him equally, though; to me, he and Issa were the cavalry that had come in to save my so very tired ass. And I appreciated it.

When I saw these guys in that conference room at the Phoenix Westin, I felt a surge of relief. Not only were they getting my full statement on record, but they were also getting the other agents who were willing, after being subpoenaed, to testify as well, which meant I was no longer the lone agent from the Phoenix Field Division speaking up. Alt, Casa, and Forcelli would all end up going on the record.

We did the transcribed interview along with my entire three-member legal team. We started early in the morning and went until around three in the afternoon. The committee's minority staffers were all still in D.C. and attended via conference call. Their plane was heading out later that day. At several times during the interview, they voiced their desire to postpone until after they actually had arrived and repeatedly argued with Castor that it was unfair that they hadn't had the opportunity to talk to or interview me ahead of time as he and majority staff had done. Finally, near the end, Joy made a declaration for the record that she had previously, the very day that she had begun to represent me, emailed every member of the committee on the minority side and notified them of her representation of me and offered to make me available to any of them at any time they wanted to speak to me. Joy finished by saying that not a single minority member or staffer ever reached out to her in any way.

When we finished, everyone was starving. We had skipped lunch to get done faster, so Joy, Jameson, Shannon, and I went to a restaurant near the Westin and they bought me lunch.

During lunch conversation, Shannon brought up the predominantly poor questioning by the Democratic committee staff, even describing it as "awful." Joy agreed that their questions were horrendous and a sign they had no clue what they were talking about. But then she volunteered, "It was so bad I was emailing them while they were talking, telling them what questions they should be asking you."

I wasn't comfortable hearing that. *You're my zealous advocate,* I thought. *You're supposed to be looking out for me.* I wondered for the first time where her allegiance truly lay. Still, I wanted to give her the benefit of the doubt. Maybe she just wanted to ensure some questions and their answers were on the record; providing the questions could perhaps help both them and me. That's how I rationalized it anyway—it still bothered me, though.

Joy continued. "I have no idea how the government is going to get out of this one," she said. "The Democrats are looking really bad. The only way they'll save themselves here is if the president himself calls you to the White House, shakes your hand, apologizes, and pins a medal on you."

I didn't want any medals. I just wanted my life back and to be allowed to do the job that I had been sent to Phoenix to do.

We left it there and I headed home. I filled Keri in on all the details. Then I got a call from Foster. "Hey, we're going out for dinner and some of the other guys may have a beer or two," he said after I picked up. "Want to join us?"

"Sure."

Seamus is an Irish pub in downtown Phoenix. Keri came with me, and we walked in and found Foster, Castor, and the rest of his crew all seated around a couple of tables that had been pushed together. I introduced Keri to everyone and then ordered a beer for each of us. Five minutes later, I noticed a man walk in and stand at the door, as if looking for someone. He was a black guy, late twenties to early thirties, stocky, wearing slacks and a button-down.

As he scanned the room, his head stopped when he saw all of us at the table and he nodded in acknowledgment. Castor waved him over to sit down next to us. As he walked our way, Foster explained to me that his name was Sherman, and that he was an attorney with Maryland Democratic representative Elijah Cummings's staff. Cummings was the ranking member of the House Oversight Committee, which Issa chaired, and Sherman was one of the staffers who had been on the conference call during my interview.

After introductions were made, we all sat down. Nobody had to say it: we all knew the rules. We couldn't talk about the case or the investigation. Either way, it felt good to get out of the house. Nobody had invited me out for a beer—or asked me to do *anything*—in quite some time. We talked about old television shows and sports and other happenings in the world. We laughed. We joked. It was the first time since this all began that I could relax. People who were all trying to do the right thing surrounded us, and Keri and I enjoyed the company.

I liked Sherman, and with him at the bar with us that night, I wondered if it was a positive omen that the Democrats might just help out in the coming weeks and months. They were starting to get involved, it looked like, and they were beginning to understand the flaws of Operation Fast and Furious and how the Justice Department had lied to Congress—to them—about it.

Driving into work at the FBI building the next morning, I called Joy's number. As much as she'd probably be pissed about it, I thought I had to tell her how I had a beer with the group the night before.

On the other end of the phone, as I expected, she went thermonuclear—we weren't supposed to be meeting outside of official settings.

"I'll have their bar cards!" she screamed into the phone. "They violated all sorts of legal codes of ethics."

I mentioned how Cummings's staffer was there, too, so it wasn't just the Republicans, and I made clear to her we didn't talk about the case at all.

"I'm only telling you so as my attorney you'll know," I said in response to Joy's rage. "I don't want you to do anything about it and don't say a word to anyone."

We hung up and a few minutes later, Jameson called me. He was upset as well. I told him the same thing.

Within a half hour, Foster called me up: "Hey, what's going on?"

The other two Democratic staff lawyers had shown up in Phoenix: a scrawny, arrogant guy named Scott with oversized ears, and a young woman, Susanne, who reminded me of a federal probation officer that I had dated back in Virginia before leaving for Phoenix. Foster explained how the two newly arrived staffers had somehow found out about us getting together the night before and now they were making a big deal out of nothing.

"Joy is threatening to file a complaint against us and a grievance with the bar association," he said.

"I already talked to her," I answered, referring to Joy. "I told her not to say anything to anyone; I told her as my attorney and in confidence. I ordered her and Jameson to untie the knots in their panties and I'm going to reiterate that to them as soon I get off the phone with you."

I called Joy back and gave the order again.

– 13 –

A SHADE OF
THE TRUTH

One of the rules in Washington is that if you don't like the truth or it doesn't match up to what you want the truth to be, then simply alter it or change it entirely. This holds especially true if it comes from the other party—regardless of what "they" say, what "we" now say has to be 180 degrees the opposite. One of the best ways to do this is to cast the accusing finger at the other side of the aisle and scream, "They're playing a political game!"

Once politics are injected into it, the search for the truth gets thrown off track. Everyone picks up their shields and defends their side's assertion of what is the given truth. Whichever side is victorious, their "truth" now prevails, while the real truth is so often lost somewhere along the way.

So polarized have ideologies become that any communication coming from the opposite party is considered "incoming fire" and anything directed to them should strictly be "outgoing fire." Our country's forefathers, having lived through tyranny, and knowing its perils, designed our government to be free from religious rule. However, political ideology, free of moral or ethical constraints and bound only by the two commandments "My side can do no wrong" and "Your side can do no right" has become the new religion that now infests our government and permeates the masses. Not as fortunate are we as our nation's founders, for I believe our perils are yet to come.

The irony is that "politics" may play no role whatsoever in the issue at hand. It may actually be a legitimate search for the truth, or another cause with absolutely no political motive at all. However, as soon as someone makes the declaration "they're playing a political game," politics are now thrust upon it, the label latches hold, and the unfortunate events that I described above are all played out before us on the largest stage in the land, all actors sticking to the script and the ensemble cast all marching in time.

Applying the "political" banner has become a very effective tool and is far overused. Whenever someone, a side, or a party, is challenged by something real and genuine, and they defend that challenge by declaring it is "only a political game," they have then themselves injected politics into the issue and the real meaning of and the intent behind it are lost.

As there are exceptions to all generalizations, so too are there politicians who only play a shallow game of gotcha and partisanship. Senator Grassley and his staff I believe are notable exceptions in my experience. As the Hatch Act forbids me to publicly support any political candidate, I speak now only from my own personal experience, of my opinions and my own personal beliefs. I would be saying the exact same thing if Senator Grassley were of the Democratic Party. Grassley and his staff listened to me, guided me, and helped me when nobody else would. They did it not because of any political favor or gain to be drawn from it. They did it because they believed it to be the right thing to do.

I've heard many say that Chairman Issa's involvement in the investigation of Fast and Furious was "politically motivated." I wasn't as close with his staff as I was to Senator Grassley's, but I can say that Issa's helped me many times, looked out for me, gave me cover, and carried the torch that I was clinging to—and again, without even the hope of any compensation or political benefit.

Maybe I had been naïve to think my own lawyer would represent only my interests, but after that it was clear I needed a different one. A friend that I had worked with in Virginia had given me a call to offer her support. She was an assistant U.S. attorney in Alexandria. While on the phone, I asked her if she knew any attorneys who would be able to help me out. Through a friend, she got me the name of Robert Driscoll, with Alston & Bird, out of Washington, D.C. I contacted him and he was willing to help me. I notified Joy that I had obtained new counsel. The communication was brief.

In late May and early June 2011, the FBI sent me to Quantico, Virginia, for two weeks of training. The timing was good because it gave me a chance to meet with Driscoll and describe the whole situation face-to-face. When I arrived in Virginia, I heard from Grassley's and Issa's staffers that the minority staff for the House Oversight Committee wanted to meet with me for another interview. They didn't know why, exactly. I made the hour-and-a-half drive up to Washington from Quantico for the interview.

When I got to the Rayburn House Office Building, Driscoll and the staffers escorted me down to a small conference room. The room was packed. I sat on the end of a small little table and the others lined the rest of the table and stood along the walls, all eyes on me.

Scott, the Democratic staffer with outsized self-assurance and ears to match, started grilling me. Castor made several demands to be told what this was about or what the line of questioning was hoping to get to, but the minority staffers refused to say. They asked me if I knew Andre Howard and how many times had I met with him since the CBS interview had aired in March.

"Twice," I told them.

Scott asked me to recount what was said at those meetings. I did so to the best of my recollection.

Scott asked me if Senator Leahy's name had come up at either meeting and if I had ever met Leahy or spoke to a member of his staff. I told him that Andre had mentioned the name at both meetings and that I had not met or spoken to Leahy or anyone on his staff. His tone now dripping with condescension, Scott asked, "So, you *never told* Andre that you were working with Senator Leahy and talking to his staff?"

I have testified many, many times in my career. I knew when a defense attorney was walking me down a road he believed led to some big *a-ha!* moment. I had been "in the box" and cross-examined by some of the best defense attorneys in this country and I had enough experience to know when he might actually have that "a-ha," and more important, when he didn't. And I also knew that this moron didn't have shit, nor was he even that good of an attorney.

"No, I *never* said I talked to Leahy, I *never* said I was working with him or his staff, and I *never* said that I had met the man. Truth is, I wouldn't know him if he was standing in this room right now with the rest of you."

Scott then began to ask me about "recorded conversations" with Andre. I only knew of three. The first was the recording that I had made during my second meeting with Andre at his home. It had been solely for my protection, not for the investigation. I had shared it with Foster under the agreement that it was just for his benefit, a prelude to what Andre might have to say if they got the chance to interview him. I trusted Foster and was certain he hadn't told anyone of its existence. When the committee got involved with the investigation, Foster called me and asked permission to share it with Castor. I had granted his doing so but under the same caveats—it was not to be part of the investigation and no one else was to know. Foster and Castor respected my wishes and hadn't even shared the existence of the recording with the other members of their staff. Downey and Donovan didn't even know about it. The only other people who did were my former attorneys Joy, Jameson, and Shannon.

Because Joy was my lawyer and supposedly my zealous advocate, I had filled her in on all the details. I spoke in the belief that everything I had said to her, Jameson, and Shannon was all privileged information. I had made it explicitly clear to all three that no one was to know about that recording. I didn't want Andre to find out about it and think he couldn't trust me.

The other two conversations with Andre that had been recorded were ones he had recorded. He explained to me how he had recorded two of his conversations with Hope after he realized that they were trying to set him up and coerce him to testify against me. To my knowledge at that time, only Andre, his attorney, Castor, Foster, and I knew that those recordings existed. Andre told me that his attorney had provided them to Castor.

"Was that first meeting with Andre recorded?" Scott asked.

"I don't know," I answered.

"What do you mean you don't know?"

"I mean I don't know. I know I didn't record it but Andre may have."

"So your testimony is that you don't know if that meeting was recorded?"

"Yes, that is my testimony. And for the record, I wish it had been."

"Why do you wish that?"

"Because if it had been, you wouldn't have to ask me all these questions about it."

"What about the second meeting?" he asked.

"I don't know if Andre recorded that one, either," I answered

Acting like he had just scored some big victory, Scott looked at Susanne and gave her the facial equivalent of a high-five. She whispered something to him and then he turned back at me and asked. "So, your testimony is that none of your two meetings with Andre were ever recorded?"

"No, sir, that's not my testimony."

He sat up quickly; so confident in his victory yet confused in his facts, he was surprised by my answer. "What do you mean 'that's not your testimony'?" he barked. "That's what you just said."

"No, what I said was I didn't know if Andre had recorded the first meeting or not and didn't know if he recorded our second meeting, either."

"But you said you didn't record them," he said, trying to frantically bail out the water that was rushing in through the hull of his ship.

"No, you asked me if I knew whether that 'first meeting' with Andre was recorded and I said that I didn't know if he had done so or not, but that I knew I didn't record it—it being the 'first meeting.'"

He now realized that he sprung his trap before he had set it properly. It wouldn't have worked regardless; I would have never lied to them. But they were hoping that I would or that they could confuse me enough to get me to make a mistake, blur the meetings so as to ask about one and I answer for another. Anything to get a lie, an untruth, omission, or even an inconsistency in my testimony so that they could argue to have it all disregarded as "inconsistent." But my testimony, everything that I had said to anyone, was candid, truthful, and complete.

"What about the second meeting?" he asked.

I looked at Driscoll, he nodded, and I told them about my recording it. The minority staff already knew about it and they knew that I didn't want it on the record. They figured this as a perfect chance to catch me omitting something or outright lying, anything to impeach me as a witness. Not because anything that I said wasn't true, but because what I said was embarrassing to their side.

There were only six other people on the planet that knew about that recording. I knew Foster and Castor hadn't said anything; they were equally as pissed by the minority's failed attempt to impeach me. Driscoll had just found out probably an hour before when I was bringing him up to speed on everything before heading over to the Rayburn Building. So that left only Joy, Jameson, and Shannon. And to be honest, I never got the feeling from Shannon that she would do something like that.

The minority staffers had brought me there that day only to try to discredit me, and I am convinced they had used privileged information from my former attorney to try to do it. If they did, what happened was immoral, unprofessional, unethical, and against the rules of the bar association, and potentially even criminal.

This was a huge eye-opener for me. I really thought that once the Democrats saw the evidence and heard the story, there would be a political cease-fire and then an effort to remedy the situation.

I was wrong. It seemed the political battle would just keep heating up and the Dems were going to use every dirty trick in the book to try to make the story—and me—go away.

While I was back east, I was also interviewed by the inspector general's office again. I had filed a complaint in late February, and supposedly from the attorney general's testimony, he had ordered they do an investigation on February 28, but it was late May before they really got knee-deep in it. They were going to interview everyone involved, but they wanted to interview me first before they went to anyone else. In a marathon six-hour interview in Driscoll's office, we went over everything and then went over it all again.

After the interview, I was cautiously optimistic. One of the investigators really seemed like he "got it." He asked the right questions. He and I were the only cops in a room full of lawyers. Knowing the huge political machine that everything was operating under, I still had doubts as to whether or not the higher-ups in the OIG could really be objective. There were several people who had warned me to not have too many hopes riding on their investigation.

Back in Phoenix, Tom Brandon had been sent by ATF to fill in as the Special Agent in Charge replacing Newell. Newell had been set to transfer to Mexico, but now that his plans were thwarted, he got a temporary assignment at headquarters. ATF also replaced Gillett and sent Tom Atteberry in as the acting ASAC. I was hearing good things about the new leadership from Alt and Casa. They told me how Brandon and Atteberry were talking with them and listening to what they had to say and how Dave, Hope, and Tonya were apparently on the outs. Wanting my chance to finally be heard by anyone at ATF who had put forth any attitude of actually giving a shit whatsoever about the problem, I contacted Brandon and requested a meeting.

The first meeting he had, included Atteberry and division counsel. He was rightly cautious. He didn't know anything about me and wanted to make sure someone else heard everything that was said. I just wanted an opportunity to tell my side, to be heard, to say, "Look, I've had to take a huge bite of this shit sandwich not because I wanted to, not because I want to get back at anybody, not because I hate ATF, but because I believed it was the right thing to do and we owed it to the Terry family." I would have said it at a podium in front of every ATF agent if given the chance, or publicly debated it with anyone.

Brandon seemed to get it. He understood where we were coming from and the hell we had been through. At our next meeting, it was just him and me, no counsel in there with us, which made me feel that I had come across as not a guy to fear, but someone trying to get the truth out. Brandon was later chosen to replace Billy Hoover as the number-two man at ATF, the deputy director. In spite of all that happened to me, I respect Brandon for being the one and only guy at his level or any level who took the time to sit down and look into the situation. That was the only time I saw any leadership at ATF during this whole ordeal.

Pressure from Washington only ramped up in the spring of 2011. Forcelli, Casa, and I were all served with subpoenas to testify in front of Congress on June 15, 2011. Brandon completely supported us and said simply, "Go and tell the truth. Be one hundred percent honest." He even told us that ATF would pay for our trip; just turn in a travel voucher.

Since our kids had gone away again for the summer, I was lucky enough that Keri accompanied me to D.C. She had been by my side during this whole thing and I appreciated having her there for that. The day before the hearing, I spent more than eight hours at Driscoll's office preparing my written statement with one of his associates, Michael Chapman, making sure I didn't state something that would inadvertently make me look like an ass. Chapman was a former Special Forces guy who for some reason had become a lawyer in D.C. He being a lawyer, and me being a cop, we would have to butt heads for a while before we reached a compromise, which is one of the things I really grew to like about him.

Many times during our almost daily phone conversations over

the next few months, Chapman and I could be heard screaming at each other. I could call him "a want-to-be big-time D.C. lawyer that doesn't know shit about being a cop" and he would call me "just an agent whose dumb ass needs to shut up and listen." Then we'd laugh and shake it off. At times, Chapman would hang up on me, so after a while I'd email him something like "The counselor said we should never go to bed angry at each other." He'd send me an equally awkward reply and then all would be fine. We never took it personally.

I had five minutes to read a written statement that would be submitted, so it was quite the challenge to strongly and succinctly say all the things that I felt it pertinent to say. To make matters worse, Driscoll's office received a letter from ATF that day—a gag order. The day before I was to testify before Congress, ATF lawyers sent my attorney (and no one else's) a letter making it clear that although I had been subpoenaed, I wasn't authorized to say shit. That just motivated me more.

On June 15, Keri and I woke up early to get ready for the hearing. As I was putting on my suit, I couldn't help but think, *How the hell did I wind up here doing this?* It was not a place I had ever pictured myself being.

I was a little anxious, but not nervous, because the wonderful thing about telling the truth is that you don't have to worry about it—it's the same every time you say it. I knew that Brian Terry's family was also going to be there that day and I would have to look into their eyes and greet them knowing I had been a part of a plan that ultimately contributed to his death.

Brian's cousin, Robert Heyer ("Bobby"), an agent with the Secret Service, had reached out to me after my CBS News appearance to thank me for coming forward, and to talk to me more about the situation over the phone. Before the hearing, he wanted to meet me in person, so Keri and I waited for them outside the Rayburn Building.

Bobby; Brian's mother, Josephine Terry; Brian's sister; and two of Brian's closest friends from Michigan all arrived there together. They all greeted me with hugs, handshakes, and thank-yous. I was humbled by their warm greeting. I still had guilt from ever being a part of any of this. I wouldn't have blamed them if they had been less than cordial.

There was something simultaneously troubling and reassuring about looking into the eyes of Josephine Terry. She bore the burdens of any grieving mother. I could tell the past six months, since the time she had received that early-morning call that her son had been killed, had been difficult. Her dark hair was graying. Her eyes were heavy, weighted down by the tears and stress she had undoubtedly endured. Still, there was no sense that she felt put upon, no feeling that the world had wronged her, even though she had every right to feel that way. She wasn't seeking attention, only answers.

We still had some time before the hearing, and everyone was hungry, so we wandered downstairs to the building next door and into the cafeteria for breakfast. Brushed aluminum serving counters ringed several walls on one side of the big room, with a selection of fruits, hot breakfasts, and bagels. We grabbed some food and coffee, and paid the cashier before sitting down at a big table on the other side of the huge room.

It was emotional to string together words and answers to their questions. As we all sat there together, conversation began to flow more easily between us. Keri and I both enjoyed their company. They were just normal, everyday, hardworking people who like me had unexpectedly and unwillingly found themselves colliding with an unknown world.

Still unaware of many of the details, Bobby was very interested in some of the specifics of the case. As I filled him in on certain things, he had what had become the all-too-familiar look when I told the story. The mind just doesn't want to go there. It's so hard to comprehend and make sense of it that it takes a little bit for your brain to finally rest at the conclusion of . . . yes, this really did happen.

As we chatted, I had the nagging feeling that maybe it would have all been easier for them had I just not said anything. At least they would have closure, knowing only that Brian had been killed in a shootout with dangerous drug traffickers and then given the honors accorded to a hero. That way they wouldn't have had to go through the agony of congressional hearings, a press corps hounding them for interviews, and most of all, the outrage that their own government had been responsible for his death.

After breakfast, we made our way over to the Committee Hearing Room. We were then taken to a waiting room. Forcelli and Casa got there about the same time. They were also humbled and emotional upon meeting the Terry family. Grassley and Issa came in and introduced themselves to everyone and expressed their condolences to the Terry family. I had been formally introduced to both on my previous trip to D.C., so I greeted them and introduced them to Keri.

After greetings and basic pleasantries, it was time to get down to business. The first part of the hearing consisted of Grassley testifying alone.

After Grassley, it was the Terry family, me, Casa, and Forcelli. As I walked into the hearing room, it was surreal with all the people, reporters, microphones, and cameras. ATF brass and Justice Department officials were present as well. I found my place at the table and Keri, Driscoll, and Chapman sat directly behind me. I was comforted in that I was sitting there with Casa and Forcelli and knowing that all three of us were going to get the opportunity to tell everyone the truth.

I was no longer alone. That snowball that I had pushed for so long by myself now had a crowd behind it and it was cresting over the hill.

Casa and Forcelli both had very strong opening statements. At first, as the members of the committee started firing questions our way, we would all look at each other, yielding to one another to give an answer. By the end, however, our comfort level greatly increased and we were all but fighting over the chance to push the mic button first and finally be heard. Getting it all out in front of people who were willing to do something about it was a huge relief.

Every one of the members of the committee was respectful to all of us and both sides expressed their appreciation in our coming forward. The Democrats and Republicans did some sparring back and forth between each other. It was about the normal stuff that gets feathers ruffled . . . more laws, less laws, more gun control, less gun control . . . same shit, different day on Capitol Hill.

After the questioning of our panel ended, the lawmakers came up to thank us for what we were doing. Democratic representative William Lacy Clay from Missouri walked up to me and shook my hand. "We're going to work to get you those new gun laws you need so this doesn't happen again," the congressman told me. While I appreciated his kindness, I felt the need to point something out.

"With all due respect, sir, I didn't ask for any new laws," I responded. "All I ask for is the opportunity to go back to Phoenix and enforce the ones we have. When I've had a chance to do that, if I think we need any more, I'll let you know."

The third panel of the hearing included the testimony from the Justice Department's Weich. He was the one who had sent the infamous February 4 letter outlining how ATF had done nothing wrong and that there was no way the agency would have participated in an operation walking guns to drug cartels. Issa was visibly excited to question him. He backed off the whole February 4 letter and started doing the ambiguous dance that we had expected to see months ago. Weich said that the department didn't lie, but as it turns out, he may not have been accurate in the letter, and it was being further investigated. He touted how the Inspector General was now doing a full investigation and when it was completed, corrective measures would be taken if necessary.

A few weeks later, the committee held another hearing. This one included Bill Newell and William McMahon, who was Newell's boss; Darren Gil, Carlos Canino, and Jose Wall, who were agents in Mexico during the case; and Lorren Ledman, a senior intel analyst from ATF headquarters. Although approaching it from another angle, Gil, Canino, Wall, and Ledman all backed up what Forcelli, Casa, and I had said at our hearing.

The real nail in the coffin, though, was Newell's and McMahon's testimony. It was painful to see how inept they were at their jobs. Only in government can two men, who cannot even properly express their own defense, make it to highest levels of supervision and management.

Keri and I were watching the hearing live on our computer at home.

She was actually yelling at the computer, "Oh, my God! And the American taxpayers are actually paying you a decent salary to be this oblivious and idiotic?" She then turned to me and said, "John, if nothing else ever comes of this whole thing and no one is ever held accountable, the American people owe you a huge thanks just for the fact that Newell will not be the attaché to Mexico. I can only imagine the disaster that could have followed that man around."

I couldn't help but think that if these guys had known the secret weapon in my corner, they would never have entered into battle with me. When you have a strong woman with strong convictions in your corner, you are about three strides ahead of the other guy and he doesn't even know it.

The efforts to discredit me continued, this time through the press. Someone leaked some of the Fernandez case documents in an effort to smear me. The leak was illegal and in violation of my rights under the Privacy Act. At this point the truth was out there and well substantiated. The only point of smearing me was petty vengeance. They were trying to say that I was just covering my own ass and that the Republicans had used me to start a big political war with the Democrats.

The Fernandez case had become a double-edged sword for me. When I first talked with Grassley's office, it was that case that gave me credibility. I wish I had never gone through with it and I had made every effort that I, working alone, could have possibly made to recover those six guns. However, there was no better proof that the Justice Department's February 4 letter was a complete lie.

In August, I found out that U.S. Attorney Dennis Burke, a long-time confidant and former chief of staff to Homeland Security secretary Janet Napolitano, had admitted to the leak.

Brandon began talking to Forcelli, Casa, Alt, and me about transferring out of Phoenix. The shit storm had become so huge that it made it difficult for us to work not only with our fellow agents, but also with the U.S. attorney's office. It was important for the Phoenix Field Division to start moving forward under new leadership, so removing the polarizing figures was probably the best way to do that. Even though leaving Phoenix was not what I wanted—after all, I had spent a good portion of my life wanting to get there—I felt like moving was probably the best way to go forward with my life, get away from all this mess, and save what career I had left.

Brandon said there was an opening in Greenville, South Carolina, where he personally knew the supervisor. Greenville wasn't too far from where both Keri and I were from. Being closer to family after all we had been through seemed appealing. Also, it was a smaller office, which to me meant greater odds of getting a fair shake.

In late August, Keri and I went to a justice of the peace and got married. We had both known that we were committed for life and very happy together. But due to the pain of our previous relationships, marriage certainly was not top on either of our priority lists. However, to make the move more financially viable, getting married seemed the sensible thing to do. Therefore I asked if I could always say that "I married her for the money." Her sense of humor intact, she agreed, and we did it.

In November, Congress had another hearing with Attorney General Eric Holder, who discussed the February 4 letter. He stated that the Department of Justice knew that the letter was now no longer "accurate." However, Weich and others who had drafted and sent the letter thought it to be accurate when they had done so. A few weeks later, the Justice Department formally "withdrew" the February 4 letter and released at least 1,300 documents that related to its drafting. Justice admitted that they could no longer stand behind it because it contained inaccurate and false information.

The documents released by the department were revealing in what they didn't say. The overwhelming majority of them were emails between countless people giving their opinions and advice. Interestingly enough, in these emails between all of these higher-ups, not one time did anyone ask, "Hey, did anyone ask anybody who is actually making these allegations?" They didn't give a rat's ass about me or Styers, who had submitted a memo the day before Weich sent his false letter to Congress. The Justice Department and ATF brass simply called down to Newell and asked him if this happened and essentially his answer was "Hell no!" They then readily accepted that I must be a "disgruntled" dumbass field agent who was taking advantage of political games to get back at somebody.

I don't care if the people who drafted that letter didn't "mean" for it to be false. I understand that Newell et al. may have given them erroneous information, but it's Investigations 101 that if you're trying to run something to ground, you don't just ask the guy at the heart of the allegations. I expect more from my government and my superiors than the first order of business being to protect their own asses by having a mentality, whether purposeful or not, of "don't ask the field agents because they can't wrap their brains around these vast international conspiracies." Maybe, just maybe, this lowly GS-13 from the hills of Virginia who has served and protected his community with countless blood, sweat, and tears for so many years isn't such a dumbass after all.

If it were me, had I been anywhere in that chain of command and had heard that a field agent was making these allegations, my ass would have been on the first plane to Phoenix to have a face-to-face with him, especially since his chain of command was telling me a completely different story.

AFTERMATH

In September 2012, I found myself back in Arizona, at the Tucson airport. It was a very different feeling being back out west. So much had happened in my life since I loaded up my truck and bought a house I'd never seen in Phoenix.

I had flown out for the Brian Terry Memorial Benefit and the subsequent dedication of the new Border Patrol station in Naco, Arizona, in his honor. I had again met with and spent time with the Terry family. It was a wonderful event aimed at turning tragedy into something worthwhile. Although joyful at the honor being bestowed upon Brian, I'm always reminded of their pain from having lost him.

I was on my way back to the airport when I received a notification on my cell phone. The long-awaited report from the Office of the Inspector General finally had been released. For nineteen months senior officials at the Justice Department and ATF had deferred action on a number of matters, citing "the ongoing OIG investigation." It was made clear to me on many occasions that my fate was tied directly to its findings. The year and a half of anticipation was at times almost too much to handle.

Maybe it was fitting that I was in Arizona again when the report came out. Back at the scene of the crime.

I was warned many times that in drawing conclusions the inspector general would more than likely "split the baby." They would criticize the agency, but also whistle-blowers like me as well. I braced myself for what was to come.

I had just boarded the plane, my knees feeling like they were crushed against my chest back in steerage. My Droid started downloading the file. Five percent. Ten percent. Twenty percent. I had been one of the last to board and the flight attendants were making their final checks through the cabin. It was a race between one bar of weak cellular signal and the cabin door closing. My hands grew sweaty as I peered at the screen in anticipation. I stole a glance down the aisle. The last thing I wanted—or needed—was an Alec Baldwin moment.

Eighty percent. Ninety percent. Download complete. Just as the thump of the cabin door closing reverberated, even down into the cheap seats in the back.

Here we go. I clicked the file. "Conversion failed." My heart sank.

After the five-hour flight back to South Carolina, as soon as I got home I rushed in the house, ran to the computer, and spent the next several hours going over what it said.

The inspector general, to my surprise, largely seemed to understand what had happened. The report criticized most of those in the chain from Phoenix ATF all the way up to Weinstein at main Justice:

Our review of Operation Fast and Furious and related matters revealed a series of misguided strategies, tactics, errors in judgment, and management failures that permeated ATF Headquarters and the Phoenix Field Division, as well as the U.S. Attorney's Office for the District of Arizona. In this report, we described deficiencies in two operations conducted in ATF's Phoenix Field Division between 2006 and 2010—Operation Wide Receiver and Operation Fast and Furious. In the course of our review we identified individuals ranging from line agents and prosecutors in Phoenix and Tucson to senior ATF officials in Washington, D.C., who bore a share of responsibility for ATF's knowing failure in both these operations to interdict firearms illegally destined for Mexico, and for doing so without adequately taking into account the danger to public safety that flowed from this risky strategy. We also found failures by Department officials related to these matters, including failing to respond accurately to a Congressional inquiry about them.

Although deficient in some ways (like giving Deputy Attorney General Breuer a pass when he undoubtedly knew that ATF Phoenix was walking guns—the affidavits alone spelled this out), the report supported what I had complained about from the start of the case. We knew where those guns were headed and not only failed to stop it, but facilitated the continuation of it.

In some ways, it was a great relief, a validation of what I and others had been saying. I felt vindicated, at least in part.

Nobody involved in the death of Brian Terry or potentially hundreds if not thousands of others was truly held accountable. Sure, Jason Weinstein, a deputy assistant attorney general in the Criminal Division, ultimately resigned. And Arizona U.S. Attorney Dennis Burke resigned from his post after admitting to illegally leaking documents in an attempt to smear me.

But Burke quickly found a new job, landing another high-caliber position with a private political strategy company. Newell, Gillett, and Dave were all transferred to positions in Washington, D.C., before the report was released. Some months afterward, I understood that Newell and Dave received government-paid transfers to other locations with a lower rank, but the same salary. ATF's Melson, Hoover, and Chait—ATF's numbers one, two, and three during this debacle, all quietly retired, their full pensions intact. McMahon, who was Newell's direct supervisor in the chain of command, initially went out on terminal leave pending his retirement date, with a full pension, of course, but when Senator Grassley and Chairman Issa called ATF out on the fact that while McMahon was still an ATF employee he had assumed a lucrative position in the Philippines with JPMorgan Chase (which just happens to be ATF's new credit card company), he was subsequently terminated.

As far as I know, Hope and Tonya are still working in the Phoenix Field Division. I don't know exactly what they are doing now, but we can all hope it has nothing to do with working cases.

No one has ever been fired or truly held accountable for the strategy or for retaliating against the whistle-blowers. The Justice Department still refuses to turn over subpoenaed documents—citing a claim of "executive privilege" and culminating with the attorney general being the first ever to be held in contempt of Congress. And the Terry family still has many questions that remained unanswered. What really happened in Peck Canyon that night and why the huge cover-up protecting all the information surrounding it?

I do take some comfort that the Phoenix Field Division is no longer run by the most incompetent leaders that ATF has to offer. But has the agency really learned its lesson? Or will there be other misguided adventures undertaken out of hubris, the desire for recognition, or to impress the brass? The utter dysfunction and incompetence of our government had been exposed, very publicly, for everyone to see. The disheartening part is that only a few people did see and fewer yet seemed to even care about it. Many of the same agencies implicated are run by the same people who are now asking for more money and more resources to respond to some other crisis of the day.

We did at least stop gun walking. The senselessness of Fast and Furious has been recognized by almost everyone (I hear Dave Voth and Bill Newell still argue what a great case it was) and hopefully such a thing will never be allowed to happen again. If we hadn't spoken up, I have no doubt the Phoenix operation would be replicated elsewhere.

Hopefully, for all the injustices we suffered, if we made it a little easier for others to speak out against the actions of their government then what we did was worth it. I believe there are still plenty of us out there who believe the unarmed truth is ultimately worth more than any job or accolade. I want my story to be known to anyone willing to take a stand, so they will know that they don't stand alone.

Acknowledgments

So many have helped Keri and me that the words and pages needed to acknowledge them all, detail their contributions, and to express my appreciation for them would more than double those contained between these covers. Some, however, cannot go unrecognized: Paul de Souza, who had the vision to turn a professional and personal nightmare into a book; Keith Urbahn and Matt Latimer with Javelin, whose contributions and dedication helped make it possible; Matthew Boyle, whose comments, questions, and fearless reporting to this day are so very much appreciated; Chairman Issa and Senator Grassley for pursuing the truth rather than politics, neither asking for or expecting anything in return; staffers Jason Foster, Brian Downey, Rob Donovan, and Steve Castor, who listened to me, looked out for me, provided air cover for me, counseled me, consoled me, and most of all, befriended me when no one else would; Tristan Leavitt and the many other staffers who put in all those hours and worked so tirelessly to uncover the facts wherever they led; Larry Alt, Lee Casa, Pete Forcelli, and Darren Gil, who because of their own convictions openly spoke out as well; Sharyl Attkisson, William La Jeunesse, Katie Pavlich, Lori Jane Gliha, Maria Henao, and Jorge Ramos, who did their jobs by being intrepid journalists rather than mere mouthpieces and who are rare exemplars of integrity and tirelessness in their profession; Robert Driscoll and Michael Chapman of Alston & Byrd, who helped me navigate the deep and treacherous waters inside the Beltway; the Greythorne group, whose friendship and support helped us through many difficult times. And then there are all of those, many of whom I have never even met, who reached out to me and offered their encouragement and support. You have my deep appreciation for strengthening my resolve when I doubted it most. Brian Terry, for your service and sacrifice, and Brian's family and close friends, for showing such grace in a time of such tragedy all the while embracing and supporting me. Last, and perhaps most important, there is family. My father, John M. Dodson; my brother; my in-laws, Hugh and Sandra Smith; and so many others in our family have always been and will continue to be there for us. My children, you inspire me to be a better person, a better man, a better father.